WordPerfect® Suite 8 For Dummies

Cheat Sheet

Universal Shortcuts

Tip: These shortcuts work in most Windows 95 programs, as well as in WordPerfect Suite 8.

To Do This	Press This	Or Click This Button
Create a new document	Ctrl+N	
Open an existing document	Ctrl+O	
Close the current document	Ctrl+F4	
Cut data to the Clipboard	Ctrl+X	
Copy data to the Clipboard	Ctrl+C	
Paste Clipboard data	Ctrl+V	
Print the current document	Ctrl+P	
Save the current document	Ctrl+S	
Undo the last thing you did	Ctrl+Z	
Cancel an Undo (or Redo)	Ctrl+Shift+R	
Quit the current program	Alt+F4	
Make text boldface	Ctrl+B	
Italicize text	Ctrl+I	
Underline text	Ctrl+U	
Get help about a feature	F1	

Shortcuts for Moving around Documents

Tip: These shortcuts work in most Windows 95 programs, including those in WordPerfect Suite 8.

To Do This	Press This
Jump to the beginning of a document or to the top of the first page in a spreadsheet	Ctrl+Home
Jump to the beginning of the current line or to the top of the current spreadsheet page	Home
Jump to the end of the document	Ctrl+End (Ctrl+End+Home in Quattro Pro)
Jump to the end of the current line (not available in Quattro Pro)	End
Move to the next option in a dialog box	Tab
Move to the previous option in a dialog box	Shift+Tab
Scroll display up one screen	PgUp
Scroll display down one screen	PgDn

For more information about IDG Books, call 1-800-762-2974.

...For Dummies: #1 Computer Book Series for Beginners

COMPUTER
BOOK SERIES
FROM IDG

WordPerfect® Suite 8 For Dummies®

Cheat Sheet

WordPerfect 8 Shortcuts

To Do This	Do This
Select a word	Double-click the word
Select a sentence	Triple-click the sentence
Select a paragraph	Place cursor in left margin of paragraph and double-click
Select entire document	Press Ctrl+A
Find and replace text	Press Ctrl+F
Insert a page break	Press Ctrl+Enter
Insert a line break	Press Ctrl+Shift+L
Open the Font dialog box	Press F9
Indent the current paragraph	Click at the beginning of the paragraph and press F7
Center the current line	Press Shift+F7
Display/hide ruler	Press Alt+Shift+F3

Presentations Toolbar Shortcuts

To Do This	Click This Button
Create a text box	
Add a new slide	
Open the Master Gallery	
Display the Slide Properties dialog box	
Display the Object Properties dialog box	
Open the Scrapbook	or press F11
Play a slide show	
Change the formatting of a bullet chart	
Skip the current slide in playback list	
Animate the selected object	

Quattro Pro Toolbar Shortcuts

To Do This	Click This Button
Display the Active Cells dialog box	or press F12
Insert a row or column	
Delete a row or column	
Adjust the size of a row or column to fit data	
Create a chart	
Find the sum of cells in a selected row or column	
Use QuickFill to fill selected cells	
Format the selected block using SpeedFormat	

WORDPERFECT®
SUITE 8
FOR
DUMMIES®

WORDPERFECT® SUITE 8 FOR DUMMIES®

by Julie Adair King

IDG Books Worldwide, Inc.
An International Data Group Company

Foster City, CA ◆ Chicago, IL ◆ Indianapolis, IN ◆ Southlake, TX

WordPerfect® Suite 8 For Dummies®

Published by
IDG Books Worldwide, Inc.
An International Data Group Company
919 E. Hillsdale Blvd.
Suite 400
Foster City, CA 94404
http://www.idgbooks.com (IDG Books Worldwide Web site)
http://www.dummies.com (Dummies Press Web site)

Library of Congress Catalog Card No.: 97-72407

ISBN: 0-7645-0187-9

Printed in the United States of America

10 9 8 7 6 5 4 3 2 1

1B/QZ/QX/ZX/IN

Distributed in the United States by IDG Books Worldwide, Inc.

Distributed by Macmillan Canada for Canada; by Transworld Publishers Limited in the United Kingdom; by IDG Norge Books for Norway; by IDG Sweden Books for Sweden; by Woodslane Pty. Ltd. for Australia; by Woodslane Enterprises Ltd. for New Zealand; by Longman Singapore Publishers Ltd. for Singapore, Malaysia, Thailand, and Indonesia; by Simron Pty. Ltd. for South Africa; by Toppan Company Ltd. for Japan; by Distribuidora Cuspide for Argentina; by Livraria Cultura for Brazil; by Ediciencia S.A. for Ecuador; by Addison-Wesley Publishing Company for Korea; by Ediciones ZETA S.C.R. Ltda. for Peru; by WS Computer Publishing Corporation, Inc., for the Philippines; by Unalis Corporation for Taiwan; by Contemporanea de Ediciones for Venezuela; by Computer Book & Magazine Store for Puerto Rico; by Express Computer Distributors for the Caribbean and West Indies. Authorized Sales Agent: Anthony Rudkin Associates for the Middle East and North Africa.

For general information on IDG Books Worldwide's books in the U.S., please call our Consumer Customer Service department at 800-762-2974. For reseller information, including discounts and premium sales, please call our Reseller Customer Service department at 800-434-3422.

For information on where to purchase IDG Books Worldwide's books outside the U.S., please contact our International Sales department at 415-655-3200 or fax 415-655-3295.

For information on foreign language translations, please contact our Foreign & Subsidiary Rights department at 415-655-3021 or fax 415-655-3281.

For sales inquiries and special prices for bulk quantities, please contact our Sales department at 415-655-3200 or write to the address above.

For information on using IDG Books Worldwide's books in the classroom or for ordering examination copies, please contact our Educational Sales department at 800-434-2086 or fax 817-251-8174.

For press review copies, author interviews, or other publicity information, please contact our Public Relations department at 415-655-3000 or fax 415-655-3299.

For authorization to photocopy items for corporate, personal, or educational use, please contact Copyright Clearance Center, 222 Rosewood Drive, Danvers, MA 01923, or fax 508-750-4470.

is a trademark under exclusive license to IDG Books Worldwide, Inc., from International Data Group, Inc.

About the Author

Julie Adair King has been wrestling with computers since 1976, when she stood in line with all the other first-year geeks at Purdue University to type programming commands into now-antiquated keypunch machines. Since then, she has churned out documents using almost every type of word processor, spreadsheet, and office utility program to grace the computer-store shelves.

A longtime writer and editor, King has contributed to many computer books published by IDG Books Worldwide, including *CorelDRAW! 7 For Dummies, PerfectOffice 3 For Dummies, PageMaker 6 For Macs For Dummies,* 2nd Edition, and *PageMaker 6 For Windows For Dummies,* 2nd Edition.

When not fiddling around with computers, King writes business and career books and frequently speaks about career issues on radio and television talk shows. Her work has been published in *Cosmopolitan* and other national magazines.

ABOUT IDG BOOKS WORLDWIDE

Welcome to the world of IDG Books Worldwide.

IDG Books Worldwide, Inc., is a subsidiary of International Data Group, the world's largest publisher of computer-related information and the leading global provider of information services on information technology. IDG was founded more than 25 years ago and now employs more than 8,500 people worldwide. IDG publishes more than 275 computer publications in over 75 countries (see listing below). More than 60 million people read one or more IDG publications each month.

Launched in 1990, IDG Books Worldwide is today the #1 publisher of best-selling computer books in the United States. We are proud to have received eight awards from the Computer Press Association in recognition of editorial excellence and three from *Computer Currents'* First Annual Readers' Choice Awards. Our best-selling *...For Dummies®* series has more than 30 million copies in print with translations in 30 languages. IDG Books Worldwide, through a joint venture with IDG's Hi-Tech Beijing, became the first U.S. publisher to publish a computer book in the People's Republic of China. In record time, IDG Books Worldwide has become the first choice for millions of readers around the world who want to learn how to better manage their businesses.

Our mission is simple: Every one of our books is designed to bring extra value and skill-building instructions to the reader. Our books are written by experts who understand and care about our readers. The knowledge base of our editorial staff comes from years of experience in publishing, education, and journalism — experience we use to produce books for the '90s. In short, we care about books, so we attract the best people. We devote special attention to details such as audience, interior design, use of icons, and illustrations. And because we use an efficient process of authoring, editing, and desktop publishing our books electronically, we can spend more time ensuring superior content and spend less time on the technicalities of making books.

You can count on our commitment to deliver high-quality books at competitive prices on topics you want to read about. At IDG Books Worldwide, we continue in the IDG tradition of delivering quality for more than 25 years. You'll find no better book on a subject than one from IDG Books Worldwide.

John Kilcullen
John Kilcullen
CEO
IDG Books Worldwide, Inc.

Steven Berkowitz
Steven Berkowitz
President and Publisher
IDG Books Worldwide, Inc.

Eighth Annual Computer Press Awards ≥1992

Ninth Annual Computer Press Awards ≥1993

Tenth Annual Computer Press Awards ≥1994

Eleventh Annual Computer Press Awards ≥1995

IDG Books Worldwide, Inc., is a subsidiary of International Data Group, the world's largest publisher of computer-related information and the leading global provider of information services on information technology. International Data Group publishes over 275 computer publications in over 75 countries. Sixty million people read one or more International Data Group publications each month. International Data Group's publications include: **ARGENTINA:** Buyer's Guide, Computerworld Argentina, PC World Argentina; **AUSTRALIA:** Australian Macworld, Australian PC World, Australian Reseller News, Computerworld, IT Casebook, Network World, Publish, Webmaster; **AUSTRIA:** Computerwelt Osterreich, Networks Austria, PC Tip Austria; **BANGLADESH:** PC World Bangladesh; **BELARUS:** PC World Belarus; **BELGIUM:** Data News; **BRAZIL:** Annuário de Informática, Computerworld, Connections, Macworld, PC Player, PC World, Publish, Reseller News, Supergamepower; **BULGARIA:** Computerworld Bulgaria, Network World Bulgaria, PC & MacWorld Bulgaria; **CANADA:** CIO Canada, Client/Server World, ComputerWorld Canada, InfoWorld Canada, NetworkWorld Canada, WebWorld; **CHILE:** Computerworld Chile, PC World Chile; **COLOMBIA:** Computerworld Colombia, PC World Colombia; **COSTA RICA:** PC World Centro America; **THE CZECH AND SLOVAK REPUBLICS:** Computerworld Czechoslovakia, Macworld Czech Republic, PC World Czechoslovakia; **DENMARK:** Communications World Danmark, Computerworld Danmark, Macworld Danmark, PC World Danmark, Techworld Denmark; **DOMINICAN REPUBLIC:** PC World Republica Dominicana; **ECUADOR:** PC World Ecuador; **EGYPT:** Computerworld Middle East, PC World Middle East; **EL SALVADOR:** PC World Centro America; **FINLAND:** MikroPC, Tietoverkko, Tietoviikko; **FRANCE:** Distributique, Hebdo, Info PC, Le Monde Informatique, Macworld, Reseaux & Telecoms, WebMaster France; **GERMANY:** Computer Partner, Computerwoche, Computerwoche Extra, Computerwoche FOCUS, Global Online, Macwelt, PC Welt; **GREECE:** Amiga Computing, GamePro Greece, Multimedia World; **GUATEMALA:** PC World Centro America; **HONDURAS:** PC World Centro America; **HONG KONG:** Computerworld Hong Kong, PC World Hong Kong, Publish in Asia; **HUNGARY:** ABCD CD-ROM, Computerworld Szamitastechnika, Internetto online Magazine, PC World Hungary, PC-X Magazin Hungary; **ICELAND:** Tolvuheimur PC World Island; **INDIA:** Information Communications World, Information Systems Computerworld, PC World India, Publish in Asia; **INDONESIA:** InfoKomputer PC World, Komputek Computerworld, Publish in Asia; **IRELAND:** ComputerScope, PC Live!; **ISRAEL:** Macworld Israel, People & Computers/Computerworld; **ITALY:** Computerworld Italia, Macworld Italia, Networking Italia, PC World Italia; **JAPAN:** DTP World, Macworld Japan, Nikkei Personal Computing, OS/2 World Japan, SunWorld Japan, Windows NT World Japan; **KENYA:** PC World East African; **KOREA:** Hi-Tech Information, Macworld Korea, PC World Korea; **MACEDONIA:** PC World Macedonia; **MALAYSIA:** Computerworld Malaysia, PC World Malaysia, Publish in Asia; **MALTA:** PC World Malta; **MEXICO:** Computerworld Mexico, PC World Mexico; **MYANMAR:** PC World Myanmar; **NETHERLANDS:** Computer! Totaal, LAN Internetworking Magazine, LAN World Buyers Guide, Macworld Netherlands, Net, WebWereld; **NEW ZEALAND:** Absolute Beginners Guide and Plain & Simple Series, Computer Buyer, Computer Industry Directory, Computerworld New Zealand, MTB, Network World, PC World New Zealand; **NICARAGUA:** PC World Centro America; **NORWAY:** Computerworld Norge, CW Rapport, Datamagasinet, Financial Rapport, Kursguide Norge, Macworld Norge, Multimediaworld Norge, PC World Ekspress Norge, PC World Nettverk, PC World Norge, PC World ProduktGuide Norge; **PAKISTAN:** Computerworld Pakistan; **PANAMA:** PC World Panama; **PEOPLE'S REPUBLIC OF CHINA:** China Computer Users, China Computerworld, China InfoWorld, China Telecom World Weekly, Computer & Communication, Electronic Design China, Electronics Today, Electronics Weekly, Game Software, PC World China, Popular Computer Week, Software Weekly, Software World, Telecom World; **PERU:** Computerworld Peru, PC World Profesional Peru, PC World SoHo Peru; **PHILIPPINES:** Click!, Computerworld Philippines, PC World Philippines, Publish in Asia; **POLAND:** Computerworld Poland, Computerworld Special Report Poland, Cyber, Macworld Poland, Networld Poland, PC World Komputer; **PORTUGAL:** Cerebro/PC World, Computerworld/Correio Informático, Dealer World Portugal, Mac*In/PC*In Portugal, Multimedia World; **PUERTO RICO:** PC World Puerto Rico; **ROMANIA:** Computerworld Romania, PC World Romania, Telecom Romania; **RUSSIA:** Computerworld Russia, Mir PK, Publish, Seti; **SINGAPORE:** Computerworld Singapore, PC World Singapore, Publish in Asia; **SLOVENIA:** Monitor; **SOUTH AFRICA:** Computing SA, Network World SA, Software World SA; **SPAIN:** Communicaciones World España, Computerworld España, Dealer World España, Macworld España, PC World España; **SRI LANKA:** Infolink PC World; **SWEDEN:** CAP&Design, Computer Sweden, Corporate Computing Sweden, Internetworld Sweden, it.branschen, Macworld Sweden, MaxiData Sweden, MikroDatorn, Nätverk & Kommunikation, PC World Sweden, PCaktiv, Windows World Sweden; **SWITZERLAND:** Computerworld Schweiz, Macworld Schweiz, PCtip; **TAIWAN:** Computerworld Taiwan, Macworld Taiwan, NEW ViSiON/Publish, PC World Taiwan, Windows World Taiwan; **THAILAND:** Publish in Asia, Thai Computerworld; **TURKEY:** Computerworld Turkiye, Macworld Turkiye, Network World Turkiye, PC World Turkiye; **UKRAINE:** Computerworld Kiev, Multimedia World Ukraine, PC World Ukraine; **UNITED KINGDOM:** Acorn User UK, Amiga Action UK, Amiga Computing UK, Apple Talk UK, Computing, Macworld, Parents and Computers UK, PC Advisor, PC Home, PSX Pro, The WEB; **UNITED STATES:** Cable in the Classroom, CIO Magazine, Computerworld, DOS World, Federal Computer Week, GamePro Magazine, InfoWorld, I-Way, Macworld, Network World, PC Games, PC World, Publish, Video Event, THE WEB Magazine, and WebMaster; online webzines: JavaWorld, NetscapeWorld, and SunWorld Online; **URUGUAY:** InfoWorld Uruguay; **VENEZUELA:** Computerworld Venezuela, PC World Venezuela; and **VIETNAM:** PC World Vietnam.   3/24/97

Dedication

This book is dedicated to my grandparents, George and Irene Harris, Mae King, and the late Cecil King. Thank you for a lifetime of love.

Author's Acknowledgments

Thanks to project editor Robert Wallace for making sure that everything happened when it should, how it should, in the best and most painless way possible. Thanks also to technical editor Lee Musick, who did his usual stellar job in steering me away from embarrassing technical faux pas, and to copy editors Bill Barton and Gwenette Gaddis for helping me avoid editorial missteps. I also want to acknowledge all the people in the IDG Books production department who work so hard to turn raw words and pictures into polished pages.

Last, but absolutely not least, special thanks to associate publisher Diane Graves Steele, who it has been my privilege to know these past several years. Your encouragement and support have meant more than you will ever guess.

Publisher's Acknowledgments

We're proud of this book; please send us your comments about it by using the IDG Books Worldwide Registration Card at the back of the book or by e-mailing us at feedback/dummies@idgbooks.com. Some of the people who helped bring this book to market include the following:

Acquisitions, Development, and Editorial

Project Editor: Robert H. Wallace

Acquisitions Editor: Michael Kelly

Product Development Director: Mary Bednarek

Copy Editors: William A. Barton, Gwenette Gaddis

Technical Editor: Lee Musick

Editorial Manager: Leah P. Cameron

Editorial Assistant: Donna Love

Production

Project Coordinator: E. Shawn Aylsworth

Layout and Graphics: Lou Boudreau, Angela F. Hunckler, Todd Klemme, Drew R. Moore, Mark C. Owens, Brent Savage

Proofreaders: Renee Kelty, Christine D. Berman, Robert Springer

Indexer: Richard Shrout

Special Help: Michael Bolinger, Copy Editor

General and Administrative

IDG Books Worldwide, Inc.: John Kilcullen, CEO; Steven Berkowitz, President and Publisher

IDG Books Technology Publishing: Brenda McLaughlin, Senior Vice President and Group Publisher

Dummies Technology Press and Dummies Editorial: Diane Graves Steele, Vice President and Associate Publisher; Judith A. Taylor, Product Marketing Manager; Kristin A. Cocks, Editorial Director

Dummies Trade Press: Kathleen A. Welton, Vice President and Publisher

IDG Books Production for Dummies Press: Beth Jenkins, Production Director; Cindy L. Phipps, Supervisor of Project Coordination, Production Proofreading, and Indexing; Kathie S. Schutte, Supervisor of Page Layout; Shelley Lea, Supervisor of Graphics and Design; Debbie J. Gates, Production Systems Specialist; Tony Augsburger, Supervisor of Reprints and Bluelines; Leslie Popplewell, Media Archive Coordinator

Dummies Packaging and Book Design: Patti Sandez, Packaging Specialist; Lance Kayser, Packaging Assistant; Kavish + Kavish, Cover Design

◆

The publisher would like to give special thanks to Patrick J. McGovern, without whom this book would not have been possible.

◆

Contents at a Glance

Cartoons at a Glance

By Rich Tennant

The 5th Wave — By Rich Tennant

"...AND, AS WE ALL KNOW, SAVE FOR ONE PERSON, SERIOUS DEPARTMENTAL INTEGRATION FOR SUITE SOFTWARE DEVELOPMENT IS PRACTICALLY COMPLETE."

page 7

The 5th Wave — By Rich Tennant

"THE FUNNY THING IS, I NEVER KNEW THEY HAD DESKTOP PUBLISHING SOFTWARE FOR PAPER SHREDDERS."

page 229

The 5th Wave — By Rich Tennant

"I SUPPOSE THIS ALL HAS SOMETHING TO DO WITH THE NEW MATH."

page 141

The 5th Wave — By Rich Tennant

TYPE? NAW, I JUST SORT OF HUNT AND PECK...

page 39

The 5th Wave — By Rich Tennant

NERD MOMS

Okay young man, it's time to wash your hands, brush your teeth, and defrag your hard disk.

Awwww, Mom.

page 317

Fax: 508-546-7747 • E-mail: the5wave@tiac.net

Table of Contents

. . . .

Introduction

• •

*W*hoever said "ignorance is bliss" obviously never had to use a computer. Although it's true that you're better off not knowing some things — for example, exactly *what* you just stepped in — not knowing how to use a computer program can make you decidedly unblissful, especially if someone expects you to actually do some work using that program. Even if you're lucky enough to figure out how to accomplish a certain task without any instruction — which is doubtful, given that most programs are about as self-explanatory as macroeconomics — you most certainly won't be able to do the job quickly, or well, or without a heaping dose of hair-pulling, teeth-gnashing frustration.

The problem is, working your way through the instruction manuals provided by software manufacturers takes time — more time than you've got. On top of that, software manuals are notoriously dull and obtuse. A few minutes with a typical manual not only strips you of any excitement you felt about getting a new program but also leaves you more confused than you were before.

So how do you solve this dilemma — especially now that you bought WordPerfect Suite 8, which gives you not one, but five major programs to conquer? Wait a minute . . . I think I hear . . . yes, that's definitely the sound of hoofbeats and bugles in the distance. The cavalry, in the form of *WordPerfect Suite 8 For Dummies,* has arrived to rescue you from imminent disaster. (Well, actually, you've been holding the cavalry in your hands all this time, but I didn't want to mention it earlier and spoil the dramatic build-up. Also, I was afraid you were allergic to horses.)

Okay, So What Will This Book Do for Me?

In short, this book will get you up and running with all the major programs in WordPerfect Suite 8 in the fastest and most enjoyable way possible. You don't have to wade through pages of technobabble to find out how to do something. You don't have to waste your time reading about features you'll never use in a million years. Instead, you get quick, easy-to-understand how-to's for tackling those tasks you need to do every day, whether you're using your computer at work, at home, or both.

Thanks to the philosophy of the *...For Dummies* series, you'll also have a pretty good time getting acquainted with your new software. As you probably already guessed, this series is based on the notion that you can give people the information they need and have a little fun in the process. If it's against your principles to laugh while you work, you can feel free to ignore the cartoons and other lighthearted touches throughout this book, though.

What Programs Does This Book Cover?

Like Version 7, Version 8 of the WordPerfect Suite comes in two flavors: a standard and professional version. The standard version of the Suite includes WordPerfect, Quattro Pro, Presentations, Netscape Navigator, Photo House, and several small utilities, including the Envoy Viewer. The professional version offers those programs plus a database program called Paradox and some additional tools for using the Suite in a large office network. Both versions run on Windows 95 or Windows NT 4.0 only.

This book covers the standard version of the Suite, providing information about all the major programs in the Suite. Of course, you can also use this book if you bought the professional version of the Suite, although you don't find coverage of Paradox here.

How Is Stuff Organized?

...For Dummies books are organized differently from other books in that they're not meant to be read cover to cover, starting with Chapter 1 and continuing in sequence through the last chapter. You can read the book in that fashion, of course, and it will make perfect sense to you. But the book is also designed to work like a reference book. When you encounter a situation that stumps you (or simply interests you), look it up in the Table of Contents or Index and flip to the section that contains information on that subject. You don't have to read the entire chapter to understand what's going on; you can find out what you need to know to tackle the problem at hand quickly and without any messy cleanup.

WordPerfect Suite 8 For Dummies is organized into several parts, with each part focusing on a different aspect of using the Suite. The following paragraphs give you a little preview of what's to come.

Part I: The Suite Life

Here's where you shake hands with your new programs and find out what each intends to do to justify its existence in your computer. You also discover how to do some basic things like move around inside programs, use your mouse and keyboard to make the programs actually do something, and get on-screen assistance from the Help system. (Mind you, with this book at your side, you may never need to look up information in the Help system. But the WordPerfect Suite Help system has some tools that actually complete certain computing chores for you — which makes the Help system definitely worth checking out.)

Part II: Goodbye, Typewriter . . . Hello, WordPerfect!

This part explains everything you need to know to create letters, memos, reports, and other documents using WordPerfect 8. You find out how to enter and edit text, change the type size and style, add graphics to your documents, check your spelling, and do all sorts of other things to produce professional-looking pages. Reading this section causes you to lose all respect for your typewriter.

Part III: Crunching Numbers Like a (Quattro) Pro

Part III gives you the lowdown on using Quattro Pro to create budgets, track sales and inventories, and do other number-crunching tasks. You also find out how to create and edit simple tables of information, such as a list of your favorite sports teams, their win/loss records, and the amount you lost betting that they could beat the other guys. And, to help you put your numbers in perspective, you discover how to turn data into colorful charts.

Part IV: Those Other Programs

I probably should have rethought the title for this part, because it sounds as though the programs covered in this section aren't worth much attention — which is anything but the case. Part IV explains how to use Presentations 8, a powerful tool for creating multimedia slide shows; Netscape Navigator, the leading tool for browsing the World Wide Web; and Photo House, a program that enables you to edit scanned photographs and other digital images.

Part IV also explains how to use all the programs in the Suite together to get things done more efficiently. You find out how to create text or graphics in one program and then make copies that you can use in other documents, for example. You even discover how to create copies that automatically get updated when the original data changes.

Come to think of it, a better name for this part may be "Don't Miss This Part — Important Stuff Here!"

Part V: The Part of Tens

In this part, you find three top-ten lists of tricks, tips, and techniques. One list describes ten cool features that are fun to try when you have some time to kill. Another lists ten shortcuts that you can use in any of the Suite programs to save yourself a little time and energy. And the third offers still more ways to get more done in less time, which is what owning a computer is all about, after all.

Appendix: Installing WordPerfect Suite 8

Okay, I'll admit that this part, which walks you through the steps of installing WordPerfect Suite 8, isn't exciting or entertaining. But seeing as how you can't use any programs in the Suite until you install them — except as tax write-offs, maybe — this part does contain information you really ought to read.

That Symbol Means Something, Doesn't It?

Scattered throughout the margins in this book are little symbols — known as *icons* in the computer universe. The icons flag information that's especially important, interesting, or just plain useful.

A Tip icon alerts you to a secret, easy way of doing something. Well, maybe not secret, exactly, but something that you may not discover on your own.

The Remember icon marks information that you need to tuck away in a corner of your brain for future reference. Trust me, this stuff will come in handy one day.

 When you see this icon, you're about to read information that may save you a big headache. Warning icons point out things you need to do to make sure that your day doesn't go horribly awry.

 If you're upgrading to WordPerfect Suite 8 from an earlier version of the package, look for this icon, which indicates information about things that are new or work differently in this version.

 This icon highlights technical or background information that you may or may not want to read. If you do take the plunge, you'll be better equipped to hold your own in discussions with computer geeks.

Other Conventions Used in This Book

As you can see if you flip through the pages in this book, many words have a particular letter that's underlined. As I explain in Chapter 2, the underlined letters represent keyboard shortcuts for commands. You can press the Alt key in combination with the underlined letter to choose a command quickly.

When you see two words joined by a little arrow, you're looking at commands that you're to choose in sequence. For example, if I tell you to choose File➪Print, you click the File menu and then click the Print command in the menu. Or, now that you're hip to keyboard shortcuts, you can also press Alt plus F and then press P.

 The small button icons — like the one attached to this paragraph — tell you of yet another way to choose a command. These icons represent buttons and tools available on the program's toolbar, Property Bar, or some other on-screen location. You click the button to access the command. To send a document to the printer, for example, you click the Print button shown in the margin here.

By the way, Chapter 2 covers all this stuff (plus other tips for choosing commands quickly) in more detail.

What Now?

That's entirely up to you. Turn the page and begin reading Chapter 1, or pick out a topic in the Index or Table of Contents that strikes your fancy and start there instead. But either way, do commit yourself to reading *something,* even if it's just a few paragraphs a day. I promise that you can acquire the skills you need to be successful with WordPerfect Suite 8 in no time — and it won't even hurt.

Remember, ignorance may be bliss in some areas of life, but when it comes to computers, knowledge is power.

Part I
The Suite Life

The 5th Wave   By Rich Tennant

"...AND, AS WE ALL KNOW, SAVE FOR ONE PERSON, SERIOUS DEPARTMENTAL INTEGRATION FOR SUITE SOFTWARE DEVELOPMENT IS PRACTICALLY COMPLETE."

In this part . . .

1 f computing were an athletic event — as it sometimes is — installing WordPerfect Suite 8 would be like stuffing Michael Jordan, Monica Seles, Tiger Woods, and stars from several other sports into your computer. Like these athletic greats, each of the programs in the Suite excels in a particular area.

The superstars in WordPerfect Suite 8, though, all play by the same basic set of rules so that you can easily figure out how things work. The Suite programs also know how to play together nicely, so you can get more done in less time. On top of that, they won't hold you up for millions of dollars every time their contracts expire.

This part of the book introduces you to your new team members and explains which player you use in which situations. It also covers the features that work the same way throughout the Suite and explains how to get a program to cough up inside information when you run into trouble.

In sporting terms, this part is like spring training camp for your mind: Time spent here helps you avoid brain cramps down the road.

Chapter 1

Browsing through the Big Box

● ●

In This Chapter

▶ Taking a look at what you bought

▶ Figuring out which program to use when

▶ Putting the suite concept to work for you

▶ What's new in Version 8

▶ Using all your programs together

● ●

*W*hen I got my first apartment after leaving college, I went to the hardware store and bought one screwdriver, one hammer, and one wrench. Not having had much exposure to tools when I was growing up, I thought that I could handle whatever household projects arose with those three tools.

For years, I struggled to make those three tools work in any situation, which, of course, resulted in lots of frustration. And then one day, confronted by a bolt I couldn't budge with any combination of screwdriver, hammer, and wrench, I splurged and bought a ratchet set. What a revelation! Suddenly, I had the power to overcome any bolt. I was so excited that I went around the house loosening and tightening everything I could find, thrilling to the little click-click-click sound of my new ratchet.

Lest you think that you've wandered into *Hardware For Dummies* by mistake, let me interrupt this little trip down handyman lane and explain its relevance to the topic at hand: using Corel WordPerfect Suite 8. You see, that big, colorful Corel software package is like a well-equipped toolbox. It contains powerful tools to handle just about every computing chore. But as it is with hammers, wrenches, screwdrivers, and ratchets, the key to success is using the right tool for the job.

This chapter explains which of the many programs in the WordPerfect Suite you should use to accomplish various tasks. It also explains how the programs are all designed to work similarly — and work together — so that you can use several tools in tandem to complete one project.

What Do All These Programs Do?

Packing an enormous bang for the buck, WordPerfect Suite 8 includes programs to handle just about every computing chore you can dream up. Carrying the toolbox analogy further — and some may say a step too far — it's as if someone gave you a Sears credit card, headed you toward the Craftsman tools aisle, and told you to go nuts. (Pardon the pun — *nuts,* get it?)

If you're upgrading from Version 7, you're in for a bit of a jolt when you peer inside the Version 8 box. Many of the programs included with Version 7 are gone, replaced by alternative programs. CorelFLOW, a flowcharting program, is out, for example, as are Sidekick, a personal organizer, and Dashboard, a Windows 95 control utility. Don't think of this turn of events as a loss, though — if you're really in love with those programs, you can keep using them. And you get all the new programs provided with Version 8 as well. See, life isn't as bad as you thought, is it?

Users who upgrade from Version 7 should also be impressed with the new look and feel of the Suite. The major programs — WordPerfect, Quattro Pro, and Presentations — run much more smoothly and feature more convenient, more user-friendly tools and commands than Version 7.

The following list provides an introduction to the major programs in the Version 8 Suite. Note that I reserved the Version 8 icon for programs that weren't part of the suite in its previous incarnation. The other programs are essentially new, too, however, as they're upgrades of the versions found in Suite 7.

- ✔ WordPerfect 8 is the latest incarnation of a very popular and powerful word processor. In WordPerfect, you can create any kind of text document, from a simple letter to an annual report. You can add graphics to your documents, use fancy fonts, put text into columns, and do a whole lot of other stuff that your typewriter only dreams about. Figure 1-1 shows an example of the type of document you can create in WordPerfect. Chapters 4 through 9 explain WordPerfect's many features and commands.

- ✔ Quattro Pro 8, the subject of Chapters 10 through 15, is a leading spreadsheet program. With a spreadsheet program, you can handle accounting tasks from creating a budget to tracking product inventories. Quattro Pro can also crunch any numbers you throw at it, whether you want to calculate your company's annual net profits, perform cost and price analyses, or figure out whether you can save money by refinancing a loan.

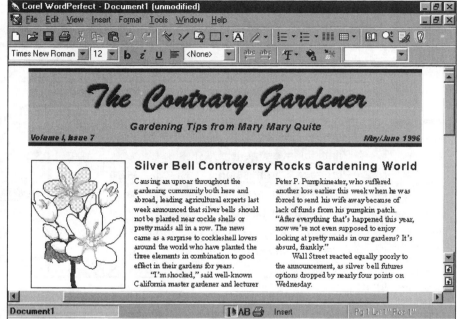

Figure 1-1:
In
WordPerfect,
you can
create
sophis-
ticated,
professional-
looking
documents
such as
this.

Figure 1-2 shows a spreadsheet that I created to calculate the potential profits for stocks bought and sold at various prices. When I see a stock that I'm interested in buying, I plug in the stock price and the estimated sell price, and Quattro Pro calculates the payoff.

✔ Presentations 8 enables you to create multimedia presentations complete with graphics, sound clips, and animation. Presentations also offers a nice selection of tools that you can use to draw and edit graphics and create organizational charts. Chapter 16 is devoted to Presentations.

✔ Envoy 7 is a nifty little program that lets a group of people view and annotate (add notes to) each other's documents, regardless of what programs they have installed on their computers. For example, if you create a WordPerfect document, you can "publish" it as an Envoy document that your colleagues can view even if they don't own WordPerfect or Envoy.

Unfortunately, you don't get the full Envoy program in the Version 8 Suite, as you did in Version 7. Version 8 includes the Envoy Viewer only. You can open and annotate Envoy documents, but you can't create your own Envoy documents as you could in Version 7. The Envoy Viewer now exists primarily to enable you to view the online user manuals provided in the WordPerfect Suite, as explained at the end of Chapter 3. (So, if you installed the version of Envoy that came with WordPerfect Suite 7, don't install this version.)

Corel Quattro Pro - C:\MyFiles\invest.wb3 (unmodified)

File   Edit   View   Insert   Format   Tools   Window   Help

Arial ▼ 10 ▼ **b** *i* <u>U</u> Normal ▼

A:E15

	A	B	C	D	E	F
1						
2	Stock Price	$50.00	$50.00	$50.00	$50.00	
3	Number Shares	25	25	25	25	
4	Principal Investment	$1,250.00	$1,250.00	$1,250.00	$1,250.00	
5	Purchase Commission	$51.50	$51.50	$51.50	$51.50	
6	Total Investment	$1,301.50	$1,301.50	$1,301.50	$1,301.50	
7	Sell Price Per Share	$65.00	$70.00	$75.00	$80.00	
8	Gross Profit	$1,625.00	$1,750.00	$1,875.00	$2,000.00	
9	Sale Commission	$55.25	$56.50	$57.75	$59.00	
10	Net Profit	$288.25	$392.00	$515.75	$639.50	
11						

‹‹ ‹ › ›› ›┃ \ A \ B \ C \ D \ E \ F \ G \ H \ I \ J \ K ┃ ◀

invest.wb3   READY

Figure 1-2:
When you have a complex math problem to solve, don't count on your fingers — use Quattro Pro instead.

✔ Corel Photo House is a basic image-editing program. You can open scanned photographs or images from a Photo CD and tweak the contrast, adjust the color balance, and crop unwanted elements out of the scene. Photo House isn't nearly as capable as programs such as Corel Photo-Paint or Adobe Photoshop, but if your image-editing needs are simple, you may find that the program has all the features you want. You can read all about Photo House in Chapter 18.

✔ Netscape Navigator Version 3, a leading program for browsing the World Wide Web, is also included. Not much is new here in the way of features — as witnessed by the lack of Version 8 icons in Chapter 17, which discusses Netscape. But the program's behind-the-scenes workings have been improved to avoid glitches that sometimes occurred with earlier versions.

✔ Version 8 also ships with a mail-in card enabling you to get a free copy of CorelCentral (well, okay, you pay for shipping and handling). CorelCentral is a personal information manager — that is, it provides tools for tracking your schedule, creating and maintaining a log of your business and personal contacts, and generally organizing all the bits and pieces of your overly complicated life. Included with CorelCentral is Netscape Communicator, which is Netscape Navigator on steroids. Communicator includes the Navigator browser plus tools for creating Web pages and getting Internet information delivered automatically to your e-mail inbox.

At press time, CorelCentral wasn't quite out of the starting gate yet. But as soon as this bonus application becomes available to you, I'll be writing a corresponding bonus chapter to show you how to use the program. The folks at IDG Books Worldwide, Inc., have generously agreed to make the chapter available to you at no charge by posting it on the World Wide Web, at www.dummies.com. You can read the chapter online, save it to your hard drive, or print it for later reference. (See Chapter 17 if you're an Internet novice and need help with any of this.)

✔ In addition to all these goodies, the WordPerfect Suite comes with tons of clip art, a nice selection of fonts, and a number of small utilities, including a font management program and a program that enables you to write *scripts,* which you use to automate certain tasks. I don't cover these utilities in this book because I think the available page space is better dedicated to programs you're likely to use on a more frequent basis.

Which Program Do I Use When?

Each program in the WordPerfect Suite specializes in handling certain tasks. But several programs enable you to handle jobs that are unrelated to the program's main function, too. Quattro Pro, for example, is primarily designed for creating spreadsheets, but it also has commands that let you use your spreadsheet data to create a slide show. It's like having a hammer that has a Swiss Army Knife attached to the handle. (Okay, okay, I'll give up on the hardware analogy now. But it was really fun while it lasted, wasn't it?)

Just because you *can* do a task in a certain program, however, doesn't mean that you *should.* Yes, you may be able to create a slide show in Quattro Pro, but you get better results if you use the tool specifically designed for creating slide shows, Presentations.

The following list offers some suggestions to help you decide which program is most appropriate for the challenge at hand. Keep in mind that you don't have to use just one program to create a document, though. As explained in the next section (as well as in Chapter 19), the programs in the WordPerfect Suite are designed so that you can use them all together to handle a single project.

✔ WordPerfect is the best choice for creating text-based documents, from letters to memos to reports. You can also use WordPerfect to create documents that contain clip art, such as advertising flyers or simple brochures.

✔ Use Quattro Pro for accounting projects such as creating budgets, recording sales, tracking inventories, and doing anything else that involves calculating data.

✔ Also use Quattro Pro for creating tables of data, such as an employee list showing each worker's name, phone number, address, department, and so on. You can create similar tables in WordPerfect, but Quattro Pro makes the job easier.

✔ To create a data chart — for example, a chart that shows your company's annual sales by region — use Quattro Pro. To create organizational charts, use Presentations.

✔ To create slide shows — whether for display on a computer or a regular projector — use Presentations.

✔ If you're feeling artistic and want to create some simple graphics to enliven your documents or slide shows, use Presentations.

✔ Want to edit a scanned photograph or image from a Photo CD? Head for Photo House. You can crop away unwanted portions of the image, touch up the image, and adjust things like color balance and contrast. Presentations also offers some image-editing tools, but Photo House has more.

✔ To create text-based graphics — for example, a company logo that presents the company name in a stylized design — use TextArt, which you can access in Presentations or WordPerfect. See Chapter 20 for a look at TextArt in action; see Chapter 16 for information on some other text effects you can create in Presentations.

Hey! These All Look Alike!

If you have a sharp eye, you'll notice right away that most programs in the WordPerfect Suite have a similar look. (Okay, so the truth is you have to be darned near asleep not to notice this fact, but I wanted to boost your self-confidence in case you were getting intimidated by all this highly technical computer talk.)

Many of the buttons, tools, and menu commands are the same from program to program. Which means that after you know what a particular button or command does in one program, you can apply that knowledge in all the other programs. You don't have to memorize a different set of buttons and commands for each individual program. (Chapter 2 covers the basic elements found in WordPerfect Suite programs, by the way.)

The beauty of the WordPerfect Suite is more than skin-deep, however. As discussed in Chapter 19, the programs are designed to interact with each other so that you can use several different programs to handle one computing project. For example, if you need to create a report that includes text, graphics, and a spreadsheet, you can create the text in WordPerfect, the graphics in Presentations or Photo House, and the spreadsheet in Quattro Pro, and then combine the different elements together into one finished product.

In many cases, you can launch another program in the Suite from within the program you're currently using. You can start up Netscape Navigator and log on to the Internet by clicking a button in Quattro Pro, for example. And you can choose a command in WordPerfect to launch Presentations so that you can create a drawing to insert into your WordPerfect document.

The cooperative nature of your WordPerfect Suite programs gives you an important computing advantage. Not only can you get up and running with all the programs quickly, but you also can use their combined strengths to get your work done in less time and with less effort. In fact, I could say that the WordPerfect Suite is a little like one of those new, many-tools-in-one power tools that are all the rage in hardware stores these days. But I swore off hardware analogies earlier in this chapter, so I won't.

Chapter 2

Basic Stuff You Need to Know

• •

In This Chapter

▶ Powering up your programs

▶ Getting acquainted with windows

▶ Using the mouse and keyboard to make things happen

▶ Figuring out which buttons do what

▶ Choosing commands from menus and dialog boxes

▶ Moving around the screen

▶ Customizing your screen

• •

*L*ife sure was simpler before computers, wasn't it? You didn't need to endure mind-numbing conversations about such things as operating systems and Internet Service Providers. You didn't need to spend oodles of cash on the latest computer gadget to keep up with the Joneses. And you didn't need to waste precious brain cells mastering the meaning of such cryptic phrases as "logging on to the network server" or "downloading a printer driver."

Well, like the situation or not, computers are here to stay. So you may as well pick up a few tricks to help you communicate with that big, glowing box on your desk — not to mention with the kids in your life. This chapter covers the basics of Corel WordPerfect Suite 8, from starting up a program to customizing your screen display.

If acquiring this information seems like a daunting (and boring) chore, take heart. First, I promise to keep it simple — telling you just what you need to know and nothing more. Second, mastering these basics not only puts you on friendlier terms with your computer but also enables you to join the legions of folks who've discovered how to use the computer as an excuse for goofing off. Pretty soon, you, too, can sound believable as you stare earnestly at your boss and say, "Sorry, I can't complete that project for you today because the network server is down and I can't download the right printer driver."

Almost everything I cover in this chapter applies to most Windows 95 programs, not only to programs in the WordPerfect Suite.

Starting Up and Shutting Down

Firing up a program in the WordPerfect Suite is a cinch. Here's the routine to follow:

1. Click the Windows 95 Start button to display the Start menu.

2. Click the Corel WordPerfect Suite 8 item in the Start menu.

3. Click the name of the program you want to start.

You can also start some programs by using the DAD icons, as explained in the section "Using DAD," later in this chapter.

Shutting down a program is just as easy as starting one. Simply click the Close button — that little square button marked with an *X* in the upper-right corner of the program window. If you haven't saved your work, the program prompts you to do so.

You can also shut down a program by choosing File⇨Exit from the menu bar or by pressing the Alt key together with the F4 key (Alt+F4). But these methods require two clicks or key presses rather than one. Who needs all that extra work?

Mastering the Mouse

If the mouse is a new entity in your world, here are some terms you need to know. (Keep in mind that this information applies to a traditional mouse. If you're using a trackball, touchpad device, or some other tool for sending signals to your computer, check its manual for instructions on how to do this stuff.)

✔ The *mouse cursor* is that little thing that moves around the screen when you move your mouse. Cursors take on different shapes and sizes depending on what program you're using and what you're trying to do.

✔ To *click* means to press and release a mouse button. If I tell you to *click* something, move your mouse so that the cursor is pointing to that something and then click the mouse button. To *double-click* is to press and release the mouse button twice very quickly.

✔ Usually, the left mouse button is the *primary button* — the one you use to accomplish most tasks. With some brands of mice, however you can switch the buttons around so that the right button is the primary button. In this book, whenever I say to click or double-click, I mean that you're to push the primary mouse button. If you need to click the secondary mouse button, I tell you to *right-click*. If you switch your mouse buttons, remember that, if I tell you to right-click, you actually left-click — and vice versa.

Right-clicking your way to fame and fortune

Although the left mouse button is the primary clicker, the right mouse button can be extremely useful, too. Right-clicking something on-screen usually displays a menu of commands or options related to that item. Some programs call these menus *context-sensitive menus;* Corel WordPerfect Suite 8 calls them *QuickMenus.* To discover what QuickMenus are available to you, just right-click your way around the screen.

> ✔ To *drag* is to move the mouse while you hold down the primary mouse button. Dragging is a handy way to move words and objects around. After you have the item where you want it, you release the mouse button to complete the drag. Releasing the mouse button is called *dropping*. The entire operation is known as *drag and drop*.

Saving Time with Keyboard Shortcuts

Sometimes, using the mouse can be cumbersome. Luckily, you have another option. You can perform most common computing tasks without ever taking your hands off the keyboard, as described in the following list:

> ✔ To open one of the menus at the top of a program window, press Alt plus the menu's *hot key* — the letter that's underlined in the menu name. Then, to choose a command from the menu, press the command's hot key. You can also use Alt+hot key combos to select options in dialog boxes. (I explain dialog boxes in the section "Digging through Dialog Boxes," later in this chapter.)

> ✔ *Keyboard shortcuts* enable you to choose a command by pressing one or two keys in combination. To open a document in WordPerfect, for example, you press Ctrl+O — in other words, press the Ctrl key along with the O key.

Shortcuts that are available in a particular program usually appear next to the command names in the menus. In Suite 8, some programs enable you to specify whether you want the shortcuts to appear on menus. For how-to's, see the section "Customizing Your View," later in this chapter.

In most programs, you can determine the shortcut for a command by pausing your cursor over the command name. If you have the QuickTips option turned on (also explained in the "Customizing Your View" section), a little box pops up to provide information about the command and show the keyboard shortcut, if one exists.

Doing Windows

Figure 2-1 shows the window you see after you first start WordPerfect. (Your screen may look slightly different than mine, depending on the default settings on your system, but the essentials are the same.) This window works much like every other window you encounter in the Suite — or in any Windows 95 program, for that matter. Here's a rundown of the basic parts of this window:

  ✔ The *title bar* tells you which program you're using. (The title bar is a great reference for the absent-minded.) If you have more than one program open, the title bar of the active program is highlighted, while title bars on inactive programs appear dimmed.

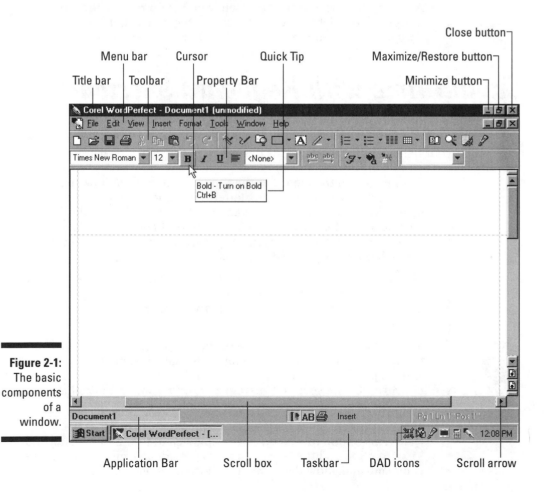

Figure 2-1: The basic components of a window.

Close button

Maximize/Restore button

Minimize button

Menu bar   Cursor   Quick Tip

Title bar   Toolbar   Property Bar

Application Bar   Scroll box   Taskbar   DAD icons   Scroll arrow

✔ The *menu bar* is simply a row of menus, each of which contains a list of commands. To display the contents of a menu, click its name in the menu bar or press Alt plus the hot key (the underlined letter in the menu name).

If you choose a command that's followed by a little arrowhead, a submenu of related options appears. Three dots trailing a command name indicate that choosing that command opens a dialog box. For clues on how to converse with a dialog box, see the section "Digging through Dialog Boxes," later in this chapter.

Whenever you see two commands joined by an arrow in this book, choose the commands in sequence. Format⇨Line⇨Spacing, for example, means to click the Format menu, choose the Line command in that menu, and then choose the Spacing command in the Line submenu.

If a command is *dimmed,* or *grayed out,* it's not available, either because it's not pertinent to the task you're trying to accomplish or because your system doesn't support the command.

✔ The *toolbar* is a strip of buttons that you can click to choose certain commands quickly and efficiently. In Suite 8, the buttons appear flat if they're inactive. After you pass your cursor over a button, it "pops up," and you can click it.

✔ The *Property Bar* is a revamped version of the old Power Bar found in some WordPerfect Suite 7 programs. Like the toolbar, the Property Bar contains buttons that provide quick access to popular commands and options. But Property Bar buttons change depending on what you're doing at the moment. If you're working with text, for example, the Property Bar contains buttons for formatting text. If you're creating a graphic, the Property Bar offers buttons for modifying graphics. (Notice that the Property Bar is not available in all the Suite programs.)

✔ Property Bar and toolbar buttons that include both an icon and a down-pointing arrowhead have two functions. If you click the arrowhead, you display a drop-down list of options. Click an option to select it. The icon for that option then appears on the button face to the left of the arrowhead. If you want to select the same option again, you can simply click the icon — you don't have to select the option from the drop-down list.

✔ Also new to some Version 8 programs is the *Application Bar*. If you're familiar with other Windows programs, you no doubt notice that the Application Bar bears a strong resemblance to the feature usually known as a *status bar*. But the Application Bar offers a convenient twist: It displays a button for each open document in the program. You can switch back and forth among open documents by clicking the buttons. (You can also switch to a different document by choosing its name from the Window menu or clicking anywhere in the document's window.)

The Application Bar also contains icons and information about the active document. Sometimes, clicking, double-clicking, or right-clicking an item in the Application Bar enables you to perform actions or commands.

✔ Lurking beneath the Application Bar is the Windows 95 *taskbar*. Click the program buttons on the taskbar to switch from one running program to another. (You can also switch to a different program by clicking the program window.) On the right end of the taskbar is the *Desktop Application Director* (*DAD*), explained in the section "Using DAD," later in this chapter.

✔ Click the up- and down-pointing *scroll arrows* in the *scroll bar* on the right side of the window to move the screen display up or down so that you can see a different part of your document. Click the scroll arrows at the bottom of the window to move left or right. Drag the *scroll box* to scroll in bigger increments.

✔ In the top-right corner of the window are the Minimize button, the Maximize/Restore button, and the Close button. If you have a document open, you get two sets of buttons. The top set controls the program window; the bottom set affects the document window. These controls are covered in the following section, "Resizing, Moving, and Closing Windows."

✔ Remembering what all the different elements on your screen do or mean isn't always easy. Luckily, you can find out with a quick move of your mouse. Just place the mouse cursor over a button or item, and a little flag — called a *QuickTip* — unfurls to give you helpful information.

Resizing, Moving, and Closing Windows

Windows 95 is nothing if not flexible. You can shrink, enlarge, reshape, and rearrange your windows until you get them just the way you like them. The keys to this heady power are the Minimize, Maximize/Restore, and Close buttons, labeled earlier in Figure 2-1. Here's how they work, moving from right to left:

 ✔ Click the Close button to close the window and the document or program that the window contains.

 ✔ The appearance and purpose of the Maximize/Restore button alternates depending on the current status of the window. If the button face shows a single box, it's the Maximize button. Clicking this button enlarges the window so that it eats up your entire screen. If the button shows two stacked boxes, it's the Restore button. Clicking this button restores the window to its former size.

✔ Click the Minimize button to hide the window temporarily. After you minimize a program window, a program button appears on the Windows 95 taskbar; click this button to make the window reappear. After you minimize a document window, it shrinks to a tiny bar at the bottom of the program window. This bar offers both a Maximize and a Restore button; click either one to redisplay the window.

You can resize a window by placing the cursor over an edge of a window. After the cursor becomes a two-headed arrow, drag the window to whatever size you deem appropriate. To move a window, drag its title bar.

Customizing Your View

Resizing and reshaping your windows isn't the only way to customize your view of the computer world. You can also change the way that certain other screen elements appear. The following techniques apply to the major Suite programs (WordPerfect, Quattro Pro, and Presentations):

 ✔ Choose Tools⇨Settings to access a dialog box full of options for customizing your screen display. (In earlier versions, you accessed these commands by choosing Edit⇨Preferences.) You can also right-click various screen elements to display QuickMenus that contain customization options.

✔ Choose View⇨Hide Bars or press Alt+Shift+F5 to hide everything but your document itself. To return to normal view, press Esc or press Alt+Shift+F5 again.

✔ You can also hide or display just the toolbar or Property Bar. The commands vary from program to program, but you typically choose the Toolbars command from the View menu, choose the Settings command from the Tools menu, or right-click the bar you want to hide and then choose the Hide command from the QuickMenu that appears.

✔ Many programs offer more than one toolbar; you can choose which ones appear on-screen. Again, try the Toolbars command or Settings command or right-click the bar to hunt down the toolbar controls on the QuickMenu.

 ✔ You can customize your toolbars and Property Bar so that they contain buttons for the commands you use most. You can find more information in Chapter 22, in the section "Create Your Own Toolbar and Property Bar Buttons."

 ✔ Right-click the Application Bar and use the commands on the resulting QuickMenu (which vary from program to program in the Suite) to specify what information you want to display on the bar.

✔ If you don't like the position of the toolbar or Property Bar, place your cursor on an empty spot in the bar until the cursor changes to a four-headed arrow. Then drag the toolbar to a new home. In some cases, the bar turns into a free-floating window, complete with a title bar and Close button. To resize the window, drag a corner of the window.

✔ Most programs offer Zoom buttons on the Property Bar or toolbar. (The button usually looks like a little magnifying glass.) Use these buttons to magnify or reduce the size of your document on-screen. Zoom options also are found under the View menu or the Zoom menu, depending on the program you're using.

✔ WordPerfect and Presentations enable you to hide and display shortcut keys on menus and turn QuickTips on and off. In WordPerfect, choose Tools⇨Settings and then click the Environment icon. The Environment Settings dialog box appears, as shown in Figure 2-2. Click the Interface tab to access the relevant options, spotlighted in the figure. A check mark in the option box means that the option is turned on.

In Presentations, choose Tools⇨Settings and click the Display icon in the resulting dialog box to access these options. In Quattro Pro, you turn QuickTips on or off by choosing Tools⇨Settings and clicking the Display tab of the Application dialog box that appears.

Figure 2-2: Version 8 gives you control over whether keyboard shortcuts and QuickTips appear on-screen.

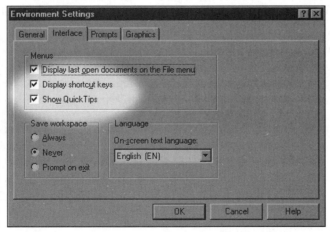

Using DAD

The *Desktop Application Director — DAD* for short — places icons for certain programs along the bottom of your Windows 95 taskbar. You can click an icon to launch the program. If you don't see the DAD icons on-screen, click the Windows 95 Start button and then choose Corel WordPerfect Suite 8⇨ Accessories⇨Corel Desktop Application Director.

To remove an icon from the taskbar, click the DAD Properties icon on the taskbar. After the DAD Properties dialog box appears, click the name of the icon you want to remove and then click the Delete button.

 To add an icon, click the Add button and choose the program execution file (the one that starts the program) from the Open dialog box. (The filename has the letters EXE tagged onto the end.) Click OK to close the dialog box. You can even add programs that are not in the WordPerfect Suite.

To turn off DAD altogether, right-click any icon and then choose Exit DAD from the QuickMenu.

Digging through Dialog Boxes

After you choose some commands, you get a dialog box similar to the one shown in Figure 2-3. By making selections in the dialog box, you tell the program how you want it to carry out a particular command. The components of a dialog box work as follows:

✔ To change a value in an option box, double-click the box or press the option's hot key (the underlined letter in the option name). Then enter a new value from the keyboard. In some cases, you can change the value by clicking the little arrows next to the option box.

✔ To display the contents of a drop-down list, click the little downward-pointing arrowhead. Then click the option you want to use.

 ✔ You can resize some dialog boxes so that you can display more of their contents. Just drag any corner of the box.

✔ To turn a radio button on or off, click the button. The option is on if a black dot appears in the middle of the button. You can turn on only one radio button in a group at a time.

✔ To turn a check box on or off, click the check box. An X or a check mark in the box (depending on the program in the Suite) means that the option is turned on. You can turn on as many check boxes as you want.

✔ Clicking the rectangular buttons — sometimes called Command buttons — initiates a command or displays a menu or second dialog box of related options.

✔ Some dialog boxes, such as the one shown in Figure 2-3, contain several layers of options. To get to a different layer, click its tab.

 ✔ You can move from option to option by pressing the Tab key. To move to the previous option, press Shift+Tab.

✔ To close a dialog box and return to your document without making any changes, click the Close button.

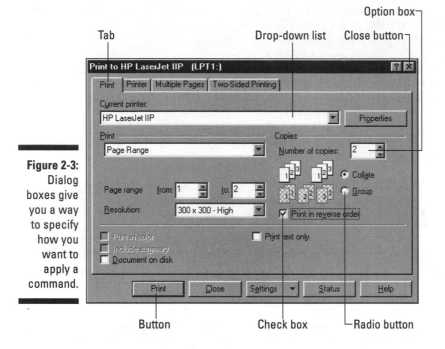

Tab   Drop-down list   Close button
                              Option box

Figure 2-3:
Dialog
boxes give
you a way
to specify
how you
want to
apply a
command.

Button   Check box   Radio button

> As I explain in Chapter 3, some dialog boxes contain a question mark button. Click this button and then click an option in the dialog box to get more information about how the option works.

Chapter 3

Can I Get Some Help, Please?

. . . .

In This Chapter

▶ Getting step-by-step advice

▶ Asking for help in plain English

▶ Navigating a Help window

▶ Using the Reference Center and Envoy

. . . .

*A*re you the sort who hates to ask for help from anyone? Do you prefer driving around in hopeless circles to stopping at a gas station for directions, for example? Is your VCR still blinking "12:00" because you refuse to let your 10-year-old show you how to set the clock?

If so, you probably want to skip this chapter. On the other hand, if you believe that nothing's shameful about asking for help — and that doing so can save you time and headaches — you're going to find the information on the next few pages invaluable.

This chapter explains the various tools offered by the WordPerfect Suite Help system. You discover where to click to get information about a particular topic, how to display step-by-step on-screen instructions for completing a task, and how to use templates that automatically create common documents with hardly a keystroke or deep thought required on your part.

Not all programs in the WordPerfect Suite offer all the advanced Help features covered in this chapter. And some use slightly different command names or hot keys than the ones mentioned here. But the basic aspects of the Help systems work the same way, and even the most simple Help system should provide some guidance if you get stuck.

If you want assistance with advanced topics not covered in this book, don't forget to check out the *...For Dummies* titles on the individual programs in the WordPerfect Suite. They're excellent, easy-to-digest references that provide more in-depth coverage on the programs than I can include in this book.

Getting Help from an Expert

The Help system in the main Suite programs has been significantly re-vamped in Version 8. The Coaches and QuickTasks features from Version 7 are now integrated into an expanded PerfectExpert feature.

Available in WordPerfect, Quattro Pro, and Presentations, PerfectExpert is sort of like having a software service representative built into your computer (only better, because you don't need to wade through a snarl of voice mail commands or cool your heels on hold for 30 minutes before you get your question answered).

The Version 8 PerfectExpert comprises three main components: One sticks close to your side and walks you through the steps in creating a document; one enables you to ask for specific information in plain English; and one provides templates that automate the process of creating common documents. The following sections describe each of these tools.

Keeping an expert by your side

If you choose <u>H</u>elp⇨Perfect<u>E</u>xpert or click the PerfectExpert toolbar button, the PerfectExpert window appears on-screen, as shown in Figure 3-1. By default, this window locks itself into position on one side of the document window. Drag the border between the PerfectExpert window and the document window to resize the two windows.

You can separate the PerfectExpert window from the document window (as I did to create Figure 3-1) if you want to make it even smaller or move it to a different location. Move your cursor toward the edge of the PerfectExpert window until the cursor turns into a four-headed arrow. Then drag the window to a location you like better. Resize the window by right-clicking the title bar, choosing Size from the QuickMenu, and then dragging one of its corners. To move the window, drag its title bar.

The PerfectExpert is supposed to help you work your way through basic tasks. After you first turn on the PerfectExpert, you see the Home page — ground zero for building a document. Click a topic button (refer to Figure 3-1) to get information about the button's subject.

After you click a topic button, you may be presented with another set of buttons that enable you to get even more specific about the information you want. If you click the Typing button in the WordPerfect PerfectExpert, for example, you see a new set of buttons: Change Font, Change Tab Settings, and other topics related to typing. Or you may be taken to the dialog box where you accomplish the task you clicked. Click the Font button, for example, and the Font dialog box opens.

Topic button

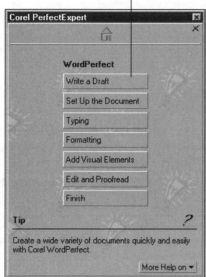

Figure 3-1:
The
PerfectExpert
window
gives you
step-by-step
assistance
in creating
documents.

After you click your way into a dialog box, you can get more information about how to use the various options by clicking the Help button in the dialog box or, in some cases, by clicking the More Help On button in the PerfectExpert window. Either way, a Help window opens with information about the topic at hand. (See the section "Navigating a Help Window," later in this chapter, for more information.) Some dialog boxes also include a question mark icon in the top-right corner; click the icon and then click an option in the dialog box to get an explanation of what that option does.

Click the Home icon at the top of the PerfectExpert window to return to the Home page. Clicking the question mark icon takes you to the Ask the PerfectExpert panel of the Help window, which I describe in the next section.

The PerfectExpert window is a good idea, but I find it a little lacking in that you're left to your own devices after you get inside the dialog box related to the topic you clicked. I suppose that the feature may be helpful for folks who can't remember what menu command to choose to perform a specific task, are brand new to computers and don't know what a menu is in the first place, or weren't clever enough to buy this book. As for you, you savvy book buyer, I suspect that you'll agree that the PerfectExpert window is a perfect waste of screen space, unless, of course, you happen to be traveling and didn't think to tuck this book in your briefcase. Click the X icon in the PerfectExpert window, click the PerfectExpert toolbar button, or choose Help⇨PerfectExpert to close the window.

Hey, I have a question!

The Ask the PerfectExpert feature enables you to ask a question of the little information fairy who lives inside the Help system. You can ask your question by using plain English, which makes Ask the PerfectExpert the ideal solution for those who haven't yet completed the full course in Computer Babble 101. Here's how it works:

1. **Choose Help⇨Ask the PerfectExpert.**

   The Ask the PerfectExpert panel of the Help dialog box appears, as shown in Figure 3-2. (You can also press F1 to open the dialog box and then click the PerfectExpert tab.)

2. **Type your question in the What Do You Want to Know? text box.**

3. **Click the Search button.**

   The dialog box displays a list of possible topics to explore, as Figure 3-2 shows. The topics are arranged as "pages" inside "books" — double-click a book icon to display the topic pages within.

4. **Click the topic that matches your interest and then click the Display button.**

   Up pops a Help window containing the information you requested. You can find out about the intricacies of the Help window in the section "Navigating a Help Window," later in this chapter.

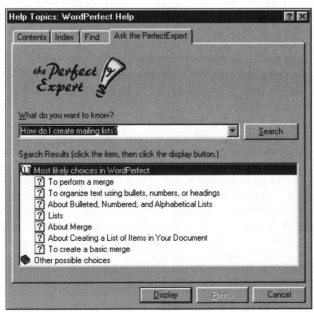

Figure 3-2: The PerfectExpert enables you to communicate with an information fairy that lives inside the program's Help system.

That bit about the information fairy isn't for public consumption, by the way. Most people don't believe in things such as fairies that live inside computers. These naysayers insist that computers are nothing more than cold, uncaring machines, a bundle of wires and chips and such. I say that's nonsense — how else can you explain data that mysteriously disappears and appears without any warning? But until the world comes around to my way of thinking, you're better off keeping this news to yourself. Look for an episode of *The X Files* focusing on this very subject soon.

Using PerfectExpert Templates

PerfectExpert templates, formerly known as QuickTasks, are templates that the WordPerfect Suite provides to speed up the process of creating common documents, from mailing labels to household inventory worksheets.

To access the templates, click the Corel PerfectExpert icon on the DAD bar. Or click the Windows 95 Start button and then choose Corel WordPerfect Suite 8⇨Corel New Project. The Corel PerfectExpert dialog box appears, as shown in Figure 3-3. Choose a category of document from the drop-down list at the top of the Create New tab and then double-click the type of document you want to create in the list below. The appropriate program for creating the document opens, along with the PerfectExpert window, which contains buttons related to the different steps in creating the document.

Typically, the templates format the document and create some appropriate text and/or graphics. You can edit the document as you would any other document. Click the different PerfectExpert buttons for help in completing the document. The first time you use some templates, you're asked to enter personal or business information (your name, address, and so on) that helps the PerfectExpert customize your document.

You can also access the templates from inside WordPerfect, Quattro Pro, or Presentations by choosing File⇨New and selecting one of the templates from the Create New tab of the New File dialog box. (See Chapter 5 for more information on this dialog box.)

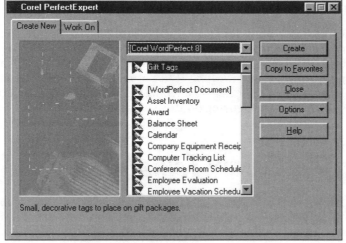

Figure 3-3:
Choose a
template
from the
PerfectExpert
dialog box
to create
common
documents
quickly.

Getting More Help

Here are still more ways to dig up information about a subject that's troubling you:

- ✔ Choose Help➪Help Topics or press F1 to display the Help Topics dialog box and then click the Index tab to display the panel of the Help Topics dialog box shown in Figure 3-4. Enter a topic in the first option box or use the scroll bar and arrows to locate the topic in the list box. Click the topic in the list box and then click the Display button.

- ✔ On the Contents tab of the Help Topics dialog box, Help information is organized by task. Double-click one of the book icons to display a list of page icons for different tasks. Double-click a page icon to display the Help information for that task.

- ✔ Some dialog boxes have a little question mark button, usually at the top of the dialog box. For information about a dialog box option, click the question mark icon and then click the option to display a pop-up information box. Click again to get rid of the information box. If the dialog box also has a button labeled Help, clicking the button displays information about that dialog box in a Help window.

- ✔ If you have a modem and are hooked into the Internet, you can get online help by choosing Help➪Corel Web Site.

- ✔ As I mention in Chapter 2, placing your mouse cursor over a button or other on-screen element displays a QuickTip box with hints about what that button or element does.

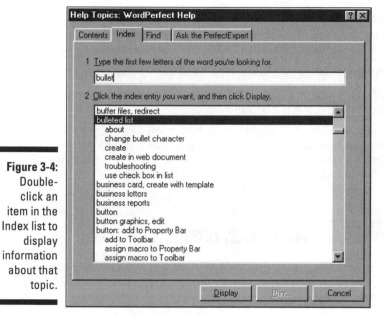

Figure 3-4:
Double-click an item in the Index list to display information about that topic.

Navigating a Help Window

Figure 3-5 shows a typical Help window that appears after you display information about a particular command or task. Here are a few tips for making your way around the Help window and performing some other useful tricks:

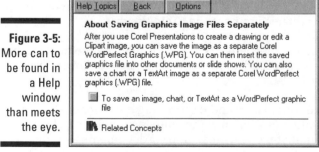

Figure 3-5:
More can to be found in a Help window than meets the eye.

✔ Click underlined words or phrases to jump to information about that topic. Clicking a word or phrase that's adorned with little icons or gray squares also jumps you to that topic.

✔ If you click a term that's underlined with dots, an explanation of the term pops up.

✔ Click the Back button to return to the previous screen.

✔ Click the Help Topics button to display the Help Topics dialog box.

✔ To print a Help screen, click the Options button and choose Print Topic from the drop-down list that appears.

✔ If you want to keep the Help window on-screen as you work in the program, click on the Options button and choose Keep Help on Top⇨On Top. You can resize the Help window as you would any window — just drag an edge or corner of the window.

Using the Reference Center

The WordPerfect Suite comes with its own digital library of reference manuals, contained in a utility called the Reference Center, for many of the programs in the Suite.

You have the option of installing the Reference Center, the reference manuals, and Envoy (the program you use to view the Reference Center documents) on your hard drive. As far as I'm concerned, you don't need to waste hard drive space on these elements. Instead, run the Reference Center from the CD, as I explain in the next few paragraphs.

To use the Reference Center, first put the CD into your CD-ROM drive. After you first slip the CD into the CD-ROM drive, the WordPerfect Suite 8 Setup window appears automatically. Click Reference Center to launch the Reference Center window. Or, if you installed the Reference Center on your hard drive, you can choose Corel WordPerfect Suite 8⇨Setup & Notes⇨Reference Center from the Windows 95 Start menu. (Unless you installed the Reference Center documents, you still need to have the CD in the drive.)

After the Reference Center screen appears, click the icon for the manual that you want to see. After a few seconds, the manual opens in an Envoy Viewer window, as shown in Figure 3-6.

Envoy is a program used for creating and distributing documents electronically — that is, by computer. In Version 7, the Suite included the full version of Envoy, which meant that you could create Envoy documents as well as view them. But in Version 8, you can view documents only. Envoy now is provided primarily as a tool for viewing the Reference Center manuals. The Suite contains many other tools for creating documents for electronic distribution, however, including commands that enable you to save documents in HTML format, the format used for publishing pages on the World Wide Web. If you want more information on this topic, turn to *WordPerfect 8 Web Publishing For Dummies,* by David Kay, available soon from IDG Books Worldwide, Inc.

To close an Envoy document, choose File⇨Close. To open another Reference Center manual, choose File⇨Open. An Open dialog box, similar to the one I explain in Chapter 5, appears; select the document that you want to open and press Enter. The Envoy documents are stored on the CD in the Corel/ Suite8/Shared/Refcntr folder (unless you installed them on your hard drive, of course). Envoy documents have the file extension EVY.

If you want to print hard copies of a Reference Center manual, open the manual and choose File⇨Print. Envoy responds with a dialog box that looks and works much like the one I discuss in Chapter 5. A word of caution: The manuals contain lots of graphics, so if your printer doesn't have a lot of memory or your computer is low on hard drive space, you may have trouble printing more than a page or two at a time.

Envoy provides many tools for "marking up" a document — highlighting important passages, adding hypertext links that jump you from one page to another, and so on. The problem is that, if you mark up a Reference Center manual, you must save the manual to your hard drive after you're done or you lose your changes at the end of your Envoy viewing session. (You can't resave the documents to the Suite CD-ROM.) I don't recommend storing the manuals on your hard drive; if you're like most mortals, you can't spare the hard drive space that the manuals consume. That's why I didn't cover the markup tools here. If you're interested, you can find more about the tools and about saving your marked up documents in — guess where! — the Envoy manual in the Reference Center.

Getting acquainted with Envoy

As do other programs in the WordPerfect Suite, the Envoy window has a menu bar, toolbar, status bar, scroll bar, and other elements common to Windows 95 screens, as Figure 3-6 shows. For information on these elements, read Chapter 2. Envoy does not offer an Application Bar or Property Bar as do some of the other Version 8 programs, however.

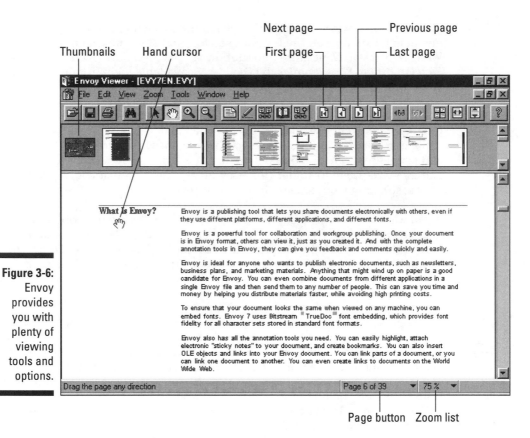

Thumbnails   Hand cursor   First page   Next page   Previous page   Last page

Figure 3-6:
Envoy
provides
you with
plenty of
viewing
tools and
options.

Page button   Zoom list

You can view document pages in several different ways, as the following list describes:

 ✔ You can display thumbnail views of the pages in your document across the top or left side of the window, as I do in Figure 3-6. To cycle quickly through the thumbnail display options — top, left, and hidden — click the Thumbnails button on the toolbar. Alternatively, you can choose the Top, Left, or Hidden command from the View⊏➪Thumbnails submenu.

✔ To see page numbers displayed with the thumbnails, choose View➪Thumbnails➪Show Page Numbers.

 ✔ Zoom in and out on your pages by clicking the Zoom buttons on the toolbar and then clicking the page. Keep clicking to keep zooming. Click the Select tool (which looks like an arrow) in the toolbar to deselect the Zoom tool and return to the regular cursor. You can also zoom by selecting an option from the Zoom menu or the Zoom list (refer to Figure 3-6).

✔ Click the Fit Page to Height button or press Ctrl+H to see the entire length of the page in the window.

 ✔ Click the Fit Page to Width button or press Ctrl+W to magnify or reduce the page so that its entire width appears on-screen.

 ✔ The Previous View and Next View toolbar buttons switch you back and forth between the last view you were using and the current view.

Flipping through your pages

Here are some of the bazillion ways you can move from page to page and move about within a page:

✔ Click the page navigation buttons on the toolbar (refer to Figure 3-6).

 ✔ Click the Select tool and then double-click a thumbnail to go to that page.

✔ Click the Page button (refer to Figure 3-6) to display the Go To Page dialog box. Enter the page number you want and press Enter or click OK.

✔ Click the scroll arrows or drag the scroll box along the right or bottom edge of the window.

 ✔ Click the Hand tool and drag with the Hand cursor to move the page around on-screen, as shown in Figure 3-6.

Finding a specific word or phrase

 Most of the Reference Center manuals are hundreds of pages long. Scrolling through all those pages to find the information you need is definitely not the way to go. Instead, choose Edit⇨Find, press Ctrl+F, or click the Find button to open the Find dialog box, as shown in Figure 3-7. Click the Text radio button and enter the word or phrase you want to find in the box below. Select the Match Case option box if you want Envoy to find only text that matches, er, the case of the text you enter (in other words, text that uses the exact same capitalization as the letters you enter). Click the Find Next button, and Envoy takes you to the first occurrence of the text. If that passage doesn't contain the information you want, click Find Next again to search for the next occurrence of the text. Click Find Previous to return to the previous passage.

In some manuals, you can also track down the content you want by clicking the hypertext link for the topic in the manual's table of contents or index. Place your cursor over the topic and click when your cursor turns into a hand with a pointing finger.

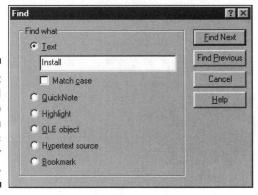

Figure 3-7:
Use the Find feature to track down a specific word or phrase.

Part II
Goodbye, Typewriter . . . Hello, WordPerfect!

In this part . . .

*B*ack in the old days (you know, before Bill Gates took over the world), producing reports, letters, and other text documents was no easy feat. Even if you had a really good typewriter, turning out professional-looking, error-free pages often required hours and hours of tedious labor — not to mention gallons of correction fluid.

Thanks to the advent of the word processor, you can now produce flawless pages of text and graphics in minutes. Okay, maybe not minutes, but certainly in a heck of a lot less time than it took using the old Smith-Corona. What's more, you can easily rearrange sentences and paragraphs, fancy up your pages with all sorts of fonts and pictures, and even get the computer to check your spelling.

WordPerfect 8 is one of the more powerful word processors on the market. In fact, the program offers so many features that you'll probably never use them all. This part introduces you to the features you'll use every day to create basic documents — as well as a few fun tricks for producing not-so-basic documents.

Chapter 4

The Process of Processing Words

*I*f you were alive in the precomputing era, when the typewriter was the primary mechanism for producing text, you will have a special appreciation for WordPerfect. No longer do you have to type and retype the same page over and over again until you get it just right. No longer do you need to spend hours dabbing at mistakes with correction fluid. And no longer do you need to strain your back hurling a heavy typewriter at the uncaring boss who asks you to add "three tiny paragraphs" to the beginning of a 20-page report that took you days to complete.

WordPerfect gives you the power to churn out page after page of great-looking (and correctly spelled) text in no time. This chapter gets you started on your word-processing adventure by explaining what's what on the WordPerfect screen, giving you basic how-to's for entering text and moving around the screen, and describing ways to make the WordPerfect interface behave just the way you want.

Getting Started

To start WordPerfect, click the WordPerfect DAD icon on the taskbar or click the Windows 95 Start button, click the WordPerfect Suite 8 item, and then click the WordPerfect 8 item. After some gurgling and wheezing by your computer, you see a screen that looks something like the one shown in Figure 4-1. Your screen doesn't display the text you see in the figure — the Corel folks foolishly declined my offer to use my poetry in the opening screen.

Margin guideline   Inspiring poetry   Mouse cursor   Shadow cursor

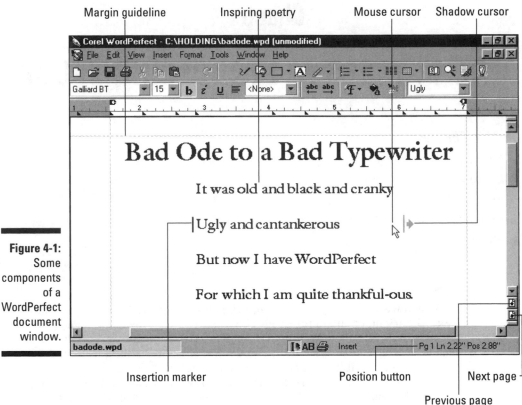

Figure 4-1:
Some
components
of a
WordPerfect
document
window.

Insertion marker   Position button   Next page

Previous page

Many elements of the WordPerfect window are the same as you find in any Windows 95 window, as I cover in Chapter 2, in the section "Doing Windows." But a few elements require some explanation, as follows:

✔ The blinking black bar is the *insertion marker*. The marker indicates where the next character you type will appear. The section "Entering Text," later in this chapter, provides more details about this all-important item.

 ✔ The nonblinking gray bar with the little arrow by its side is the *shadow cursor*. You turn the shadow cursor on and off by clicking its button on the Application Bar or by choosing View⇨Shadow Cursor. (In this book, by the way, the term *cursor* refers to the mouse cursor rather than the shadow cursor.)

 The shadow cursor hovers near your mouse cursor and shows you where the insertion marker will appear if you click. The main advantage of the shadow cursor is that it enables you to type anywhere in the white space of your document without adding tabs, spaces, or paragraph returns to position the insertion marker.

Try this exercise: With the shadow cursor turned on, type a word at the top of your page. Then click near the center of the page and type another word. WordPerfect automatically adds whatever paragraph returns, tabs, or spaces are needed to place your insertion marker at the spot you clicked. Now try the same thing with the shadow cursor turned off. Whoops, doesn't work, does it? You need to add all the paragraph returns and tabs yourself.

By default, the shadow cursor "snaps to" (aligns with) the nearest tab stop. The little gray arrow next to the shadow cursor changes depending on whether the tab stop is a regular left tab, center tab, and so on. (For more about tab stops, see Chapter 7.) You can change this behavior if you want; see the following section, "Customizing Your Workspace," for details. When the snap-to function is turned on, you can't click with the shadow cursor between tab stops; if you try, the cursor just jumps to the nearest tab stop.

✔ The dotted horizontal and vertical lines on-screen indicate page margins, as I explain in Chapter 7. If these *margin guidelines* don't appear on your screen, choose <u>V</u>iew➪<u>G</u>uidelines to open the Guidelines dialog box and click the Margins check box.

✔ Click the *page icons* at the bottom of the vertical scroll bar for a quick way to move from page to page in your document.

✔ The *Position button* on the Application Bar indicates the location of the insertion marker. The button displays the current page number, line number, and distance from the left edge of the page.

✔ If you're upgrading from Version 7, you may be wondering what happened to QuickSpots, those little gray buttons that appeared if you passed your cursor over a paragraph. The functions that you accessed by using QuickSpots are now readily available via the Property Bar, so QuickSpots are dead and gone in Version 8.

Customizing Your Workspace

You can control many things about the WordPerfect *interface* (a fancy term for how the program looks and behaves). The key to making the most of these changes is the Settings command that you find on the Tools menu. Choosing the command displays the Settings dialog box, as shown in Figure 4-2.

Double-click the Display icon to open the Display Settings dialog box, as shown in Figure 4-3. Here's a sampling of the customization options — known in the computer world as *preference settings* — that you find in this dialog box:

Figure 4-2:
Make
WordPerfect
bow to your
personal
whims by
using the
controls in
this dialog
box.

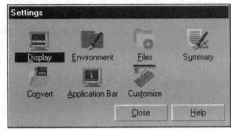

✔ On the Document tab, you can select which elements appear on-screen, change the unit of measure used on the ruler (labeled in Figure 4-4), and specify when you want the scroll bars to appear, if at all.

The Document tab also provides options for controlling the shadow cursor. You can change the shadow cursor's color and shape; make it snap to spaces, tabs, margins, or indents; and set it to be active in text only, in the white space of your document only, or both.

✔ Options on the Symbols tab determine whether so-called *hidden symbols* appear on-screen. Hidden symbols are little symbols that show you where spaces, paragraph breaks (also known as *hard returns*), tabs, indents, and other formatting instructions are located throughout your text. Figure 4-4 shows some hidden symbols scattered throughout a famous ode. You can also turn hidden symbols on and off by choosing View⇨Show ¶ or by pressing Ctrl+Shift+F3.

Figure 4-3:
You can
control how
certain
screen
elements
appear by
using the
options in
this dialog
box.

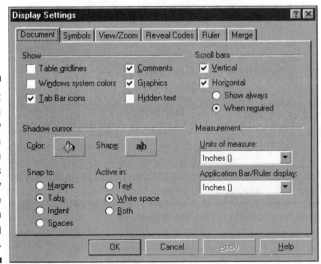

✔ On the View/Zoom tab, you can choose the default zoom ratio (magnification) and view mode for your document display. Page view mode displays your document as it appears after you print it; Two Page *view* is similar except that you see two pages side by side. Draft view displays your document close to its printed appearance but without certain formatting features such as headers and footers (which I cover in Chapter 8). Hiding these features speeds up the screen display somewhat.

✔ You can also access view modes from the View menu. The View menu offers one mode not found in the Display Settings dialog box: Web Page mode. This mode displays your document as it would appear if you converted it to HTML format for publication on the World Wide Web. Because HTML doesn't support advanced formatting options, you may lose some of your document formatting if you switch to this view.

Another way to zoom in and out on your document is to click the Zoom button on the Property Bar and select a zoom ratio from the drop-down list that appears, as shown in Figure 4-4.

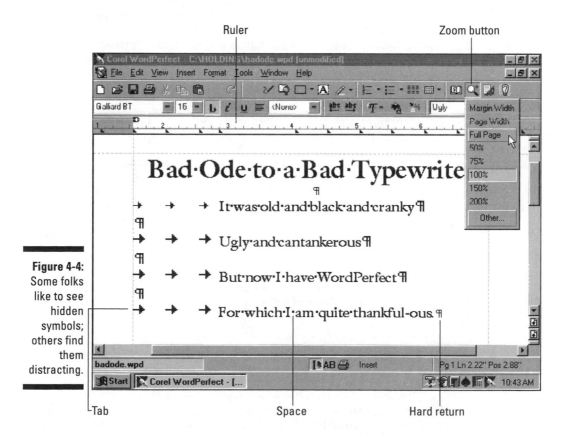

Ruler

Zoom button

Figure 4-4:
Some folks like to see hidden symbols; others find them distracting.

Tab

Space

Hard return

Other choices in the Settings dialog box enable you to customize your toolbar, Property Bar, Application Bar, menu bar, keyboard, and other screen elements. Play around with these options to see what's available and what setups best suit your needs.

The Settings dialog box isn't the only vehicle for custom-tailoring the WordPerfect interface, however. Check out these other options that you can use, too:

- ✔ Choose View⇨Toolbars to display or hide the toolbar, Property Bar, or Application Bar. Choose View⇨Ruler or press Alt+Shift+F3 to hide or display the ruler, labeled in Figure 4-4. (I discuss the ruler in Chapter 7.) Alternatively, you can right-click the element you want to hide and then choose the Hide command from the QuickMenu.

- ✔ You can also access preference settings by right-clicking the Application Bar, ruler, toolbar, or Property Bar and choosing the Settings command from the QuickMenu.

- ✔ You can control how many rows of buttons appear in your toolbar. Right-click the toolbar, choose Settings from the QuickMenu to access the Customize dialog box, and then click the Options button. In the dialog box that appears next, change the Maximum Number of Rows/ Columns to Show value. You can also change other aspects of the buttons' appearance, including whether you see just pictures on the button faces or pictures and text labels.

- ✔ WordPerfect enables you to add, remove, and rearrange toolbar and Property Bar buttons. For how-to's, see Chapter 22 (in the section "Create Your Own Toolbar and Property Bar Buttons").

- ✔ You can even customize your menu bar, moving commands from menu to menu or displaying menus as they appeared in Version 7. To do so, right-click the menu bar and choose Settings from the QuickMenu. I don't recommend mucking around with your menus, however, because the instructions I give in this book and those that you find in the WordPerfect Help system aren't going to mesh with what you see on-screen if you do make such changes.

- ✔ To hide or display margin guides, column guides, and other nonprinting guides, choose View⇨Guidelines and select the guides you want to display from the Guidelines dialog box.

Entering Text

Putting your words down on paper is easy: Just bang those keys, and WordPerfect slaps the corresponding letters onto your page. Go ahead, try it: Type **Now is the time for all good men to come to the aid of the party** or one of those other hysterical typing-class goodies.

In a lot of ways, creating text in WordPerfect is the same as creating text by typing on a typewriter. But in just as many ways, the process is quite different. And if you try to rely on the same techniques that worked so well on your typewriter, not only can you botch things up, but you're also failing to take advantage of the power that WordPerfect offers. So unless you want your computer to serve as a $2,000 typewriter, you need to remember the following things as you enter text:

- ✔ If you type a character or characters and then decide better of it, press the Backspace or Delete key to wipe out your mistake. The Backspace key gets rid of letters to the left of the insertion marker; the Delete key zaps characters to the right of the insertion marker. For a host of other editing options, see Chapter 6.

- ✔ Don't press the Enter or the Return key after you reach the edge of your page. WordPerfect automatically wraps the text to the next line whenever necessary. Pressing Enter or Return creates a paragraph break. This rule is important to remember because of the way that WordPerfect applies such paragraph formatting as line spacing, indents, and so on, as I explain in Chapter 7.

- ✔ As you reach the end of a page, WordPerfect creates a new page and then wraps the text to the new page. If you want to create a page break manually, press Ctrl+Enter or choose Insert⇨New Page.

- ✔ Don't use spaces to indent paragraphs or lines of text. If you do, you waste a lot of time, and you don't get consistent spacing, as I explain in Chapter 7.

- ✔ You can work in either of two text-entry modes. If you work in *Insert mode*, whatever you type is inserted between existing text. If, for example, you type **Bob**, click between the B and the o, and then press **l**, you get Blob. If you work in *Typeover mode*, whatever you type replaces existing characters. In the preceding example, the o gets replaced by the **l** that you type, and you get Blb. A button on the Application Bar tells you which mode is active (the button label reads either Insert or Typeover). Click the button or press the Insert key on your keyboard to switch modes.

- ✔ A red striped line underneath a word you type is WordPerfect's way of telling you that you may have a spelling problem on your hands. Similarly, a blue striped line indicates a potential grammatical error. These two features are called Spell-As-You-Go and Grammar-As-You-Go, respectively. To turn off both features, choose Tools⇨Proofread⇨Off. To turn off the grammar checker only, choose Grammar-As-You-Go from the Proofread submenu. If the grammar checker is active, Spell-As-You-Go is automatically on as well. For more information on these options, see Chapter 9.

✔ If WordPerfect changes the text you type or overrules your formatting instructions, the program's QuickCorrect features are probably enabled. For information about QuickCorrect, see Chapters 6 and 8.

✔ Don't forget that the insertion marker — not the mouse cursor or shadow cursor — controls where the next thing you type appears. Click the mouse button to position the insertion marker. If you have the shadow cursor turned on, you can click anywhere on your page and begin typing. If the shadow cursor is off, you can click inside existing lines of text only. (See the following section for additional ways to move the insertion marker.)

Moving Around in Your Document

Sophisticated programs such as WordPerfect give you lots of different ways to do the same thing. That flexibility is nice, but it can also be overwhelming. Such is the case with the topic of *navigation* — which is geekspeak for moving around in your document. WordPerfect gives you about a zillion ways to move the insertion marker and view different portions of your document. Here are your basic options:

✔ Use the scroll arrows or scroll box, as I explain in Chapter 2, to scroll through the document so that you can see the page where you want to place the insertion marker.

✔ Alternatively, click the Previous Page or Next Page icons (labeled in Figure 4-1 earlier in this chapter) to move to the page. Then click at the spot on the page where you want the insertion marker to appear.

✔ You can also move the insertion marker by pressing the arrow keys on your keyboard. If an arrow key has a number on it, however, make sure that the Num Lock feature is off. (Press the Num Lock key to turn the feature on and off.) If Num Lock is on, the arrow keys type numbers instead of moving the insertion marker.

✔ If you click the Position button in the Application bar (refer to Figure 4-1), WordPerfect displays the Go To dialog box. Enter a specific page number in the Page Number option box or select a general page position from the Position list. Then click OK to make the insertion marker jump to that location.

Just for good measure, WordPerfect gives you three — that's right, three — other ways to access the Go To dialog box: Choose Edit⇨Go To, press Ctrl+G, or right-click the scroll bar and choose Go To from the QuickMenu.

Believe it or not, these options are just the tip of the navigation iceberg. You also have all the navigation keys and keyboard shortcuts listed in Table 4-1 at your disposal.

Table 4-1	Keyboard Navigation Shortcuts
Press This Key	*To Do This*
Home	Move to the beginning of the current line.
End	Move to the end of the current line.
Ctrl+Home	Move to the beginning of the document.
Ctrl+End	Move to the end of the document.
Page Up (PgUp)	Move up one screen.
Page Down (PgDn)	Move down one screen.
Alt+PgUp	Move up one page.
Alt+PgDn	Move down one page.
Ctrl+↑	Move to the beginning of the current paragraph or, if you're at the beginning, to the beginning of the preceding paragraph.
Ctrl+↓	Move to the beginning of the next paragraph.
Ctrl+←	Move left one word.
Ctrl+→	Move right one word.

Using these keyboard shortcuts can really speed up navigation time. What's more, you can use them to navigate documents in most Windows programs, not just in WordPerfect. So why not dump some of the more useless pieces of information in your brain's memory banks — for example, maybe you don't really *need* to remember the theme song from *Gilligan's Island* anymore — to make room for these shortcuts.

Chapter 5

Open, Close, Save, Print: Dull but Vital Basics

● ●

In This Chapter

▶ Opening new and existing documents

▶ Saving time by using WordPerfect templates

▶ Getting familiar with filenames, folders, and other document storage terms

▶ Putting documents away

▶ Saving your work

▶ Making your printer spit out pages of text

● ●

Some chapters in this book are a lot of fun to explore. You discover all sorts of cool things you can do by clicking here, clicking there, and otherwise messing around with on-screen gizmos and gadgets. Other chapters — such as this one, I'm sad to say — are less action-packed but are vital to getting your money's worth from your software investment.

This chapter focuses on some of the dull but very necessary aspects of word processing: how to open and close documents, save documents to your computer's hard drive or a floppy disk, and print out your finished masterpiece. It's not the kind of stuff you can use to titillate your friends and relatives (unless you have really geeky friends and relatives), but the information is important if you want to stop fooling around and actually produce something in WordPerfect.

The good news is that, after you muddle through these yawner topics, you don't need to repeat the process for every program you want to use. Although this chapter explains concepts in terms specific to WordPerfect, you use virtually the same procedures to open, close, save, and print documents in all programs in the WordPerfect Suite — and in most other Windows programs as well.

Opening a New Document

Before you can type on a typewriter, you need to put a piece of paper in the machine. And before you can do anything in WordPerfect, you need a *document,* sometimes also referred to as a *file.* When you first start WordPerfect, you're presented with a new blank document. If you need a second blank document, you can get one by performing any of the following four actions:

✔ Choose File⇨New.

✔ Press Ctrl+Shift+N.

✔ Click the New Blank Document button on the toolbar.

✔ Press Ctrl+N.

If you click the New Blank Document button or press Ctrl+N, you get a new blank document, just as you do after you first start WordPerfect. But if you use the other two methods to open a new document, WordPerfect displays the New dialog box, as shown in Figure 5-1.

Figure 5-1:
The prefab templates in the New dialog box provide you with the basic framework for creating common documents, such as press releases.

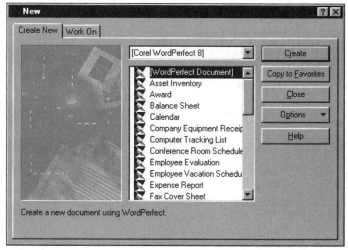

The Create New tab of the dialog box contains templates for creating common documents, such as press releases or work schedules. If you use a template, WordPerfect handles basic formatting chores for you and provides sample document text. You simply edit the text and tweak the formatting to your taste. If you want to use a template, click it in the list to select the template and then click OK.

If you decide that you don't want to use a template, choose the WordPerfect Document option from the list of templates. WordPerfect then gives you an ordinary blank document.

Opening Existing Documents

To open an existing document, you can perform one of the following actions:

- Choose File➪Open.
- Press Ctrl+O.

 - Click the Open button on the toolbar.

Whichever method you choose, the Open File dialog box appears. This dialog box, as shown in Figure 5-2, works like just about every other Windows 95 Open File dialog box. Here are the basics:

- To open a document, double-click its name in the Document List box (labeled in Figure 5-2). Or click the document name once and then click Open or press Enter.

- To split your Open File dialog box in two, revealing the Preview box shown in Figure 5-2, click the Preview button in the toolbar. Now, if you click a document name in the list box, WordPerfect displays a preview of the document. Right-click the preview and choose Page View from the QuickMenu to display the document (shown in Figure 5-2). Choose Content from the QuickMenu to get a closer look at the text. Use the scroll arrows along the side of the Preview box to scroll through your document.

 - Drag the vertical border between the Document List box and the Preview box to make one box smaller and the other larger. Drag a corner of the dialog box to make the entire dialog box larger or smaller.

- Click the downward-pointing arrow at the end of the Filename option box to display a drop-down list of the last ten documents you edited. Click a document name in the list to select that document.

- If the document you want isn't stored in the folder displayed in the Look In option box above the document list box, click the downward-pointing arrow to display a drop-down list of folders and drives. After you find the folder you want, click it to display its contents in the document list box. Double-click a folder in the document list box to display the folder's contents. Click the Up One Folder button, labeled in Figure 5-2, to back up one folder.

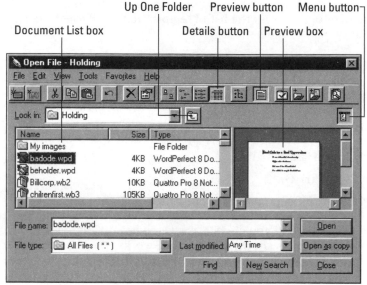

Up One Folder   Preview button   Menu button

Document List box   Details button   Preview box

Open File - Holding

File   Edit   View   Tools   Favorites   Help

Look in: Holding

Name	Size	Type
My images		File Folder
badode.wpd	4KB	WordPerfect 8 Do...
beholder.wpd	4KB	WordPerfect 8 Do...
Billcorp.wb2	10KB	Quattro Pro 8 Not...
chilrenfirst.wb3	105KB	Quattro Pro 8 Not...

File name: badode.wpd   Open

File type: All Files (*.*)   Last modified: Any Time   Open as copy

Find   New Search   Close

Figure 5-2:
The imposing Open File dialog box isn't as complicated as it looks.

✔ *Folders* are little storage compartments on your computer's hard drive. You use them just as you'd use hanging files or file folders in your file cabinet — to store groups of related documents together. Before Windows 95, folders were called *directories*. Many programs still use the old term, but the meaning is the same. You can create a new folder in the Open File dialog box by choosing File⇨New⇨Folder.

✔ In Version 8, you can choose to hide or display the menu bar inside the Open File dialog box. To toggle the menu bar on and off, click on the Menu button, labeled in Figure 5-2.

✔ If you still don't see the file you want, you may need to change the file type shown in the File Type option box. If you want to see all types of files, open the drop-down list and select All Files. If you want to see only WordPerfect documents, select the WP Documents (WPD) option.

✔ Notice the Details button at the top of the Open File dialog box. If you select this button, you can see detailed information about each file, including the date it was last modified and its size.

✔ If you click the Open as Copy button rather than the Open button, WordPerfect opens a copy of your original document. This option gives you a way to fool around with a document, secure in the knowledge that, if you screw it up, you still have the original available.

You can open any of the last ten documents you edited without opening the Open File dialog box. Just choose the document name from the bottom of the File menu. If you don't see any document names on your File menu, choose Tools⇨Settings, double-click the Environment icon, click the Interface tab, and click the Display Last Open Documents on the File Menu option. Click OK to exit the dialog box.

Another way to open your recently edited documents is to click the Work On tab of the New dialog box. (Choose File⇨New or press Ctrl+Shift+N to open the dialog box.) The left side of the dialog box lists the last documents that you had open. Click a document name to see a preview in the right side of the window. Right-click the preview to choose between Page view and Content view from the QuickMenu, just as in the standard Open File dialog box. Double-click the name of the file you want to open.

You're probably wondering what those little boxes that appear to the left of each file name on the Work On tab do (unless, of course, you have better things to do with your time). Well, if you click the little square beside a file name, a check mark appears in the square. The next time you open the New dialog box, files that have check marks appear at the top of the file list.

Closing a Document

After you're sick and tired of looking at a document, click the document window's Close button — the one marked with an X, at the far right-end of the menu bar. (Make sure that you click the Close button on the menu bar and not the one on the title bar, which closes the WordPerfect program.) Alternatively, choose File⇨Close or press Ctrl+F4.

If you haven't saved your document to disk yet, WordPerfect prompts you to do so. For specifics on saving, see the following section.

Saving Your Work (And Your Sanity)

Here's a little saying to remember while you're working in WordPerfect or in any other computer program: Save your work, save your mind.

Until you choose the Save command, everything you do in a document is temporary. If WordPerfect shuts down for any reason — the computer crashes, you have a power failure, whatever — you zap your document into the electronic abyss, and all your hard work is gone forever. So learn to save early and save often.

Saving for the very first time

To save a document for the first time, follow these steps:

1. **Choose File⇨Save, press Ctrl+S, or click the Save button on the toolbar.**

   The Save File dialog box appears, as shown in Figure 5-3 — unless some text is selected in your document. If text is selected, you see a dialog box that gives you the option of saving just the selected text or the entire file. Click the option you want and then click OK or press Enter to access the Save File dialog box.

Figure 5-3: Unless you want to lose all your hard work, make friends with the Save dialog box.

2. **Choose a storage location for your document.**

   Tell WordPerfect where you want to store the document by choosing a drive (hard drive or floppy drive) and folder from the Save In drop-down menu.

3. **Enter a document name in the File Name option box.**

   For tips on choosing a filename, see the sidebar "What's in a (Windows 95) filename?" Notice that you don't need to enter the three-letter file extension (such as WPD for WordPerfect documents); WordPerfect takes care of that business for you.

4. **Choose a file type from the File Type drop-down list.**

   The File Type drop-down list enables you to choose from many different file formats, including those used by other programs. By default, WordPerfect saves your document in its *native* (own) format; usually, this choice is the one you want. But if you want to save the document for use in some other program — for example, if you want to share the document with a friend who uses Microsoft Word — choose that program's file format from the File Type drop-down list.

5. Click the Save button.

That's it! You're protected — for now. But if you make any changes to your document after you save it, those changes aren't protected until you resave the document. So saving often during your computing sessions — and also before you close a document — is important. To resave the document, just choose the Save command again. WordPerfect saves your document, this time without bothering you with the Save File dialog box.

Saving a document under a different name or format

Sometimes, you may want to save a document under a different name than you saved it the first time. Say, for example, that you open Document A and make some changes to it. You're not sure whether your client is going to like the changes or prefer the original version. By using the Save As command, you can save the changed document as Document B, which leaves Document A intact.

You can also use the Save As command to save the document to a different folder or drive than where you originally saved it — for example, if you stored the document on your hard drive and now want to save a copy on a floppy disk. Another use for the command is saving a document in a different file format (type of file). If you're giving your document to a coworker who uses a different word processor, for example, you can save it in a format compatible with that program.

To save a document under a new name, in a different format, or to a new destination, choose File➪Save As or press the F3 key to open the Save File dialog box (refer to Figure 5-3). Choose a folder and hard drive from the Save In drop-down menu, choose a file format from the File Type drop-down menu, and enter a name in the File Name option box. Then click the Save button or press Enter.

Here's an even quicker way to save a document to a floppy disk: With the document open, choose File➪Send To and then select your floppy drive (A or B) from the Send To submenu. WordPerfect copies the document to the floppy disk without displaying the Save File dialog box.

What's in a (Windows 95) filename?

In the past, Windows insisted that you follow strict rules in naming files. A correct filename consisted of an eight-character document name, followed by a period, followed by a three-letter file extension. (The extension indicated the type of document — WPD for WordPerfect documents, TIF for a graphics file saved in the TIFF format, and so on.)

Windows 95 changes the naming rules somewhat. You can now have filenames up to 255 characters long, although why you'd want such a long name is beyond me. Filenames still have three-letter file extensions, but you don't need to add the extension if you're saving a file — the extension is added automatically for you. If, for some reason, you want to specify the extension, of course, you can.

If you want to share a document with a co-worker who doesn't use Windows 95 or Windows 95 programs, however, stick with the old eight-character, three-letter-extension naming conventions. Longer filenames are truncated (cut off) in your coworker's Open File dialog box, making it difficult to tell which file is which.

Getting extra protection through automatic saving

With all the other things you need to remember during a workday — your manager's favorite flavor of latté, the names of all the really important people in the office, the date of your next salary review — remembering to save your documents on a regular basis can be difficult. Fortunately, WordPerfect offers an option that saves your document automatically at specified intervals.

To use this feature, choose Tools⇨Settings to open the Settings dialog box and then double-click the Files item in the dialog box. The Files Settings dialog box appears, as shown in Figure 5-4. If you don't see a check mark in the Timed Document Backup Every check box, as spotlighted in the figure, click the box to turn on the option. By default, WordPerfect automatically saves your document every ten minutes; this value is usually a safe bet, but you can raise or lower the time according to your individual tolerance for risk.

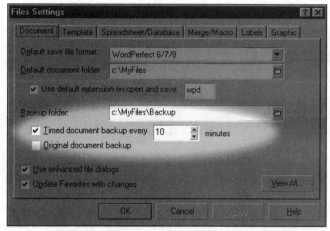

Figure 5-4:
If you
turn on
automatic
document
backup,
WordPerfect
automatically
saves your
document
at specified
intervals.

Printing Your Pages

Usually, printing is a pretty straightforward process — if your printer and your computer are correctly connected and configured to work together. If they're not, well then, printing your documents using a calligraphy pen and ink may be easier.

Because different printers and computer systems require different configurations — and because I'm not sure which printer or system you're using today — I can't give you specific instructions for setting up your printer. So the following steps assume that your printer and computer are on speaking terms and willing to cooperate in the printing process. If you have trouble, find your local printer guru (look for the person with toner-stained sleeves) and ask for help.

Having expertly dodged that responsibility, I can move on to basic printing steps. Here's how you print an open document:

1. **Choose File⇨Print, press Ctrl+P, or click the Print button on the Application Bar.**

    The Print dialog box zooms into view, as shown in Figure 5-5.

2. **Choose a printer from the Current Printer drop-down list.**

    Unless you're on a network and have access to more than one printer, you probably don't need to worry about this step. The right printer should already be selected by default. But it never hurts to check, just in case.

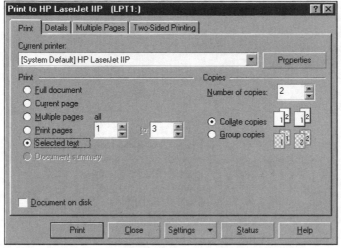

Figure 5-5:
The Print
dialog box
is the magic
window to
getting your
documents
out of the
computer
and onto
paper.

3. Specify how many copies you want to print.

Enter the number of copies in the <u>N</u>umber of Copies option box. (There's a surprise.) If you print more than one copy, the <u>G</u>roup and Coll<u>a</u>te options become available. If you choose <u>G</u>roup, the printer prints all copies of page 1 and then prints all copies of page 2 and so on. If you choose Coll<u>a</u>te, the printer prints the entire document once, prints the second copy of the document, and so on — in other words, it collates the pages for you.

4. Specify which pages you want to print.

Here are your options:

- To print your entire document, select the Full Document radio button.

- To print just the current page (the page on which the insertion marker is located), select the Current Page radio button.

- To print several pages that fall together (for example, pages 1 through 5), select the Print Pages radio button and then enter the first page number and last page number in the adjacent option boxes, as shown in Figure 5-5.

- To print several pages that don't fall in sequence — say, pages 1, 4, and 5 — click on the Multiple Pages radio button. Then click the Multiple Pages tab to access the options shown in Figure 5-6. Enter the numbers of the pages you want to print in the Page(s)/ label(s) option box and ignore the other options.

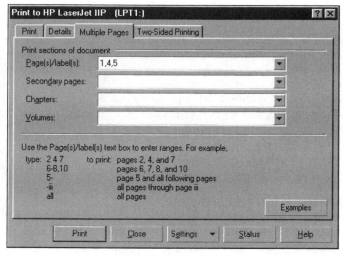

Figure 5-6:
Head for
the Multiple
Pages tab
to print
several
pages that
don't fall in
sequence
in the
document.

You can enter page numbers in several ways. You can enter each page number, separated by a comma or space, as shown in Figure 5-6. Or you can indicate a range of pages by entering the first page in the range, a hyphen, and then the last number in the range. You can also combine the two approaches by entering **1,4-5**, for example.

- If you select text before choosing the Print command, you can print just the selection by choosing the Selected Text radio button.

5. Click the Print button or press Enter.

Your pages should start shooting out of your printer momentarily. Well, maybe not shooting, exactly — they actually sort of crawl out if you have a printer like mine. May as well go get that cup of latté for your boss while you're waiting.

Here are a few additional goodies to know about printing:

✔ If you want to print your document sideways — otherwise known as *landscape* printing — click the Properties button in the Print dialog box. WordPerfect opens the Properties dialog box for your printer. Click the Landscape Orientation option on the Paper tab and then click OK. (Depending on your printer, this option may be on a different tab in the Properties dialog box.) To change the orientation of your document permanently, see the section "Choosing a Page Size and Orientation" in Chapter 7.

✔ To print a document without opening it, choose File⇨Print and select the Document on Disk check box. An option box appears to the right of the check box. Enter the complete document pathname. (See the discussion on pathnames in the sidebar "What's a pathname anyway?") Or, if you don't know the pathname, click the little white button at the right end of the option box to display the Open File dialog box, locate the file in the document list, and then click Select to put the pathname into the list box. Click Print or press Enter to express your document to the printer.

You can also print a document by right-clicking its name in the Open File dialog box and choosing Print from the resulting QuickMenu. This method, however, bypasses the Print dialog box, so you can't set any new print options.

✔ Printing graphics sometimes takes a lot of time and printer memory. If you're short on either or both and are just printing a rough draft of your document, you can print your document without graphics by selecting the Print Text Only check box on the Details tab of the Print dialog box.

If time or printer memory is limited, another option for printing graphics is to lower the Resolution setting, also found on the Details tab in the Print dialog box. Your printed piece doesn't look as good as it would if printed at a high resolution, but the output may be okay for a draft copy.

What's a pathname anyway?

Every now and then, a program demands that you enter a file's *pathname.* The pathname gives your computer all the information it needs to locate a particular file: the name of the file plus the name of the hard drive, main folder, and subfolders that hold the document.

If, for example, you store a file named FILE1.WPD inside a folder called Subfolder1, which is itself stored inside a folder called Folder1, which is stored on your C drive, the pathname is C:\Folder1\Subfolder1\FILE1.WPD.

Chapter 6

Eating Your Words and Other Editing Tasks

*T*his chapter shows you the basics of editing in WordPerfect. You find out how to delete unwanted text, how to copy and move words, sentences, and entire paragraphs, and how to use the QuickCorrect feature to automatically correct mistakes as you type.

After you get familiar with editing in a word processor, you're forever ruined as far as using a traditional typewriter. Not only do you find the limitations of a typewriter unbearable, but your typing accuracy goes to pot. WordPerfect enables you to fix mistakes so easily that you soon find yourself typing with far less regard for hitting the right keys than you used to have. You can type as fast as your thoughts can take you, knowing that you can come back later and quickly clean up any typos, bloopers, or blunders.

Don't mourn the loss of your typing accuracy, however. Look at it from the positive side: If the computer's down and someone asks you to type that letter or memo on a typewriter, you can honestly say, "Gee, I'd like to, but now that I'm a word-processing expert, I'm just no good on the typewriter. We pay a heavy price for this advancing technology, don't we?"

Make sure that you walk away quickly, before the other party has a chance to get over the shock and question your sincerity.

Selecting Stuff You Want to Edit

Before you can perform many editing and formatting tasks, you must first *select* the characters or paragraphs you want to change. Figure 6-1 shows an example of how selected text looks on-screen. You can select text in countless ways. Here are just a few:

- Drag over the characters or words you want to select.
- To select a single word, double-click that word.
- To select a sentence, triple-click anywhere within the sentence. Or move the cursor into the left margin of the sentence and click once.
- To select a paragraph, quadruple-click anywhere within that paragraph. Yikes! Who thought up that one? If this maneuver is beyond you, move the cursor to the left margin of the paragraph and double-click.
- Click anywhere in the word, sentence, or paragraph that you want to select. Move the mouse cursor to the left margin until the pointer becomes a right-pointing arrow and then right-click to display the QuickMenu, as shown in Figure 6-1. Click the selection option you want to use.

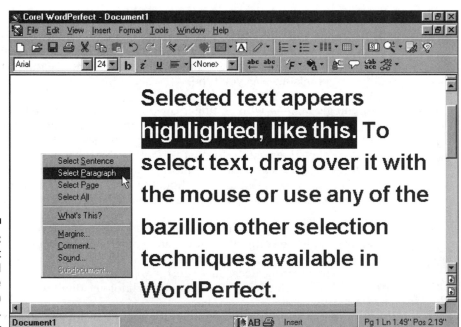

Figure 6-1:
A look at selected text and the selection QuickMenu.

- You can access the same selection commands found on the QuickMenu by choosing Edit➪Select. If you ask me, this method is the hard way to do things, but you may like doing things the hard way.

- To select everything in a document, press Ctrl+A (A for all).

- Here's one of my favorites: Place the insertion marker at the beginning of the text you want to select. Press Shift and then use the arrow keys and other cursor movement keys that I describe in Chapter 4 (End, Home, and so on) to extend the selection to the rest of the text you want to select. For example, click and then press Shift+End to select everything from the insertion marker to the end of the current line.

- If you select something and then decide that you want to add to the selection or subtract from it, just press and hold the Shift key as you use the arrow keys to move the end of the selection. Or press Shift and then click to set the new end of the selection.

- To cancel a selection entirely, click anywhere inside your text.

After you select text, you can wreak all kinds of havoc on it. You can copy it, delete it, move it, and replace it, as I cover throughout the rest of this chapter. And, as I discuss in Chapters 7 and 8, you can change the font and type size, change the line spacing and paragraph spacing, indent the text, capitalize it, number it, and make it do a little clogging dance to "Rocky Top." Oh, sorry, got a little carried away — in Windows 95, text clogs only to "Orange Blossom Special."

If you begin typing while text is selected, the selected text is replaced by the new text you type.

Deleting Selected Stuff

To get rid of unwanted text, select the text and press Delete or Backspace. As I cover in Chapter 4, you can also use Delete and Backspace to get rid of unselected text. Delete erases characters to the right of the insertion marker; Backspace erases characters to the left.

If you zap something into oblivion and then realize that you didn't want to get rid of it after all, don't panic. You can usually get it back by using the Undo or Undelete features, explained later in this chapter, in the sections "Bringing Back Lost Text" and "Undoing Changes."

Moving and Copying Text

Being able to erase unwanted text with a click of the mouse or press of a single key is pretty cool. But it's nothing compared with the editing power you gain after you discover how to cut, copy, and paste text. By using these techniques, you can quickly move and copy text from one place to another.

The cut, copy, and paste techniques described in this section work similarly in all Windows programs. You can use them to copy and move graphics as well as text. (You find more information about editing graphics in WordPerfect in Chapter 8. Make sure that you also check out Chapter 19, which discusses some special ways to move and copy data between documents and programs.)

Because of the way WordPerfect handles formatted text, you can screw up your text formatting if you rearrange text. That's why you may find that doing the bulk of your editing *before* you apply formatting commands, such as boldface, paragraph styles, and so on, is easier than formatting before you edit. For more information on this topic, see the sidebar, "Help! Everything got screwy after I moved stuff around!"

Using the Copy, Cut, and Paste commands

You can copy a piece of text and place the copy in a new location by using two methods. You can drag and drop the text, as explained in the following section, "Dragging and dropping," or you can use the Copy and Paste commands, as outlined in this section.

Which method is better depends on your dexterity with the mouse and the type of copying or moving you're doing. If you're copying a large block of text or copying from one document to another, using the Cut, Copy, and Paste commands is often easier. For small bits of text, dragging and dropping is more convenient.

To copy text by using the Copy command, follow these steps:

1. **Select the text that you want to copy.**

   Use any of the selection techniques discussed in the section "Selecting Stuff You Want to Edit," earlier in this chapter.

 2. **Press Ctrl+C or click the Copy button on the toolbar.**

   If you prefer, choose Edit⇨Copy from the menu bar, or right-click and choose the Copy command from the QuickMenu.

WordPerfect sends a copy of your text to the Windows Clipboard, which is a temporary storage shed for copied and cut text and graphics.

3. **Click at the spot where you want to place the copy.**

You can put the copy in your current document or in another open document. You can even put the copy in a document you created in another program.

 4. **Press Ctrl+V or click the Paste button.**

Alternatively, you can choose Edit⇨Paste from the menu bar or right-click and choose Paste from the QuickMenu.

Whichever method you pick, WordPerfect places your copy at the new location.

 The process for moving selected text is the same as for copying text except that you use the Cut command rather than the Copy command. You can choose the command from the Edit menu or from the QuickMenu, click on the Cut button on the toolbar, or press the keyboard shortcut Ctrl+X.

 After you cut or copy something to the Clipboard, that text stays on the Clipboard until you cut or copy something else. So you can paste the cut or copied text as many times as you need to in your document. Just keep pressing Ctrl+V.

Notice that the three shortcut keys, X, C, and V, lie right next to each other on your keyboard. Why these keys? Well, maybe because *X* sort of looks like a pair of scissors (for Cut), *C* is the first letter in *Copy,* and *V* . . . well, maybe it's supposed to bring to mind the word *Viscid,* which means sticky (like paste). Then again, maybe not.

Dragging and dropping

If you're handy with a mouse — and who isn't, these days? — dragging and dropping provides a quick, menuless way to cut and copy text. Try using the technique described in the following steps to move a piece of text:

1. **Select the text that you want to move.**

See "Selecting Stuff You Want to Edit" earlier in this chapter for help, if you need it.

2. **Place the mouse cursor on the selected text.**

3. **Press and hold the left mouse button as you drag the text to its new home.**

A little box appears next to your cursor to show that you've grabbed the text.

4. **After you've placed the text where you want it, release the mouse button.**

The text appears at its new location.

If you want to copy a piece of text rather than move it, press Ctrl anytime before you release the mouse button. A plus sign appears next to the cursor to tell you that you're copying instead of cutting the selected text.

In addition to dragging and dropping text within the same document, you can drag and drop between two open WordPerfect documents or between two different programs. The following steps explain how to drag and drop between programs:

1. **Open the document that contains the text you want to move.**

This document is sometimes called the *source*.

2. **Open the document where you want to move or copy the text.**

This document is sometimes referred to as the *destination*.

3. **Select the text and then drag it to the Windows 95 taskbar button for the destination program.**

Don't let up on the mouse button after you get to the taskbar; keep the button pressed until the window for the destination program appears. Then drag to the position in that window where you want to place the text and release the mouse button.

To drag and drop between two open WordPerfect documents, drag the selected text from the source document to the Application Bar button for the destination document. Wait until the destination document comes to life and then drop the text into the document.

Dragging text cuts it from the source document and pastes it into the destination document. To copy the text, press Ctrl before you release the mouse button.

Dragging and dropping between programs is possible through the magic of *Object Linking and Embedding,* otherwise known as *OLE* (pronounced *olé,* like at a bullfight). You can do lots of interesting things with OLE, so make sure that you check out Chapter 19, which covers the subject in excruciating detail.

Help! Everything got screwy when I moved stuff around!

If everything goes kablooey after you rearrange text — for example, all your plain text suddenly becomes bold and vice versa — you've messed up WordPerfect's hidden codes. You see, any time that you give WordPerfect a formatting instruction, whether you want to set a tab, make text bold, or change a paragraph indent, the program inserts little hidden codes into your text. And if you accidentally grab a code as you select a piece of text — or you don't grab a code that should be moved along with that text — WordPerfect gets all perplexed.

If this situation occurs, you have a couple options: One, you can reformat the text as needed. Two, you can choose View⇨Reveal Codes or press Alt+F3 to display the Reveal Codes window, as shown in the following figure. In this window, you can see and edit the hidden formatting codes.

The problem with editing codes is that the process can be confusing, especially for beginners. If you like puzzle-solving, however, and you want to become a code-cracker, check out *WordPerfect 8 For Windows For Dummies,* which dedicates an entire chapter to the subject.

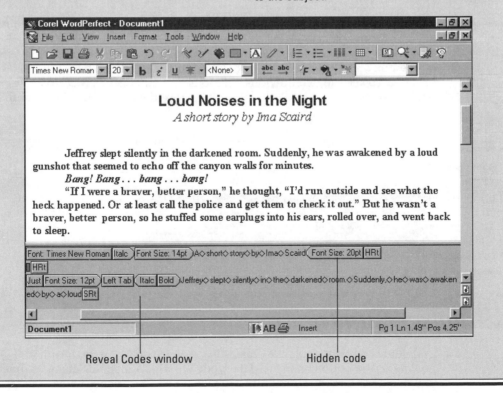

Reveal Codes window

Hidden code

Bringing Back Lost Text

Sooner or later, it happens: You delete some text and then realize with horror that you wiped out the wrong thing. The thing that's going to take you hours to re-create. The thing that your boss wants to see on her desk in 30 minutes.

Don't panic. WordPerfect has a built-in safety net just for such situations. It's called the *Undelete command.* By using this command, you can undelete the last three pieces of text you deleted.

Undelete, however, brings back only the text that you erase by using the Delete key. If you used the Cut command, you must use the Undo command, which I explain in the following section, to reverse your mistake.

Oddly enough, in Version 8, the Undelete command has been kicked out of its former home on the Edit menu. In fact, you don't find this command on any menu in Version 8. But the command still exists, and you can access it by pressing Ctrl+Shift+Z.

WordPerfect responds by displaying the Undelete dialog box, as shown in Figure 6-2, and places the last text you deleted at the insertion marker. The text is highlighted to make it easy to spot. (You may need to move the dialog box out of the way. To do so, just drag it by the title bar.) Click Previous to see the two previous deletions you made; click Next to cycle back through the three deletions. Click Restore if you see one you want to undelete.

Figure 6-2:
Pressing
Ctrl+Shift+Z
accesses
the
Undelete
command.

Undoing Changes

Undelete is a handy tool, but it pales in comparison to the restorative powers of the Undo command. Like Undelete, Undo reverses changes that you decide you really shouldn't have made. But Undo can reverse almost any editing action, not just deletions made with Delete. And whereas

Undelete restores text at the insertion marker, Undo puts it back in its original location. What's more, Undo can reverse up to your last 300 editing moves. The following list reveals the secrets to using Undo:

✔ To undo the last editing change you made, choose Edit⇨Undo, click the Undo button, or press either of two available shortcuts: Ctrl+Z or Alt+Backspace.

✔ Change your mind about that undo? Choose Edit⇨Redo, click the Redo button, or press Ctrl+Shift+R to put things back the way they were before you chose the Undo command.

✔ You must choose Redo immediately after choosing Undo. If you type new text or make any other changes to your document, Redo becomes unavailable.

✔ If you want to go further back in time than your last editing action, you have two options: You can keep choosing the Undo command, or you can choose Edit⇨Undo/Redo History to display the Undo/Redo History dialog box, as shown in Figure 6-3. The Undo list box shows your recent editing changes — albeit in rather cryptic terms. Click the action that you want to undo from the Undo list and then click the Undo button.

Figure 6-3:
You can
reverse
your edits
via the
Undo/Redo
History
dialog box.

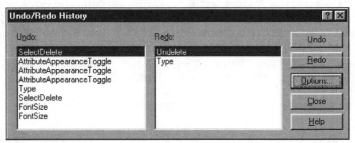

After you select an action in the Undo list box, all actions above it in the list are automatically selected and are also undone. You can't select the third action in the list, for example, without undoing the first and second actions as well.

After you click Undo, the actions you reversed appear in the Redo list box. WordPerfect makes the changes in your document, but nothing's set in stone until you click Close to exit the dialog box. If you change your mind and want to restore an action, select it from the Redo list box and click the Redo button.

✔ By default, WordPerfect enables you to undo your last ten editing changes. But if you click the Options button in the Undo/Redo History dialog box, WordPerfect displays a second dialog box, where you can raise or lower the number of undos by adjusting the Number of Undo/ Redo Items value. Keep in mind that the higher the number of undos you can perform, the more you tax your computer's memory.

✔ Undo can't undo all actions. You can't, for example, undo saving a document.

Letting WordPerfect Correct Mistakes for You

Wouldn't it be nice to have a servant that trailed around after you all the time, picking up stuff you drop, wiping up drinks you spill, and otherwise cleaning up your messes for you? What — you say that you're a mom, and *you're* the servant? Well, now's your chance to be the mess-maker and have someone else — namely WordPerfect — pick up after you.

WordPerfect's QuickCorrect feature provides as-you-type error correction. Type a word incorrectly, and WordPerfect automatically corrects it for you as soon as you hit the spacebar. Try typing *teh*, for example, and pressing the spacebar. WordPerfect assumes that what you really meant to type was *the,* so it automatically changes *teh* to *the*. It doesn't even bother you with a dialog box, beep, or other whiny complaint — it just goes quietly about its cleanup business.

Adding words to the QuickCorrect list

To determine which words need correcting, WordPerfect consults an internal list of commonly misspelled and mistyped words. You can add words to the list by choosing Tools⇨QuickCorrect or by pressing Ctrl+Shift+F1 to display the QuickCorrect dialog box, as shown in Figure 6-4.

To add a word to the QuickCorrect list, type the misspelled version in the Replace option box and enter the correct word in the With option box. Click Add Entry to make your addition official and make sure, too, that the Replace Words as You Type check box is selected. Click OK to return to your document.

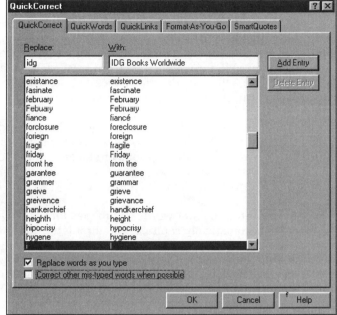

Figure 6-4:
You can
add words
to or delete
words from
WordPerfect's
QuickCorrect
list.

You can use QuickCorrect to automatically replace abbreviations with the full word or phrase. The entries shown in Figure 6-4, for example, tell WordPerfect that, whenever I type the letters **idg**, I want it to substitute the words *IDG Books Worldwide*.

The new QuickWords feature gives you an alternative way to accomplish the same thing. You can read more about this feature in Chapter 9. I don't find one method any easier to use than the other; the one you decide to use is all a matter of personal preference. QuickWords, however, does give you a few more options for when and how your abbreviations are replaced with the full text.

If you turn on the Correct Other Mistyped Words When Possible option at the bottom of the QuickCorrect dialog box, WordPerfect goes beyond the bounds of the QuickCorrect list in automatically correcting words. If you type any word that's misspelled according to WordPerfect's spell-checking dictionary, the program automatically corrects the word for you. WordPerfect doesn't make the correction, however, if it finds two or more possible ways to correct the mistyped word. If you type **knowledgable**, for example, WordPerfect automatically inserts an *e* before *able*. But if you type **thier**, no correction is made, because WordPerfect doesn't know whether you meant to type *their, thief, tier,* or some other variation of those letters.

Fixing other flubs on the fly

In addition to fixing spelling and typing errors, WordPerfect can make sure that the first letter in a sentence is capitalized, change two uppercase letters in a row into an uppercase letter followed by a lowercase letter (changing *THe* to *The,* for example), eliminate double spaces between words, and convert two spaces at the end of a sentence to a single space.

To turn these features on and off, choose T̲ools⇨Q̲uickCorrect and click the Format-As-You-Go tab in the QuickCorrect dialog box that appears, as shown in Figure 6-5. The sentence-correction options are located in the top half of the dialog box. Other Format-As-You-Go options automatically apply formatting commands and features that I discuss in Chapter 8.

Click the Exceptions button to enter words or phrases for which you don't want WordPerfect to automatically capitalize the first letter following a period or other end-of-sentence punctuation. For example, if a product name includes such punctuation — as in Corel Photo-Paint! — you may want to enter the product name as an exception. Otherwise, the first letter after the punctuation mark is automatically capitalized, as in "Corel Photo-Paint! Is the next best thing to sliced bread."

Figure 6-5:
WordPerfect can also make automatic corrections to sentences with the options in this dialog box.

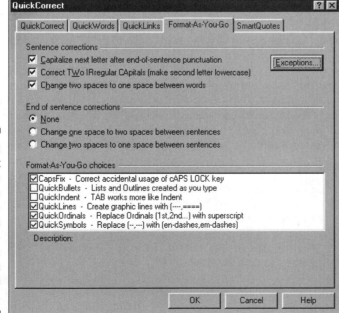

Overruling unwanted corrections

As helpful as QuickCorrect can be, it can also get in the way sometimes. Suppose that you want to use the word *august* in its adjectival sense rather than referring to the month — as in, "The king had an august nature." WordPerfect plows right ahead and changes your lowercase *august* to *August*.

You can overrule WordPerfect by deleting the word it's correcting from the QuickCorrect list. Choose Tools➪QuickCorrect (or press Ctrl+Shift+F1) to open the QuickCorrect dialog box (refer to Figure 6-4), select the word in the list box, and click the Delete Entry button.

If you want WordPerfect to substitute different text after you type a particular word or set of characters, select the original word in the list box, enter the new replacement text in the With option box, and click the Replace Entry button. (This button becomes available after you click the With option box.) Click OK to make your wish the law of the land.

To turn off QuickCorrect altogether, deselect the Replace Words as You Type check box in the QuickCorrect dialog box.

Chapter 7

Making Your Text Look Pretty

Creating professional-looking text is an artistic endeavor. And the task involves more than just turning a fancy phrase. You also need to think about things such as type style and size, the amount of spacing between words and letters, and how much to indent lines and paragraphs from the margins.

These design considerations — known collectively as *formatting* — play a significant role in whether people take the time to read your documents. Eye-catching, easy-to-read pages draw in readers and make them more receptive to your message. Poorly designed, difficult-to-read pages become receptacles for used chewing gum (or worse).

This chapter shows you the ins and outs of getting your text ready for public consumption. You find out how to make characters bold and italic, how to control text spacing, and how to perform other feats of formatting magic. In other words, this chapter gives you a chance to explore your artistic side.

If you want to feel like a real artist, make sure that you dress in weird clothes (all black is good) and drink tons of espresso as you work. You should also start describing your page designs in complex psychological and sociological terms that make sense only to you. Don't forget to look scornfully at anyone who doesn't pretend to understand what you're saying.

After you get a block of text formatted just the way you like it, you can use the QuickFormat command and paragraph styles, which I discuss in Chapter 9, to automatically copy the formatting to other text.

Playing with Fonts

One of the most noticeable ways to dress up your text is by changing the font, type style, and type size.

The *font* — sometimes called *typeface* — determines the shape and design of the characters. Each font has a distinct name, such as Times New Roman, Helvetica, and so on. Figure 7-1 shows a few different fonts for your amusement.

Type style refers to any special formatting attributes applied to the text — boldface, italics, underline, and so on. *Type size* determines, uh, well, how big the characters are. Sorry to insult you.

The following sections explain how to deal with each of these character formatting issues.

Choosing a font

The WordPerfect Suite comes with a bunch of fonts, and you may have other fonts installed on your system, too. By default, WordPerfect uses the Times New Roman font, a time-honored and traditional serif font.

A *serif* font is one that has serifs — little lines decorating the upper and lower ends of the strokes of the letters. A *sans serif* font has no serifs (*sans serif* means "without serifs" in French). The top example shown in Figure 7-1 is a serif font; the other three are sans serif fonts. Notice that the characters in different fonts can be markedly different not only in design, but also in the amount of space they take up on your page. All four lines of text in Figure 7-1 use 31-point type, but the third line is significantly shorter than the other three.

Most people love to play with fonts. But keep in mind that the more fonts you install, the more you tax your computer. So don't even think about installing all 1,000 fonts found on the WordPerfect Suite CD. Be selective, and install only those fonts that you're really going to use.

For long blocks of text, use a serif font, which is easier to read. Sans serif fonts are best used for headlines, subheads, and other short blocks of text.

Before you dig into the methods for changing fonts, you need to understand a bit about how WordPerfect applies your changes. If you select a piece of text before choosing a font, the font is applied to the selected text only. If you don't select any text, the font is applied to all text from the insertion marker forward, up to the point where you previously applied a font change.

To change the font for a single word, you can just click anywhere in the word instead of selecting it.

Font menu ⌐Type Size menu   QuickFonts button   Serif

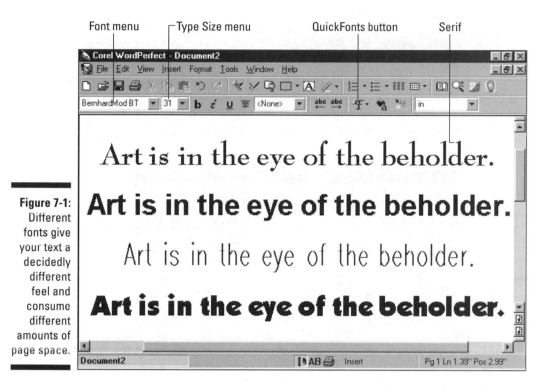

Figure 7-1:
Different
fonts give
your text a
decidedly
different
feel and
consume
different
amounts of
page space.

With those little tidbits of information under your belt, you're now ready to start playing with your fonts. To choose a new font, you can use any of the following tactics:

- ✔ Click the arrow at the end of the Font drop-down menu on the Property Bar (refer to Figure 7-1) to display a list fonts installed in your system. As you pass your cursor over each font name, WordPerfect displays a preview that shows you how the font looks. Click the font you want to use.

- ✔ Choose Format➪Font, press F9, or right-click anywhere in the document window and then choose the Font command from the QuickMenu. The Font dialog box appears, as shown in Figure 7-2. The Font dialog box gives you one central location for applying a variety of text formatting attributes, including type size, style, color, and shading.

- ✔ Click the QuickFonts button on the Property Bar to display a menu of the 20 most recent font combinations (font, size, and style) you've used.

If you want to change the default font that WordPerfect uses, first make sure that no text is selected; then open the Font dialog box and click the Default Font button. You get a miniature version of the Font dialog box in which you can specify the default font, size, and style. If you select the Use as Default check box, WordPerfect uses your settings as defaults for the current document and for any new documents you create. If you don't select the check box, the defaults apply to the current document only, and the previously set defaults are used for any new documents.

Regardless of whether you select the check box, WordPerfect applies the new defaults to any text in the current document that used the original defaults. If you previously applied a different font, size, or style to a piece of text, however, WordPerfect leaves that formatting intact.

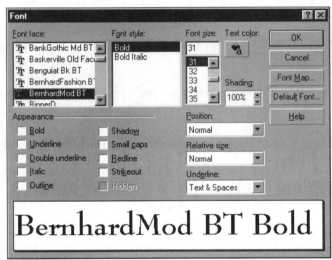

Figure 7-2:
The Font dialog box gives you a way to set several type options at once.

Changing the type size and style

As with font changes, changes to type size and style affect any text from the insertion marker forward *except* for text you previously formatted. If you want to change the size or style for a specific portion of text, select the text and then apply your formatting changes.

The quickest way to change the type size is to use the Type Size drop-down menu on the Property Bar (refer to Figure 7-1). If you want to use a size not on the menu — for example, you want 12.5-point type — double-click the drop-down menu, enter the size you want, and press Enter. Alternatively, you can change the type size in the Font dialog box (press F9 or choose Format⇨Font).

Fonts are measured in *points*. A point is roughly equivalent to $1/72$ inch. If you want people to be able to read your text easily, don't use type smaller than 10 points.

Why won't WordPerfect do what I tell it to?

If you can't get a particular formatting command to work the way it's supposed to — or applying a formatting command gives you unexpected results — it's probably because you've messed up the hidden codes that WordPerfect inserts in your text as you apply formatting. Moving text around, deleting text, and removing and reapplying formatting can sometimes mess up these hidden codes.

If things get screwy, one solution is to open the Reveal Codes window (by pressing Alt+F3 or choosing View⇨Reveal Codes). (Chapter 6, gives you a look at the Reveal Codes window, in the sidebar "Hey, everything got screwy when I moved stuff around!") If you're familiar with WordPerfect's codes, you can take a stab at sorting out the formatting codes to figure out what went wrong. If you want to become a hidden code guru, check out *WordPerfect 8 For Windows For Dummies* (IDG Books Worldwide, Inc.), which offers an in-depth explanation of the subject.

If playing in the Reveal Codes Amusement Park makes you queasy, however, simply try selecting the text you want to format and reissuing the formatting command. If you still don't get the results you want, check the style applied to the text. (I explain styles in Chapter 9.) Try applying the None style and then applying your formatting again. If things still don't work right, you need a WordPerfect guru to help you clean up your hidden codes.

Three type style options — boldface, italics, and underline — are available on the Property Bar. The **b** button makes text bold, the *i* button makes it italic, and the u button underlines the text. The Property Bar buttons *toggle* the styles on and off — click the button once to turn the style on; click again to turn the style off. You can also use the shortcut keys for these styles: Ctrl+B, Ctrl+I, and Ctrl+U, respectively. Pressing the shortcut once turns the style on; pressing the keys a second time turns the style off.

For other style attributes, open the Font dialog box (by pressing F9 if you want speedy results). You can tweak your text style in a variety of ways, as follows:

- ✔ The Appearance attributes apply special effects to your type. In addition to bold, italic, and underlined type, you can create shadowed type, outlined type, double-underlined type, and more. You can apply as many attributes to a piece of text as your conscience allows. (***Hint:*** Unless you want people to run away screaming after taking one look at your text, use these effects sparingly.)

- ✔ You may have noticed that italic and bold options are also sometimes available in the Font Style list box at the top of the dialog box. What gives? Well, some font designers create specific bold and italic versions of their type. The available versions appear in the Font Style list box.

Whenever you have the option, always use a built-in style (by selecting it from the Font Style list box) rather than applying the style via the Appearance check boxes. That way, the font appears as the font designer intended — which is not always the case when you apply the bold or italic Appearance attributes. Also, the styles applied by WordPerfect may not work correctly if you send your text document to a service bureau for commercial printing.

✔ The Position drop-down list offers superscript and subscript options. Leave the setting on Normal for normal text. (Did you guess that one already?)

✔ You can use the Relative Size option to make your text proportionally larger or smaller than the current font size. The option stays in effect until you change the font back to Normal. You probably aren't going to have much use for this option.

✔ The Underline options tell WordPerfect whether you want to underline the spaces in your text. If you choose the Text & Spaces option, the space between words is underlined. If you choose the Text & Tabs option, WordPerfect underlines across tabs as well.

✔ The Text Color and Shading options enable you to add color and shading to text. Remember that these colors don't print unless you have a color printer.

 You can change the font color quickly by clicking the Font Color button on the Property Bar. WordPerfect displays a selection of color swatches; click the swatch that you want to use. Click the More button to access a color wheel that enables you to create a custom color. Drag the little square in the color wheel to choose the basic hue; drag the square in the neighboring slider bar to make the color darker or lighter.

 Ever had one of those neon yellow, orange, and blue highlighter pens? The kind people use to mark important stuff in reports, textbooks, and such? You can create a similar highlighting effect in WordPerfect by clicking the Highlighter button on the toolbar or by choosing Tools➪Highlight➪On. The cursor changes to a little highlighter pen. Drag across the text you want to highlight. Turn on the Print/Show option on the Tools➪Highlight submenu to see the highlighting on-screen and in your printed document. (If you see a check mark next to the Print/Show command, the option is turned on. Click on the command to toggle the feature on and off.) After you're done highlighting text, click the highlighter button or choose Tools➪Highlight➪On to put the highlighter pen away.

Choosing a Page Size and Orientation

After you start a standard new document, WordPerfect gives you an 8½-x-11-inch page size, with text oriented in *portrait* position — that is, with text running parallel to the short edge of the paper. This position is called portrait, by the way, because portraits normally use this same orientation. If you turn the page on its side, you get *landscape* orientation — so-named because landscape paintings typically use this layout.

If you choose one of the templates that I discuss in Chapter 3 to create your document, WordPerfect selects a page size that's appropriate for the document. You can change the page size and/or orientation at your whim, however. Here's how:

✔ To change the page size, choose File➪Page Setup. The Page Setup dialog box opens, as shown in Figure 7-3. Choose a page size and orientation (known collectively as a *page definition*) by making a selection from the Page Information list box on the Size tab. Click the Portrait or Landscape radio button to set the page orientation.

Select the Following Pages Different from Current Page check box to display a second set of page size and orientation options, as in Figure 7-3. These options affect the pages following the current page, just as the name implies.

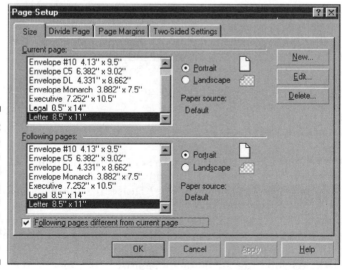

Figure 7-3:
Choose your page size and orientation on the Size tab of the Page Setup dialog box.

✔ If one of the preset page definitions isn't sufficient, you can choose the New button to create a new page definition or choose Edit to edit an existing page definition.

Any page definitions that you apply take effect from the insertion marker through the end of your document or to the point where you previously set a new page definition.

Your printer may or may not be capable of printing the page sizes you define. In addition, the printer may have difficulty applying two or more different page definitions in the same document. The types of pages available through the Page Setup dialog box also depend on the capabilities of your printer. Check the instructions that came with your printer to find out how much flexibility you have. If you're on an office network and have several printers at your beck and call, go tug on the sleeve of your network administrator and ask for the inside scoop on your printing options.

If you want to create and print labels, choose Format⇨Labels. WordPerfect displays a dialog box that enables you to choose from a whole slew of preset page definitions that mesh with labels from major label manufacturers. After you enter the information on your first label, press Ctrl+Enter to move on to the next. Use the Format⇨Page⇨Center command to center text vertically on the labels. (I discuss this command later in this chapter, in the section "Justifying text.")

You can also insert into your labels the names and addresses stored in the Corel Address Book, which I explain at the end of Chapter 9. Choose Tools⇨Address Book to open the Address Book window, click the name you want to add to the label, and click Insert. To create labels for several people or organizations at once, click the first name, Ctrl+click the other names, and click Insert.

Keep in mind that each label is a separate page in your document. So you can print individual labels by printing just the pages that contain those labels. For how-to's on printing, see Chapter 5.

Setting Page Margins

WordPerfect 8 provides a speedy way to set the top, bottom, left, and right margins of your pages. See those dotted lines running across the top, bottom, left, and right sides of your page? Those are *margin guidelines*. (If the guidelines don't appear on-screen, choose View⇨Guidelines, select the Margins check box in the Guidelines dialog box that appears, and click OK.) To change a margin, move your cursor over the guideline until it changes into a two-headed arrow, as shown in Figure 7-4. Then drag the guide to a new position. As you drag the guideline, a little box appears to show you the cursor's distance from the edge of the page.

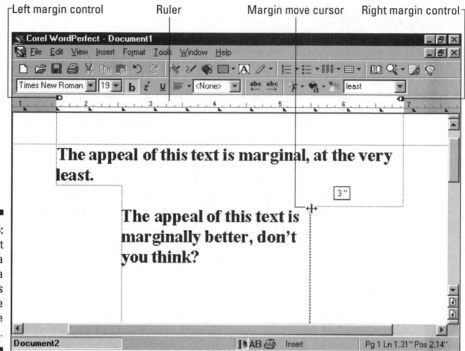

Left margin control   Ruler   Margin move cursor   Right margin control

Figure 7-4:
WordPerfect
gives you a
cornucopia
of ways
to change
page
margins.

If you prefer, you can use the following methods for setting margins instead:

✔ Press Ctrl+F8 to open the Page Setup dialog box with the Page Margins tab active. Enter your margin settings and click OK.

✔ Choose View⇨Ruler or press Alt+Shift+F3 to display the ruler (if the ruler isn't already visible, that is). Then drag the left and right margin controls (refer to Figure 7-4). Make sure that you drag the margin controls — the left- and right-most black thingies on the ruler — and not the diamonds beside the margin controls, which set margins only for individual paragraphs.

Left and right margin settings affect text from the point of the insertion marker forward and remain in effect until WordPerfect encounters another margin setting that you previously established. Top and bottom margin settings affect the current page and any subsequent pages up to the point where you previously changed the margins. If you want, you can also apply margin settings to selected text only.

Most desktop printers can't print all the way to the edges of a page. Being the protective sort that it is, WordPerfect prevents you from setting margins that are smaller than your printer can handle. WordPerfect makes its judgment based on the currently selected printer; see the section "Printing Your Pages" in Chapter 5 for information on how to select a printer.

Setting Tabs

Please place your left hand on your computer monitor — on the top, not the screen, please (fingerprints, you know) — and repeat this pledge: "I hereby swear to always use tabs instead of spaces to line things up in columns." Why? Well, for one thing, it's a heck of a lot easier to press the Tab key once instead of hitting the spacebar a zillion times to shove text across the page. But more important, your text may not line up correctly if you use spaces, as Figure 7-5 demonstrates. The entries in the Class and Age columns are slightly misaligned in the top example.

This alignment problem happens because many fonts aren't fixed-width fonts — in other words, different characters vary in width. (This kind of font is known as a *proportional* font, by the way.) So if you type Mary and press the spacebar four times, you don't end up at the same spot as you do if you type Jill and press the spacebar four times. In addition, the width of a space varies depending on the font you're using. Tabs, on the other hand, move the insertion marker to a specific spot on the page, so everything lines up as it should.

Don't use tabs to indent the first line of a paragraph, however. Instead, use the first-line indent option explained in the section "Indenting the first line of your paragraphs," later in this chapter

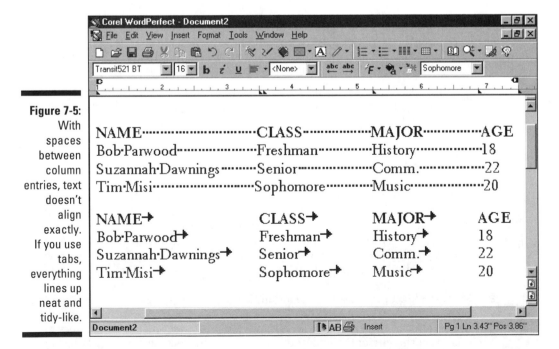

Figure 7-5: With spaces between column entries, text doesn't align exactly. If you use tabs, everything lines up neat and tidy-like.

If you're new to tabs, here's how they work: Each time you press the Tab key, WordPerfect moves the insertion marker to the next available tab stop to the right. Press Shift+Tab and you move the insertion marker to the previous tab stop — a procedure known in WordPerfect clubs as *back tabbing*.

By default, WordPerfect gives you a tab stop every half inch across the page. In many cases, you need to override the default tab stops and set your own custom tab stops. The following sections tell you what you need to know to work with tabs.

Adding, moving, or deleting a tab stop

If you add, move, or delete a tab stop, the new setting takes effect from the current paragraph forward to the end of the document or to the point where you previously changed tab settings. If you select a paragraph before changing a tab stop, the change affects the selected paragraph only.

The easiest way to set a tab is to use the ruler. (If the ruler doesn't appear on-screen, choose View⇨Ruler or press Alt+Shift+F3.) The little black triangles at the bottom of the ruler represent the tab stops (for a look at a tab stop, flip ahead to Figure 7-7). To set a standard left tab, just click the ruler; for information on how to see other tabs, such as decimal tabs, see the following section.

To move a tab stop, drag it along the ruler. To delete a tab stop, drag it down off the ruler.

You can also set tab stops in the Tab Set dialog box, as shown in Figure 7-6. To open the dialog box, choose Format⇨Line⇨Tab Set or right-click the bottom of the ruler and choose Tab Set from the QuickMenu. In the dialog box, enter the tab stop position in the Tab Position option box and click Set. Click OK to close the dialog box.

Here's some more stuff you need to know about changing your tab stops:

✔ You can choose from four major tab types, each of which aligns and formats tabbed text differently, as explained in the following section.

✔ Normally, WordPerfect measures tab stops from the left margin of your page. But you can tell the program to measure them from the left edge of the page, if you prefer. WordPerfect calls tabs measured from the left margin of the page *relative tabs*; tabs measured from the edge of the page are called *absolute tabs*. You can specify which option you want by selecting one of the Tab Position radio buttons in the Tab Set dialog box.

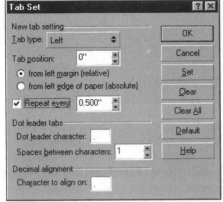

Figure 7-6:
The Tab Set
dialog box
lets you get
specific
about how
you want
tabbed text
to appear.

✔ After you add, delete, or move a tab stop, WordPerfect displays an icon in the left margin of the screen (see Figure 7-7). If you click the icon, you get a tab bar, which is a miniature version of the ruler. You can use the tab bar to change the tab settings for the paragraph just as you do on the ruler bar. Click outside the tab bar to hide it again. (If the tab stop icons don't appear, choose Tools⇔Settings to open the Settings dialog box, double-click on the Display icon to open the Display Settings dialog box, and turn on the Tab Bar Icons check box on the Document tab.)

✔ If you see a little balloon with quotation marks instead of the normal tab set icon, you've inserted more than one formatting instruction or another element, such as a sound clip (as explained in Chapter 21). Click the icon to display the individual formatting icons and then click the tab icon to display the tab bar.

✔ You can tell WordPerfect to space tabs at a specified increment across the page — for example, setting a tab stop every 3 inches. To do so, set the position of the first tab in the Tab Position option box of the Tab Set dialog box, check the Repeat Every check box, and specify the distance between tabs in the adjacent option box (refer to Figure 7-6).

✔ To clear all tab stops, right-click a tab stop on the ruler and choose Clear All Tabs from the QuickMenu. Or choose the Clear All button in the Tab Set dialog box.

✔ To return to the default tab stops — a left tab every half inch across the page — right-click the ruler and choose Default Tab Settings from the QuickMenu or choose the Default button in the Tab Set dialog box.

✔ If the QuickIndent feature is turned on, pressing Tab creates a paragraph indent instead of an ordinary tab in some situations. For more information about this feature, see the section "Indenting entire paragraphs," later in this chapter.

Figure 7-7:
Text aligns
differently
depending
on whether
you use a
left, right,
center, or
decimal tab.
(I added the
gray line in
the figure to
show the
alignment
with the tab
stop; you
don't see
the line on-
screen.)

Tab set icon   Tab bar   Tab stop

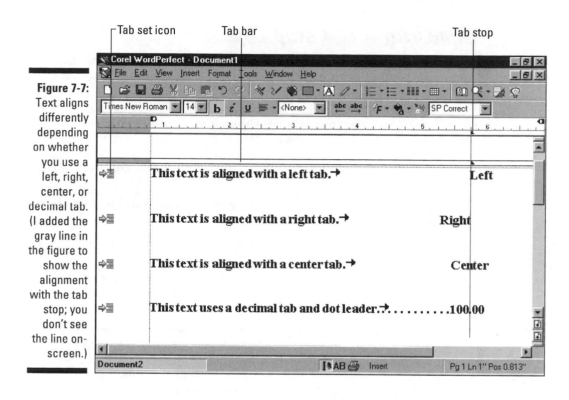

This text is aligned with a left tab.→   Left

This text is aligned with a right tab.→   Right

This text is aligned with a center tab.→   Center

This text uses a decimal tab and dot leader.→ 100.00

✔ The Tab key functions differently in Typeover mode than it does in Insert mode. (See Chapter 4 for an explanation of these editing modes.) In Typeover mode, pressing Tab moves the insertion marker across a line of text from one tab stop to the next but doesn't insert a tab. If no text is present, pressing Tab does insert a tab.

✔ By default, you can position a tab stop directly on a tick mark (gray dividing line) on the ruler or exactly between two tick marks. If you want to position a tab somewhere else, you have two options. You can set the tab by entering a specific position in the Tab Position option box of the Tab Set dialog box, or you can change the way the ruler works. Right-click the ruler bar and choose Settings from the QuickMenu to open the Ruler tab of the Display Settings dialog box. Deselect the Tabs Snap to Ruler Grid item and click OK.

Choosing a tab stop type

WordPerfect gives you four major types of tab stops, which you choose either from the Type drop-down list in the Tab Set dialog box or by right-clicking a tab stop (or the area where the tab stops appear), choosing a tab type from the resulting QuickMenu, and then clicking the ruler to insert the tab. (Click an existing tab stop to change the type of stop.) Your options, as shown in Figure 7-7, are as follows:

- **Left:** Text aligns to the right of the tab stop. A left tab stop on the ruler looks like this:

- **Right:** Text aligns to the left of the tab stop. A right tab stop looks like this:

- **Center:** Text is centered on the tab stop. A center tab stop appears like this:

- **Decimal:** The decimal point lines up with the tab stop. This setting is normally used to align columns of numbers. A decimal tab stop looks like this:

By default, decimal tabs align text by the decimal point (period). But you can change the character on which text aligns by entering a new one in the Character option box of the Tab Set dialog box. If, for example, you have a column of numbers that incorporate commas but no decimal points — such as $95,000 — you can set the align character to a comma. If the align character is a decimal point, but your numbers don't have decimal points, the numbers align by the last digit.

- You can put a dot leader into your tabbed text by choosing the Dot Left, Dot Right, Dot Center, or Dot Decimal options from the Tab Type drop-down list of the Tab Set dialog box. (On the QuickMenu, these options appear as ...Decimal, ...Right, and so on.) Dot leaders help guide the reader's eye across columns of text, as you can see in the last example shown in Figure 7-7. You can change the character used for the dot leader by entering a new one in the Dot Leader Character option box in the Tab Set dialog box. You can also vary the amount of space between each dot leader by changing the Spaces Between Characters value.

When should I take a paragraph break?

As you're entering text, don't press the Enter key after you get to the end of a line, as you do on a typewriter. WordPerfect automatically wraps your text to the next line for you. Pressing Enter inserts a *hard return.*

A hard return tells WordPerfect that one paragraph ends and another begins. If you select a paragraph, WordPerfect grabs everything from the paragraph break preceding the insertion marker to the next paragraph mark after

the insertion marker. WordPerfect also relies on the hard returns to tell it which text to change after you apply certain paragraph-level formatting, such as line spacing, paragraph indents, and paragraph spacing.

The moral of the story: Press Enter at the end of a line of text only if you want to end the paragraph. If you want to break text at the end of a line but don't want to start a new paragraph, press Ctrl+Shift+L.

Indenting and Aligning Text

Pressing the Tab key isn't the only way to shove your text across the page. You can also use WordPerfect's indent and justification options to change the way that text fits between the left and right margins of your page.

Indenting the first line of your paragraphs

If you want to indent the first line of each paragraph in your document, use indents instead of tabs. Why? Well, suppose that you use a tab to indent every paragraph in a long document. Then you decide that you don't want to indent those paragraphs after all. If you use tabs, you must remove the tab from every paragraph. If you use indents, on the other hand, all you need to do is change the indent setting to zero.

If you apply a first-line indent without any text selected, WordPerfect indents the first line of every paragraph after the insertion marker, up to the point at which you previously indented a paragraph. If you select text before applying a first-line indent, only the selected paragraphs are affected.

To indent the first line of a paragraph, follow these steps:

1. **Choose Format⇨Paragraph⇨Format.**

   WordPerfect displays the Paragraph Format dialog box, as shown in Figure 7-8.

2. **Enter the amount of the indent you want in the First Line Indent option box.**

3. **Click OK or press Enter.**

Figure 7-8:
Use the
Paragraph
Format
dialog box
to indent
the first
line of
paragraphs.

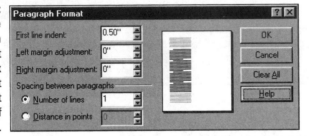

Alternatively, you can simply drag the first-line indent control on the ruler (see Figure 7-9). To remove first-line indents, just change the First Line Indent value back to zero.

Indenting entire paragraphs

As Figure 7-9 shows, you can also indent the entire paragraph from the left margin, indent the paragraph from both the right and left margins (called a double indent), and indent all but the first line of a paragraph (called a hanging indent). In addition, you can create what WordPerfect calls a *back tab*, which shoves the first line of a paragraph one tab stop to the left.

To apply these indents, first select the paragraphs you want to indent. If no text is selected, the indenting is applied from the current paragraph forward, up to the point where WordPerfect encounters any previously set indents. Then choose Format⇨Paragraph and choose an indent option from the Paragraph submenu. Or, to bypass the menus, use the keyboard shortcuts listed in Table 7-1 or drag the paragraph indent controls on the ruler bar (shown in Figure 7-9).

First-line indent   Left indent   Right indent

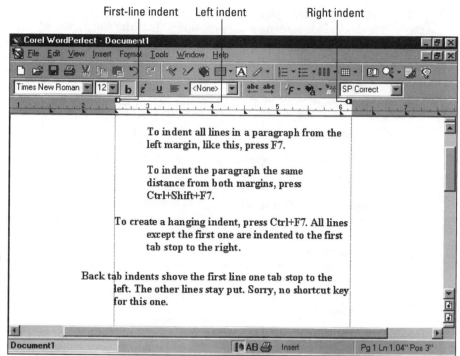

Figure 7-9:
Examples of
different
kinds of
indents.

With the exception of the first-line indents, WordPerfect indents your text according to the tab stops you set. To change the amount of indent, you have to change the tab stops, as explained earlier in this chapter.

Table 7-1	Indent Options and Shortcuts	
Indent Type	*Shortcut*	*What It Does*
First Line Indent	None	Indents the first line of a paragraph.
Indent	F7	Indents all lines of a paragraph one tab stop to the right.
Double Indent	Ctrl+Shift+F7	Moves all lines of a paragraph inward one tab stop from the left margin and an equal distance from the right margin.
Hanging Indent	Ctrl+F7	Indents all lines of a paragraph except the first line one tab stop to the right. The first line moves to the first tab stop to the left.
Back Tab	None	Moves the first line of a paragraph one tab stop to the left.

The QuickIndent option enables you to create indents a few additional ways. If QuickIndent is turned on, pressing Tab at the beginning of any line in the paragraph except the first line creates either a hanging indent or a standard indent. If the first line in the paragraph doesn't begin with a tab, WordPerfect gives you a hanging indent. Press Tab to indent the paragraph one more tab stop; press Shift+Tab to move it back one tab stop to the left. If the first line does begin with a tab, the tab is simply converted to a standard indent.

Note: QuickIndent is turned on by default. If you want to turn it off, choose Tools⇨QuickCorrect to open the QuickCorrect dialog box, click the Format-As-You-Go tab of the QuickCorrect dialog box, and deselect the QuickIndent check box.

To remove a regular indent, double indent, or back tab, place the insertion marker just before the first character in the paragraph and then press Backspace. To remove a hanging indent, press Backspace twice. If this technique doesn't work, press Alt+F3 to open the Reveal Codes window and drag the indent codes out of the Reveal Codes window. The codes appear right in front of the first character of the paragraph. (For a look at this technique in action, see "Removing styles" in Chapter 9.) For a hanging indent, you need to remove two codes: Hd Left Ind and Hd Back Tab.

Justifying text

Another way to change the amount of space between the edges of a paragraph and the left and right margins is to change the *justification*, sometimes referred to as *alignment*. Figure 7-10 shows the five available alignment options: Left, Right, Center, Full, and All, which are explained in the following list:

- ✔ *Left justification* aligns all lines in a paragraph to the left margin. This alignment is sometimes called *ragged right* because the right edge of the paragraph has an uneven look.

- ✔ *Right justification* aligns the paragraph to the right margin and is sometimes known as *ragged left* because of the appearance of the left edge of the paragraph.

- ✔ *Center justification* centers each line between the left and right margins.

- ✔ *Full justification* spaces the text so that all lines align perfectly with both the left and the right margin — except for the last line of the paragraph, which simply aligns with the left margin. Sometimes, WordPerfect needs to add spaces throughout the text in a line to justify it; sometimes it needs to cram the text closer together.

✔ *All justification* is the same as Full justification except that the last line of the paragraph is fully justified along with all the other lines. As you can see from the last example in Figure 7-10, this option can result in awkwardly spaced text.

As with other formatting commands, justification affects all paragraphs from the insertion marker forward through the rest of the document, up to the point where you previously changed the justification. If you select text before applying a justification command, the justification affects the selected paragraph only.

Justification button

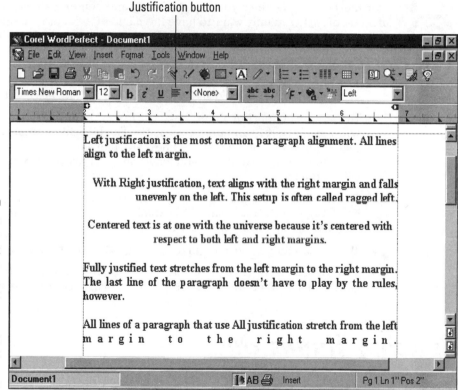

Figure 7-10:
Use the alignment options to align text in different ways in relationship to the left and right margins.

Here's a rundown of the various and sundry ways to change the justification:

- ✔ Click the Justification button on the Property Bar and select an option from the drop-down list.

- ✔ Choose Format➪Justification and choose an option from the Justification submenu.

- ✔ Press the justification shortcut keys: Ctrl+L for Left justification; Ctrl+R for Right justification; Ctrl+E for Center justification; and Ctrl+J for Full justification. The fact that there is no shortcut key for the All justification option should be a clue that this isn't a terrific option in most cases.

WordPerfect also enables you to right-justify and center a single line or part of a line of text. You may want to have the name of a document align with the left margin of the page, for example, and have the day's date align with the right margin. Your options are as follows:

- ✔ To right-justify an entire line, place the insertion marker at the beginning of the line and choose Format➪Line➪Flush Right or press Alt+F7.

- ✔ To right-justify part of a line, place the insertion marker before the text you want to justify and then choose the Flush Right command. This technique works only on single lines; you can't right-justify one line in a multi-line paragraph unless you insert a line break (Ctrl+Shift+L) at the end of the line.

- ✔ To add dot leaders before the justified text, choose Format➪Line➪ Flush Right with Dot Leaders. (I explain dot leaders in the section "Choosing a tab stop type," earlier in this chapter.)

- ✔ To center a line, choose Format➪Line➪Center or press Shift+F7.

- ✔ You can also right-click anywhere in the document window to display a QuickMenu that contains the Center and Flush Right commands.

Spacing Things Out

The amount of space between lines and paragraphs in your text has a dramatic effect on how readable and attractive your document appears. Text that's all crammed together is difficult to read and looks intimidating (just take a look at any legal document). On the other hand, text that's too spaced out is also difficult to read because the reader's eye must work too hard to get from one character to the next. Examples of some too-tight text, too-loose text, and just-right text are shown in Figure 7-11.

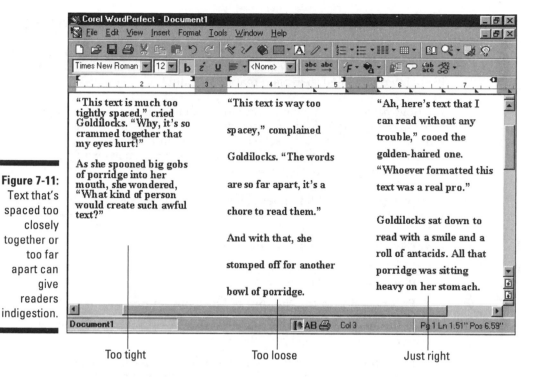

Figure 7-11:
Text that's
spaced too
closely
together or
too far
apart can
give
readers
indigestion.

Too tight   Too loose   Just right

Adjusting line spacing

To adjust the amount of space between lines in a paragraph — a value known in typesetting circles as leading (pronounced *ledding*)— click at the point where you want the line spacing to change or select the paragraph you want to format. Then choose Format⇨Line⇨ Spacing to display the Line Spacing dialog box, as shown in Figure 7-12. Enter the value you want to use in the option box and click OK or press Enter.

Version 8 doesn't give you a Property Bar button for setting line spacing. Because this formatting attribute is one you're likely to use a lot, you may want to add a line spacing button to your Property Bar, as explained in Chapter 22 (in the section "Create Your Own Property Bar and Toolbar Buttons").

Figure 7-12:
Set line
spacing
in this
dialog box.

Adjusting the space between paragraphs

Just as line spacing sets the amount of space between lines in a paragraph, paragraph spacing sets the amount of space between paragraphs. (Sorry, I probably didn't need to explain that to you, did I?)

Anyhow, paragraph spacing works similar to line spacing in that, if you select a paragraph before adjusting the spacing, your changes affect only that paragraph. If you don't select anything, your changes apply from the insertion marker forward, up to the point at which you inserted any previous paragraph spacing changes.

After you ponder that bit of news, here's how to move forward to adjust the paragraph spacing:

1. **Choose Format➪Paragraph➪Format.**

   The Paragraph Format dialog box opens. (You probably remember this dialog box from Figure 7-8.)

2. **Enter a value in the Number of Lines option box.**

   You can enter custom values, such as 1.25, by double-clicking the option box and then typing the number.

   If you prefer to make your paragraph spacing measurements in points instead of lines, select the Distance in Points radio button and enter the spacing value in that option box instead.

3. **Click OK or press Enter.**

Centering text on a page

If you want your document text to be perfectly centered between the top and bottom margins on your page — you perfectionist, you — move the insertion marker to the beginning of the text you want to center. Choose Format➪Page➪Center to open the Center Page(s) dialog box and choose a radio button to specify whether you want to center the current page of text or the current page and any subsequent pages. Press Enter to scoot your text smack-dab in the vertical center of the page.

If you later want to remove the centering, choose the Center command again and select the Turn Centering Off radio button in the Center Page(s) dialog box.

Making Text Fit on a Page

WordPerfect has a nifty little feature called *Make It Fit* that automatically adjusts your margins, font sizes, and line spacing so that your text fits neatly on the page. To try it out, choose Format➪Make It Fit to open the Make It Fit dialog box, as shown in Figure 7-13. (Notice that this command isn't available if you have any text selected.)

In the dialog box, specify how many pages you want the text to consume and which formatting items WordPerfect can play with in laying out the pages. Click the Make It Fit button to see what WordPerfect can do. If you don't like the results, click the Undo button or press Ctrl+Z to put things back the way they were.

Figure 7-13:
Use the
Make It Fit
dialog box
to reformat
your text
so that it
fits onto a
specified
number
of pages.

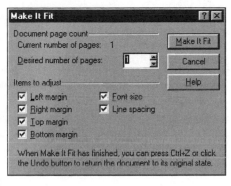

Chapter 8
Doing the Fancy Stuff

* *

In This Chapter

▶ Creating bulleted and numbered lists

▶ Inserting page numbers, dates, and special characters

▶ Adding headers and footers

▶ Putting text into columns

▶ Inserting graphics

▶ Creating lines, borders, and fills

* *

*I*n their earliest incarnations, word processors did little more than, well, process words. You could cut, copy, and paste text, make words italic or bold, and play with margins and paragraph indents — but that was about it. If you wanted to do anything more complicated — say, add a graphic to a page or put your text in columns — you turned the work over to the publishing department or sent it out to a printing company.

Today, WordPerfect and other high-end word processors give you the power to handle many page layout and design tasks right at your desk. As you find out in this chapter, you can create bulleted and numbered lists with ease, add headers and footers, and even get WordPerfect to number your pages automatically. And, if you need even fancier pages, you can insert graphics, put text in columns, and add borders and backgrounds to elements on the page.

Creating Bulleted and Numbered Lists

One of the most common design devices used in everyday documents is the bulleted or numbered list. WordPerfect gives you several ways to create these lists easily.

Bullet basics

To add bullets before paragraphs that you've already typed, follow these steps:

1. **Select the paragraphs to which you want to add bullets.**

2. **Choose Insert⇨Outline/Bullets & Numbering.**

   The Bullets and Numbering dialog box appears, as shown in Figure 8-1.

3. **Click a bullet style from the Bullets List.**

4. **Click OK.**

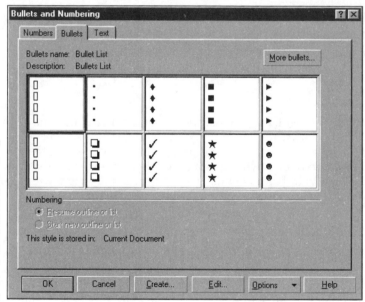

Figure 8-1:
You can select from several different styles of bullets and numbers for your lists.

 For an even quicker way to apply bullets, click the arrow on the Bullets button on the toolbar to display a drop-down list of bullet styles. Click the bullet style you want to use; or, to display the Bullets and Numbering dialog box, click More. After you select a bullet from the drop-down list, the bullet icon appears on the Bullets button face. To use that same bullet again, just click on the bullet face — no need to display the menu again.

To create a bulleted list on the fly, choose your bullet style from the Bullets and Numbering dialog box or from the toolbar menu. WordPerfect inserts a bullet and then creates a hanging indent for the bulleted text. (I explain hanging indents in Chapter 7.) Type the text for the first bulleted item and then press Enter to create the next bullet. After you type the last item in the bulleted list, press Enter and then press Backspace to discontinue the bullets.

If the QuickBullets feature is turned on, you can also use the keyboard shortcuts listed in Table 8-1 to create a bullet character. Type the shortcut and then press Tab or Indent to start your bulleted list. To turn QuickBullets on, choose Tools⇨QuickCorrect to open the QuickCorrect dialog box, click the Format-As-You-Go tab, select the QuickBullets check box to put a check mark in the box, and click OK.

Table 8-1	QuickBullets Shortcut Keys
Press these keys	*To create this bullet character*
>	▶
o or *	•
0	●
^	◆
-	—
+	★

To insert a standard bullet regardless of whether QuickBullets is turned on, press Ctrl+Shift+B.

Numbered lists

The steps for numbering items in a list are pretty much the same as for adding bullets to a list. To apply numbers to existing text, follow these steps:

1. **Select the paragraphs that you want to number.**

2. **Choose Insert⇨Outline/Bullets & Numbering.**

   The Bullets and Numbering dialog box, as shown back in Figure 8-1, appears. But this time, the Numbers tab is open. You're presented with several different numbering styles.

3. **Click the numbering style that you want to use.**

4. **Click OK.**

You can also apply numbering by clicking the arrow on the Numbering button on the toolbar and choosing a numbering style from the resulting drop-down menu. To open the Bullets and Numbering dialog box, choose the More option from the menu.

If you add or delete an item in the list after you create it, WordPerfect renumbers the list automatically. To add an item, click just before the paragraph break for the preceding item and press Enter to get the number for the new item. To delete a numbered item, just delete the paragraph as you normally would.

If QuickBullets is turned on, as explained in the preceding section, you can create a numbered list by typing the first number and a period and then pressing Tab. You can type letters (a, b, c) or Roman numerals (I, ii) instead of regular numbers, if you prefer. WordPerfect automatically formats your paragraph for a numbered list. After you type the first item in the list, press Enter, and WordPerfect presents you with the next number. After you type the last item in the list, press Enter and then press Backspace to return to regular paragraph formatting.

More news about bullets and numbers

Just for good measure, here are a few other juicy tidbits about creating bulleted and numbered lists in WordPerfect Version 8:

✔ To move a list item up or down in the list, click at the beginning of the paragraph and then click the Move Up or Move Down button on the Property Bar. These buttons appear if you're editing or creating a bulleted list.

To shove a list item one tab stop to the right, click the Demote button on the Property Bar. To move it one tab stop to the left, click the Promote button. In numbered lists, WordPerfect may change the item's number to reflect its new position in the list, depending on the numbering style you select.

✔ To delete a bullet or number from a paragraph, click before the first letter in the paragraph and press Backspace. If you want to remove bullets or numbers from a whole bunch of paragraphs, select the paragraphs you want to reformat and choose the None style from the Styles drop-down list on the Property Bar. (For more information about styles, see Chapter 9.)

✔ By default, WordPerfect places the bullet or number at the left margin and indents the bulleted text to the first tab stop to the right. To change the amount of space between the bullet and the text, move the tab stop. To indent the entire paragraph without changing the amount of space between the bullet or number and the text, change the first-line indent, as explained in Chapter 7.

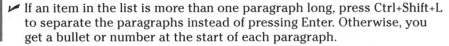

✔ If an item in the list is more than one paragraph long, press Ctrl+Shift+L to separate the paragraphs instead of pressing Enter. Otherwise, you get a bullet or number at the start of each paragraph.

Numbering Your Pages

WordPerfect can automatically number the pages in your document — and renumber them if you add or delete pages. To turn on automatic page numbering for a document, walk this way:

1. **Click anywhere in the page on which you want the page numbering to begin.**

2. **Choose Format⇨Page⇨Numbering.**

   The Select Page Numbering Format dialog box appears, as shown in Figure 8-2.

Figure 8-2: Don't number your pages manually — have WordPerfect do the job for you.

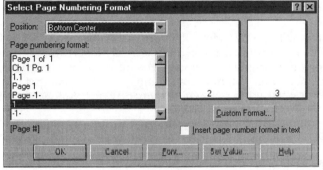

3. **Select the placement and format of the page numbers.**

   Choose the placement from the Position drop-down list and the format from the Page Numbering Format list box. The preview at the bottom of the dialog box shows you how and where the page numbers appear.

4. **Choose the font and size for your page numbers.**

   Page numbers normally appear in the same font as the default document font. If you want to use a different font, click the Font button to open the standard Font dialog box, which I discuss in Chapter 7. After you specify the font, size, style, and other font attributes, click OK.

5. **Set the starting page number.**

   Normally, WordPerfect numbers pages according to their positions in your document. Suppose that, in Step 1, you click the third page of your document to tell WordPerfect that you want page numbering to begin on that page — maybe pages one and two are your title page and table of contents. If you want that third page to be numbered Page 1, you need to click the Set Value button to open the Values dialog box. Enter the starting page number in the Set Page Number option box of that dialog box and click OK.

6. Click OK.

The page numbers appear as you requested. (You must be working in Page view or Two Page view, however, to see them.)

To remove page numbers, click the first numbered page, choose Format⇨Page⇨Numbering and choose No Page Numbering from the Position drop-down list.

To prevent a page number from printing on a particular page, click that page, choose Format⇨Page⇨Suppress, and select the check box for the Page Numbering item.

Inserting the Current Date and Time

Here's a tool you're going to love if you're never sure what day it is, let alone what the time is. WordPerfect can automatically insert the current date and/ or time into your text and even update the information each time you open or save the document. You may, for example, want to use this feature to add the date to form letters that you use frequently. Just follow these steps:

1. **Place the insertion marker at the spot on the page where you want to insert the date/time.**

2. **Choose Insert⇨Date/Time from the menu bar.**

   WordPerfect opens the Date/Time dialog box.

3. **Select a date and time format.**

   Just click on a format in the scrolling list. You can select from a wide range of formats, from the traditional month/date/year style (for example, August 30, 1996) to the downright odd (31Jan97). You can also choose to insert just the date, just the current time, or the date and time together.

   If you want the date and time to update automatically every time you open or save the document, select the Automatic Update check box.

4. **Click OK or press Enter.**

   WordPerfect inserts the date and time according to your computer's system clock. If the date or time is incorrect, update it in the Windows 95 Control panel.

To insert the date or time in the format currently selected in the Date/Time dialog box, just press Ctrl+D. Press Ctrl+Shift+D to insert the date/time and have it automatically updated whenever you open or save the document.

Tracking Down Special Characters

You're typing up your annual holiday letter to friends and relatives, thoughtfully recounting the details of your two-week vacation in France, and you realize with horror that your computer keyboard doesn't have any of those little accent marks you need to type foreign words. How ever will you tell that hilarious story about that quaint café in Chalôns, let alone mention your upcoming second honeymoon in Curaçao?

Relax — all those foreign accent marks and other special typographical symbols are yours for the taking. They reside in the Symbols dialog box, as shown in Figure 8-3. To grab a symbol and put it in your document, follow these steps:

1. **Position your insertion marker where you want the symbol to appear.**

2. **Choose Insert⇨Symbol or press Ctrl+W to open the Symbols dialog box.**

   Or click the Symbol button on the Property Bar to accomplish the same thing.

3. **Locate the character you want to insert from the Symbols list.**

   Each of the symbol sets in the Set drop-down list offers a different selection of special characters. (*Hint:* For foreign characters, choose the Multinational option.) Use the scroll arrows alongside the Symbols list box to hunt through the available characters in the current character set. After you find the one you want, click to select it.

4. **Click Insert.**

   Or just double-click the character. WordPerfect inserts the character in your document where your insertion point is located.

Figure 8-3:
If you feel compelled to add a smiley face or some other fun symbol to your document, WordPerfect obliges.

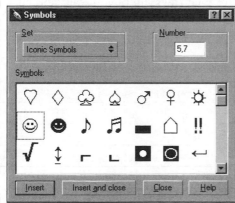

You can leave the Symbols dialog box on-screen as long as you need it. The dialog box operates the same as any other open window — click it to make it the active window; click your document to make the document the active window. After you finish inserting your special characters, click the Close button.

You can insert some commonly used symbols, such as em dashes (—) and the registered trademark symbol (®), by using the keyboard shortcuts listed in Table 8-2. For these shortcuts to work, the Replace Words as You Type option box must be selected in the QuickCorrect dialog box. (Press Ctrl+Shift+F1 to open the dialog box and turn on the option.) Remember that WordPerfect doesn't change your keystrokes into the corresponding symbol until after you press the spacebar.

QuickCorrect can also automatically replace so-called straight quotes (") and straight single quotes (') — otherwise known as apostrophes — with curly quotes ("") and curly single quotes (''). This substitution is a good thing — straight quotes are considered gauche in professional typesetting circles. But if you're typing measurements, such as 9'5", you need those straight quotes. No worries — if you type a number, WordPerfect uses the straight quotes instead.

All this quotation-mark-substituting depends, however, on the settings in the QuickCorrect dialog box. Press Ctrl+Shift+F1 to open the dialog box, click the SmartQuotes tab, and select all three check boxes on that tab to turn on these options.

If you use a special symbol frequently and WordPerfect doesn't offer a QuickCorrect shortcut for it, you can create your own. Here's how: In the Replace option box of the QuickCorrect dialog box, enter the shortcut you want to use — for example, you may want to use the shortcut **tm** for a trademark symbol. Then, click the With option box and press Ctrl+W to open the Symbols dialog box. Find the symbol you want and click Insert and Close to put the symbol in the With option box. Click Add Entry in the QuickCorrect dialog box and then click Close.

Table 8-2	Shortcuts to Common Symbols
Symbol	*Shortcut*
©	(c or (c)
®	(r
— (em dash)	- - - (three hyphens) or m- (m, hyphen)
– (en dash)	- - (two hyphens) or n- (n, hyphen)

Creating Headers and Footers

Headers and footers provide a quick and convenient way to create text that repeats on every page (or almost every page) in your document. A *header* contains text that appears at the top of every page — for example, the document title or chapter title. A *footer* contains text that appears at the bottom of your pages. The current date and the page number are two common footer elements.

The advantage of using headers and footers is that you don't need to retype the same text, page after page. You create the text once and use the Header/Footer command to place it automatically on every page.

Before you create a header or footer, make sure that you're working in Page view (which you access by choosing View⇨Page or pressing Alt+F5) so that you can see what you're doing on-screen. Then follow these steps:

1. **Click at the top of the first page on which you want the header/footer to appear.**

2. **Choose Insert⇨Header/Footer to open the Headers/Footers dialog box, as shown in Figure 8-4.**

Figure 8-4:
Choose the header or footer you want to create from this dialog box.

3. **Select the header/footer you want to create by clicking the appropriate radio button.**

   If you need only one header/footer for your document, select Header A or Footer A. If you need two different sets of headers/footers — as you do if you want a different header/footer for your left-hand pages than for your right-hand pages — select A for one header and B for the other.

4. **Click Create.**

   WordPerfect displays several header/footer buttons on the Property Bar, as shown in Figure 8-5. (More about what those buttons do in the list that follows these steps.) The name of the title bar also changes to display the name of the current header/footer.

5. Create your text.

You can enter as much text as you want and even add graphics (as I explain later in the section "Adding Graphics"). Figure 8-5 shows the header text that I created for my next blockbuster screenplay.

 6. Click the Header/Footer Close button on the Property Bar.

Or just click anywhere in your main document. You're now back in the regular document-editing mode, as you can see by the changes to the title bar and the Property Bar.

Header/Footer close button ⌐

Figure 8-5:
This header appears at the top of every page in my screenplay.

Here's some additional info about headers and footers:

✔ You can edit a header/footer by clicking it on any page on which it appears. The title bar of the document window changes to show that you're working on the header/footer. Click outside the header/footer to return to your main document.

 ✔ To move from one header or footer to another quickly, use the Previous Header/Footer and Next Header/Footer buttons on the Property Bar.

✔ If you want to include the page number on pages that have a header/ footer, the best way to do so is to insert them in the header/footer instead of using the Numbering command covered earlier in this chapter. Otherwise, your header/footer text may overprint your page numbers. To insert the page number, click the Page Numbering button on the Property Bar and choose Page Number from the drop-down list.

 ✔ You can specify whether you want a header/footer to appear on every page, on every even page, or on every odd page. Choose the Header/ Footer Placement button on the Property Bar to open the Pages dialog box, click the radio button for the option you want to use, and click OK or press Enter.

 ✔ Click the Horizontal Line button to insert a line that stretches from the left margin to the right margin. If you click on the line to select it, you can then drag it to a different position if needed.

 ✔ To adjust the spacing between the header/footer and the main docu- ment text, click the Distance button and set the distance value in the dialog box that appears.

✔ If you don't want a header/footer to print on a particular page, click the page, choose Format⇨Page⇨ Suppress to open the Suppress dialog box, and select the check box for the header or footer that you want to suppress.

✔ If you want to discontinue the header/footer after a certain page, put the insertion marker on that page, choose Insert⇨Header/Footer to open the Headers/Footers dialog box, select the radio button for the header/footer that you want to discontinue, and click the Discontinue button. To get rid of the header/footer on all pages in the document, do the exact same thing, but put the insertion marker at the beginning of the first page where the header/footer appears.

Putting Your Text in Columns

WordPerfect enables you to divide your pages into columns — as you may want to do if, say, you're creating a newsletter article. Here are the steps:

1. **Put the insertion marker at the point in your document where you want the columns to begin.**

   If you want to format just certain paragraphs in columns, select the paragraphs instead.

2. **Choose Format⇨Columns from the menu bar.**

 Or click the Columns button on the toolbar and choose Format from the drop-down list. Either way, the Columns dialog box appears, as shown in Figure 8-6.

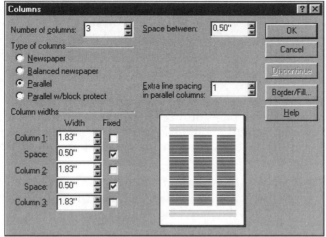

Figure 8-6:
You specify
the number,
type, and
spacing of
your
columns in
this dialog
box.

3. **Specify the number of columns you want in the Number of <u>C</u>olumns option box.**

4. **Choose a column format by clicking one of the Type of Columns radio buttons.**

   Following are your options:

   • *<u>N</u>ewspaper* fills the first column on the left all the way to the bottom of the page, fills the next column to the bottom of the page, and so on, until all the text is placed in columns.

   • *<u>B</u>alanced Newspaper* fills the columns the same way that <u>N</u>ewspaper does, except that WordPerfect attempts to make all the columns the same length.

   • *<u>P</u>arallel* groups text across the page in rows, similar to what you find in a table. You may want to use this option if you're creating a script, for example, in which you want the video portion of the scene to run down the left side of the page and the audio to appear on the right side, as shown in Figure 8-7.

   • *P<u>a</u>rallel w/Block Protect* works the same way as <u>P</u>arallel does, except that WordPerfect makes sure that no row of text is split across two pages. If the text in one column in the row is too long to fit on the page, the entire row moves to the next page.

   As you make your choices, the preview page in the dialog box changes to show you how your columns are going to appear.

5. If necessary, adjust the column width and spacing.

By default, WordPerfect spaces your columns evenly across the page and puts a half-inch space between each column. If you want some other spacing, change the values in the <u>S</u>pace Between and Column Widths option boxes. If you're not sure what spacing or width values you want, don't sweat it; you can easily change the values later.

Use the <u>E</u>xtra Line Spacing in Parallel Columns option to add more space between the rows of text in parallel columns.

6. Add a border or fill if you want.

Clicking the Bo<u>r</u>der/Fill button takes you to the Column Border/Fill dialog box, where you can add a border and/or background to your columns. The options in this dialog box are explained in the section "Adding borders and fills," later in this chapter. After adding your border or fill, click OK to return to the Columns dialog box.

7. Click OK or press Enter to create your columns.

You can also create newspaper columns by clicking the Columns button on the toolbar and choosing the number of columns you want from the drop-down list. WordPerfect creates your columns based on the default settings in the Columns dialog box.

Column guide   Columns button

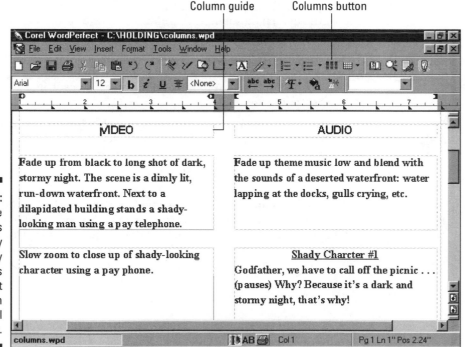

Figure 8-7:
Oliver Stone no doubt is going to pay big money for this script formatted in Parallel columns.

As you see in Figure 8-7, WordPerfect displays dotted guidelines to indicate the boundaries of each column. (If you don't see the guidelines, choose View➪Guidelines and turn on the Columns option in the Guidelines dialog box.) You can resize your columns by dragging the guidelines or by dragging the space between columns (in publishing terms, that space is called a *gutter*).

Entering and editing text in columns involves a few special techniques:

✔ If you're typing text in a Newspaper column, WordPerfect automatically moves the insertion marker to the next column after you fill up the current column. To break the column before that point, press Ctrl+Enter or click the Columns button and choose New Column from the drop-down list.

✔ If you're typing text in Balanced Newspaper columns, WordPerfect continually shifts text back and forth between the columns to balance the column length. Press Ctrl+Enter to begin a whole new block of balanced columns.

✔ In Parallel and Parallel with Block Protect columns, Ctrl+Enter moves you across the row to the next column. If you press Ctrl+Enter at the end of a row, WordPerfect creates a new row and moves the insertion marker to the leftmost column in that row.

✔ To move from column to column, just click to reposition the insertion marker. You can also use the following keyboard shortcuts: Alt+Home moves you to the top of the current column; Alt+End moves you to the end of the current column; Alt+← takes you one column to the left; and Alt+→ takes you one column to the right.

✔ To change the column type, put the insertion marker where you want the different column formatting to begin. Then choose Format➪Columns and establish your new column settings as outlined in the preceding steps.

If all you want to do is change the number of columns, you can click the Columns button and choose a number from the drop-down list. (Notice that the last item on the toolbar's Columns drop-down list shows you the type of columns you're creating. The button doesn't actually do anything.)

✔ To turn off column formatting, put the insertion marker at the point where you want to get rid of the formatting, choose Format➪Columns, and click Discontinue in the Columns dialog box. Or click the Columns button on the toolbar and choose Discontinue from the drop-down list.

Adding Graphics

Ah, here's the really fun part: adding pictures to your pages. The WordPerfect Suite comes with a bunch of clip art — pictures, borders, and other graphic elements — that you can use to add zest to your documents. You can also create simple shapes, such as arrows and boxes, by using WordPerfect's simple drawing tools.

Inserting a piece of clip art

To place a clip-art graphic from the WordPerfect Suite 8 clip art collection on a page, follow these steps:

1. **Position the insertion marker at the spot in the document where you want to put the graphic.**

2. **Click the Clipart toolbar button or choose Insert⟹Graphics⟹Clipart.**

   WordPerfect opens the Scrapbook, new to Version 8. The Scrapbook is shown and described fully in Chapter 16, in the section "Using ready-made art."
3. **Drag or copy the graphic from the Scrapbook to your page.**

   After you locate the graphic you want to use, click it and then drag it from the Scrapbook onto your document page. Or right-click the graphic, choose Copy from the QuickMenu, right-click the document page, and choose Paste from the QuickMenu.

   WordPerfect plops the graphic onto your page and surrounds the graphic by little black boxes, as shown in Figure 8-8. These boxes are *selection handles,* and they indicate that the graphic is selected and ready to be moved or edited.

You aren't limited, however, to just the pictures in the Scrapbook. You can use graphics from any source, as long as they're stored in a graphics format that WordPerfect can handle. To insert a graphic not in the Scrapbook, choose Insert⟹Graphics⟹From File. WordPerfect displays the Insert Image dialog box, which looks suspiciously like the Open File dialog box discussed in Chapter 5 — and works just like it, too. Click the Preview button to see a preview of a selected image, just as you preview documents in the Open File dialog box. Check the File Type drop-down list to see the graphics formats that WordPerfect accepts. After you locate the graphic you want, double-click it to place it in your document.

Move cursor   Selection handle

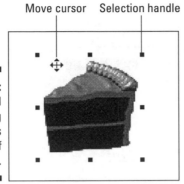

Figure 8-8:
Moving and
resizing
graphics is
a piece of
cake.

If you don't get the Insert Image dialog box but instead get a little hand cursor, choose Tools⇨Settings to display the Settings dialog box, double-click the Environment icon to open the Environment Settings dialog box, and click the Graphics tab. Then deselect the Drag to Create New Graphics Boxes option and click OK. This option enables you to set the size of your graphic before you insert it by drawing a box to hold your picture. (WordPerfect creates the box for you automatically if the option is turned off.) You can always resize your graphic later, however, even if you don't use this option.

Graphics in the Pictures and Textures folders of the Graphics folder that installs with WordPerfect are bitmap images, which behave differently than do the graphics you find in the other folders. Ditto with the images found in the Photos folder on the Suite CD-ROM. For more on this topic, see Chapter 16, in the section "Working with bitmap images."

If you want to create your own custom graphics, take a gander at Chapter 16 for information on the drawing tools offered in Presentations. You can create a graphic in Corel Presentations and then insert it into your WordPerfect document, as I explain in Chapter 16. Or you can open up the Presentations window inside WordPerfect by clicking the Draw Picture button on the toolbar or by choosing Insert⇨Graphics⇨Draw Picture. For more information on using Presentations inside WordPerfect, see Chapter 19.

To create simple shapes — boxes, arrows, and such — choose one of the shape tools from the Insert⇨Shape submenu. Or click on the Shape button on the toolbar and select the tool you want to use. These tools work just like their Presentations counterparts, discussed in the section "Creating simple graphics" in Chapter 16.

Editing graphics

WordPerfect offers a whole slew of graphics editing possibilities. But if you want to do very much editing to a graphic, you should use Presentations, which offers better drawing and editing tools.

In fact, if you double-click a clip-art graphic, the Presentations window opens inside WordPerfect, making all the Presentations tools available. (For more about using Presentations, see Chapter 16. Also check out Chapter 19, which explains how this program-within-a-program stuff works.)

But you can perform some simple editing tricks by using WordPerfect's own artistic capabilities. After you select a graphic, the Property Bar offers a bunch of graphics tools. Right-clicking a graphic uncovers additional graphics-editing options. After clicking a graphic to select it, you can perform all the following actions on it:

- ✔ To resize a graphic, drag a selection handle. Drag a corner handle to retain the graphic's original proportions as you resize. If you want to get specific in resizing the graphic, click the Graphics drop-down list on the Property Bar, choose Size, and enter new height and width values in the Box Size dialog box.

- ✔ Don't enlarge bitmap images. Doing so makes them fuzzy and unattractive, like that four-week-old bagel in your bread box.

- ✔ To move a selected graphic, place the cursor on the graphic until you see a four-way arrow (as in Figure 8-8) and then drag the graphic to the new position. Ctrl+drag to copy and move the graphic.

- ✔ To draw a border around the graphic, click the Border button on the Property Bar and choose a border style from the drop-down list. To place a *fill* (background) behind the graphic, click the Fill button and click a fill style on the drop-down list.

- ✔ WordPerfect *wraps* text around graphics — that is, it shoves lines of text out of the way to make room for the image. Click the Wrap button to display a drop-down list that enables you to change the placement of the graphic relative to the text.

- ✔ You can stack graphics one on top of the other to create layered images, as shown in Figure 8-9. To change a graphic's placement in the stack, select it and then click on the Object Forward and Object Backward buttons on the Property Bar or choose one of the stacking order commands in the Graphics drop-down list. To create the image in Figure 8-9, I placed the cattails image at the back of the stack, the cheetah in the middle, and the dragon on top. The result is a delightful cheetah-towing-a-dragon-through-cattails scene. Or is it a cheetah-about-to-become-lunch scene? Depends on your outlook on life, I guess.

Figure 8-9:
You can stack graphics on top of each other to create intriguing scenes such as this one.

✔ If you have several graphics stacked on top of each other, selecting an individual graphic with the mouse can prove difficult. That's why the Property Bar offers the Next Box and Previous Box buttons. Click these buttons to cycle through all the graphics in your document.

✔ To flip a selected graphic about its horizontal or vertical axis, click the Flip Left/Right or Flip Top/Bottom buttons, respectively.

✔ If you select a shape that you drew by using WordPerfect's shape tools, the Property Bar offers buttons for adding shadows, changing the thickness and color of the shape outline, and making other changes. Notice that double-clicking shapes doesn't take you to Presentations; you must do all your editing with WordPerfect's tools.

✔ To get rid of a selected graphic, press Delete.

✔ To save a graphic in its own file, without the rest of the document, select the graphic, choose File⇨Save As, and select the Selected Image radio button in the Save dialog box. Then, give your image a name and save it as you would any other document.

Creating Borders, Fills, and Lines

Another way to jazz up your pages is to add borders, lines, and fills to selected text. *Fill,* by the way, is a computer-art term that means "background" — loosely translated, of course.

Adding borders and fills

You can add a border or fill to a page, paragraph, or column. To do so, select the text you want to dress up. Or, if you want to apply the effects to all your pages, paragraphs, or columns, don't select any text. Your formatting then affects all text from the insertion marker forward.

To apply borders or fills to paragraphs or pages, choose the Border/Fill command from the Format⇨Paragraph or Format⇨Page submenu. To apply a border or fill to columns, click the Border/Fill button inside the Columns dialog box (which you access by choosing Format⇨Columns), as I discuss in "Putting Your Text in Columns" earlier in this chapter. Regardless of where you choose the Border/Fill command, you open a Border/Fill dialog box that looks something like the one shown in Figure 8-10. (The dialog box name and options change slightly depending on whether you're formatting columns, paragraphs, or a page.)

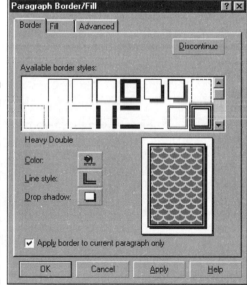

Figure 8-10:
You can apply a border and background to paragraphs, pages, and columns inside the Border/Fill dialog box.

Border options are found, appropriately enough, on the Border tab of the Border/Fill dialog box. Click a border style in the Available Border Styles list and then play around with the Color, Line Style, and Drop Shadow options until you create an acceptable border. If you're applying a border to a page, choose the Line option from the Border Type menu to access these options. As you mess with the options, the preview box shows you how your border is going to look.

Apply a fill to your text by using the options on the Fill tab of the Border/Fill dialog box. When applying fills to pages, you must choose the Line option from the Border Type menu to access fill options. You can create solid-colored backgrounds or wacky-patterned backgrounds, as shown in the preview box in Figure 8-10.

The options on the Advanced tab of the Border/Fill dialog box are available only after you select certain options on the other tabs. If you select a fill from the Fill tab, for example, you can use the options at the bottom of the Advanced tab to create a *gradient fill* — that is, one that blends from one color to another in a geometric pattern. Choose any option but None from the Gradient drop-down list to create a gradient fill.

After you change the settings on any tab, click Apply to preview the border or fill on your text. If you want to apply the effect to more than the current paragraph/page/column, make sure that the check box at the bottom of the Border tab isn't selected. After you're satisfied with how things look, click OK.

To remove a border from selected text, choose the Border/Fill command to open the Border/Fill dialog box and then click the Discontinue button. To delete a fill, choose the blank (white) fill on the Fill tab instead of using the Discontinue button.

Adding lines

To draw a straight line from the left margin to the right margin, click at the spot where you want the line to appear and choose Insert⇔Shape⇔ Horizontal Line or press Ctrl+F11. You can also type four hyphens or four equal signs and then press Enter to create a single or double horizontal line, respectively. (The QuickLines check box on the Format-As-You-Go tab of the QuickCorrect Options dialog box must be selected. Choose Tools⇔QuickCorrect to open the dialog box.)

To create a vertical line from the top margin to the right margin, click the spot where you want to position the line and then choose Insert⇔Shape⇔Vertical Line or press Ctrl+Shift+F11.

To move a line, click it to display its selection handles (little black squares) and then drag it to the new position. To resize the line, drag its handles. Depending on which handle you drag, you can make the line fatter, skinnier, longer, or shorter. To delete a line, click it to display the selection handles and then press Delete.

After you select a line, buttons for changing the color, thickness, style, and orientation of the line appear on the Property Bar.

Chapter 9

Tools to Save You Time (And Embarrassment)

....

In This Chapter

▶ Using styles to speed up formatting

▶ Copying character and paragraph formatting

▶ Finding and replacing words and phrases

▶ Checking your spelling

▶ Using QuickWords

▶ Using Address Book

....

*H*ave you heard the expression, "The hurrieder I go, the behinder I get"? No? Well, my Grandma King says it all the time, and she's nobody's fool. Loosely translated, this time-honored saying means that, if you rush to get a job done, you make mistakes that put you even further behind schedule than if you had taken a slow, methodical approach. At least, I think that's what it means.

At any rate, going slow isn't always possible in our speed-it-up, get-it-done-yesterday world. Your boss wants that report now, your client wants that project done yesterday, and the IRS wants all your money this very minute — with a hefty interest penalty for any delay whatsoever.

Fortunately, WordPerfect has some tools that not only help you work faster, but also help make sure that your documents don't contain any embarrassing spelling or formatting mistakes. This chapter shows you how to use these tools so that you can go hurrieder without getting any behinder.

Using Styles to Speed Up Formatting Chores

Without a doubt, one of the better ways to save time is to use *styles*. Styles are like templates that you can use to quickly apply character and paragraph formatting to your text.

Here's how it works: You create a style that contains all the formatting instructions for a specific text element — for example, a headline style that uses 14-point, bold Helvetica type; centered alignment; and double-line spacing. To format your headlines, you just select the headline text and apply the headline style. WordPerfect applies the right font, type size, alignment, and paragraph spacing in one fell swoop.

Using styles not only saves you time but it also ensures that your formatting is consistent throughout your document. You don't need to worry about what font, type size, or spacing you're supposed to use each time you create a new headline — all the formatting information is contained in the style. And if you want to change the formatting of your headlines (for example, you decide to use 13-point type instead of 14-point type), you don't need to search through your document looking for headlines and changing them manually. You just edit the style, and WordPerfect automatically applies the new formatting to any paragraphs that use the style.

Choosing a style type

You can create three types of styles in WordPerfect:

- *Character styles* contain formatting related to individual characters of text — font, type size, type style, and so on. They can't contain paragraph-level formatting, such as indents and line spacing.

- *Paragraph styles* contain paragraph-level formatting plus character-level formatting.

- *Document styles* can contain paragraph-level formatting, character-level formatting, plus document-level formatting such as page size. I don't cover this option because, frankly, creating and editing document styles is complicated, and you probably don't have much reason to use them, anyhow.

WordPerfect assigns a standard document style, called *DocumentStyle*, to every document you create. You can't delete this style, although you can edit it if you're a WordPerfect hidden codes aficionado (or know someone who is), as I explain in the section "Editing a style," later in this chapter. You really shouldn't need to delete or edit the DocumentStyle style, however, because any formatting you do inside the document overrides the style's formatting instructions.

Creating character and paragraph styles

WordPerfect comes with some prefab styles that you can select from the Styles drop-down list on the Property Bar (labeled in the upcoming Figure 9-3). But you probably want to define your own styles, because the prefab styles aren't likely to meet your specific formatting needs. You can create styles from scratch, but an easier method is to create some text, apply the formatting you want to use, and then use the QuickStyle feature to create a style based on your formatted text.

To create a character or paragraph style by using QuickStyle, follow these steps:

1. **Format and select the text you want to use as the basis for the style.**

2. **Click the Styles drop-down list on the Property Bar and choose QuickStyle.**

   The QuickStyle dialog box appears, as shown in Figure 9-1.

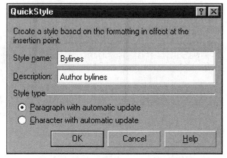

Figure 9-1: Use the QuickStyle command to create a style based on existing text.

QuickStyle

Create a style based on the formatting in effect at the insertion point.

Style name: Bylines

Description: Author bylines

Style type
- ◉ Paragraph with automatic update
- ○ Character with automatic update

OK   Cancel   Help

3. **Give your style a name and a description.**

   Enter the name into the Style Name option box. (You can't use a style name that already exists.) In the Description box, enter some descriptive text that reminds you what sort of text you plan to format with the style.

4. **Choose a Style Type radio button.**

   The differences between the style types are explained in the preceding section.

5. Click OK or press Enter.

You should see your new style listed on the Styles drop-down list.

Applying styles

Applying styles to your text is easy. To apply a character style, select the text you want to format, click on the Styles drop-down list, and then select the style from the list. To apply a paragraph style, click in the paragraph you want to format and select the style. To apply a style to several paragraphs, select the paragraphs before selecting the style.

If you're not sure what style you applied to a particular paragraph, click in the paragraph and then take a look at the Styles drop-down list. The current style is displayed. If no style is applied, you see the word <None>.

Editing a style

Suppose that you create a paragraph style named Byline for all the author bylines in your monthly newsletter. You originally specify that you want the bylines to be left-justified. You later decide that you want them to be centered instead. All you do is click one of the bylines and change the justification, as I explain in Chapter 7. WordPerfect automatically makes the same change to all text that uses the Byline style.

If you don't want WordPerfect to perform this automatic updating, change the style type from Paragraph (paired auto) to Paragraph (paired). You make this change inside the Styles Editor dialog box, as I describe in the upcoming steps.

By default, character styles are now created as paired auto styles as well, which means that, if you click in a word that uses the style and change the font or other character formatting, WordPerfect changes the formatting for all other text that uses that style as well. In previous versions, you needed to edit character styles by using the Reveal Codes window.

If you select text before reformatting it, your changes apply to that text only, even if the text uses a paired auto style.

If you want to make changes to all text that uses a plain paired style — that is, one that doesn't offer automatic updating — head for the Style Editor dialog box. This dialog box is also the place for changing the style type from paired to paired auto and vice versa. To access this dialog box and change your styles, follow these steps:

1. **Choose Format⇨Styles or press Alt+F8 to open the Style List dialog box.**

2. **Click the style you want to edit and then click the Edit button.**

   WordPerfect displays the Styles Editor dialog box, as shown in Figure 9-2.

3. **Make your edits to the style.**

   The dialog box has a menu bar and a mini-toolbar that offer many of the same commands as the regular WordPerfect window. If you want to add a formatting attribute, choose the appropriate command from the menus or toolbar.

   To delete a formatting attribute, drag its code out of the Contents window at the bottom of the Styles Editor dialog box. To get rid of the italic attribute in the Byline style, for example, you'd drag the Italc code (at the end of the Contents line in Figure 9-2) out of the window.

   If you want to *replace* a formatting attribute — say, to substitute 10-point type for 12-point type — drag the old code out of the window before you set the new attribute.

4. **Click OK or press Enter to return to the Style List dialog box.**

5. **Click the Close button.**

   WordPerfect closes the Style List dialog box and applies the updated formatting to any text that uses the style.

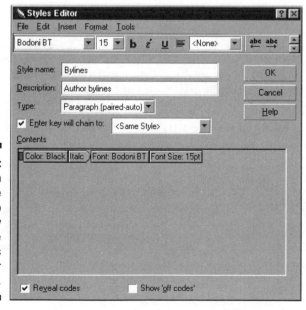

Figure 9-2:
You can make changes to a style by using the Styles Editor dialog box.

Removing styles

If you want to remove a style from a paragraph, click inside the paragraph and select <None> from the Styles drop-down list on the Property Bar.

Removing character styles is dicier — it requires deleting hidden codes in the Reveal Codes window. So take a big breath and follow these steps:

1. **Click the space to the left of the first character in the text that you want to "destyle."**

2. **Press Alt+F3 to open the Reveal Codes window.**

   In the Reveal Codes window, you can see your document text along with all the hidden formatting codes. To the left of the first character in the text that you want to unformat, you should see a code that begins with Char Style (the character style code), as shown in Figure 9-3. A similar code appears at the end of the text that uses the style.

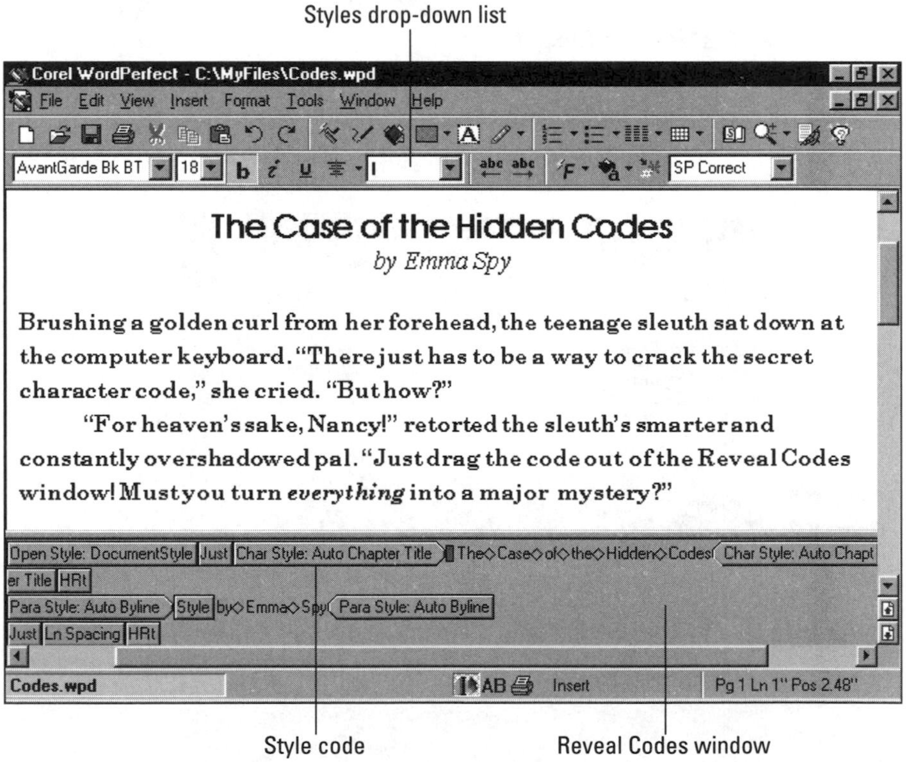

Styles drop-down list

Figure 9-3:
To remove
a character
style, drag
either of the
Char Style
codes out
of the
Reveal
Codes
window.

Style code   Reveal Codes window

3. Drag either of the Char Style codes out of the Reveal Codes window.

Deleting one code deletes both.

If things don't look right after you remove the style code, press Ctrl+Z to undo your edit. Then go make nice with the WordPerfect guru in your office to get some help sorting out your codes.

Alternatively, you can simply select the text and apply new formatting without deleting the original character style code. But leaving in old formatting codes can lead to hidden-code buildup, which can occasionally cause problems if you move or otherwise edit text. So a good idea is to delete the code entirely.

Another trick for removing character style codes is to click just to the left of the text you want to reformat and then press Backspace. No change? Press Ctrl+Z and then press Delete. See, the hidden character style code resides somewhere in the space between the first character in the text and the preceding character. But determining exactly where the code is hiding is difficult. Your cursor may look like it's poised to wipe out the first character in the text, but it may actually be on the code — something to remember if you really want to delete the character but you end up destroying formatting instead. Try this procedure out a few times with the Reveal Codes window open to get a feel for how WordPerfect does things.

To completely remove a style from the document, follow these steps:

1. Press Alt+F8 or choose Format➪Styles to display the Style List dialog box.

2. Click on the style you want to remove, click the Options button, and select Delete from the drop-down list.

WordPerfect presents the Delete Styles dialog box, which contains just two options: Leave Formatting Codes in Document and Including Formatting Codes. If you want to delete the style but leave the formatting it applied intact, choose the former. If you want to erase both the formatting and the styles, choose Including Formatting Codes.

3. To complete your mission, click OK and then click Close.

Copying Formats with QuickFormat

WordPerfect offers another tool to speed up your formatting life: *QuickFormat*. QuickFormat copies the formatting from one chunk of text to another. You can copy the formatting of a selected word, block of text, or paragraph. To see how it works, follow these steps:

1. Select the text that has the formatting you want to copy.

If you want to copy paragraph formatting, you can just click inside the paragraph.

2. Choose Format➪QuickFormat or click the QuickFormat button on the toolbar.

The QuickFormat dialog box appears, as shown in Figure 9-4.

Figure 9-4: You can copy character or paragraph formatting from one spot to another.

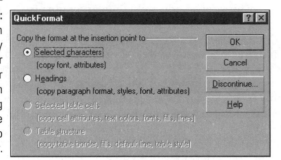

3. Choose a copy option from the group of radio buttons in the dialog box.

If you select the Selected Characters radio button, you copy the formatting of the selected characters only — font, type size, type style, and so on. If you choose the Headings button, you copy both the text formatting and the paragraph formatting (styles, indents, borders, and so on).

4. Click OK or press Enter.

Your cursor turns into a little paint roller.

5. Drag the cursor over the text you want to format.

If you're copying paragraph formatting to a single paragraph, you can just click inside the paragraph instead. The paint roller cursor remains visible, and you can keep "painting" the formatting onto as much other text as you want.

6. After you finish painting your text, turn off QuickFormat.

For the fastest results, just click the QuickFormat button again.

If you copy formatting by using QuickFormat — whether character or paragraph formatting — WordPerfect creates a QuickFormat style based on your formatting. (I explain styles in the preceding section.) The style then appears on the Styles drop-down list, just as a regular style does. The first

QuickFormat style you create is called QuickFormat1; the second one is called QuickFormat2 — and so on. So if you want to copy the formatting to any subsequent text after you put away the QuickFormat paint roller, you can just apply the QuickFormat style from the Styles list. If you want, you can rename the style by changing its name in the Styles Editor dialog box, as I explain in the section "Editing a style," earlier in this chapter.

QuickFormat styles are paired auto styles, which means that you can click inside one piece of text that uses the style, make a formatting change, and have that change automatically applied to all other text that uses the style. If you don't want this automatic updating to occur, simply select the text before you make your formatting changes. Or you may want to change the style type from paired auto to paired, as I explain in the section "Editing a style," earlier in this chapter.

For paragraphs formatted with QuickFormat, you have another option for turning off automatic updating. If you don't want formatting changes to affect a particular paragraph, click anywhere in the paragraph, choose Format⇨QuickFormat to open the QuickFormat dialog box, and click the Discontinue button. Then choose the Current Heading radio button. Now this paragraph remains untouched if you make changes to other paragraphs that carry the QuickFormat style. If you instead choose the All Associated Headings radio button, automatic updating is turned off for all paragraphs that use the style.

Finding and Replacing Errant Text

People seem to have a hard time making up their minds these days. Just as you finish typing the text for your company's 100-page annual report, the board of directors replaces all the top management. You create a catalog touting your client's new product, and just before you send the thing to the printer, the client decides that spelling the product name *ConsumerScam* instead of *Consumer Scam* would be really cool.

When these sorts of unavoidable changes happen, you could scroll through your text, hunt down all instances of outdated or incorrect information, and make the changes manually. Or you could do the smart thing and have the WordPerfect Find and Replace feature do the job for you. To go on your search and destroy mission, follow these steps:

1. **Click at the spot in your document where you want to begin searching for the incorrect text.**

2. **Choose Edit⇨Find and Replace or press Ctrl+F.**

   The Find and Replace dialog box appears, as shown in Figure 9-5.

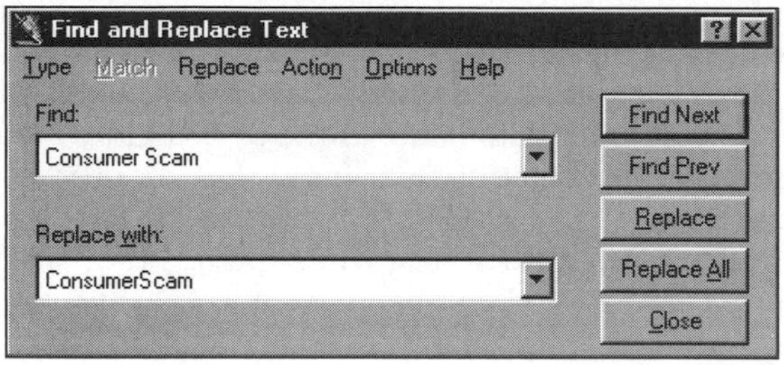

Figure 9-5:
Use the
Find and
Replace
command
to track
down and
replace
errant text.

3. **Click the Type menu and check the status of the Text option.**

   If you see a check mark next to this option in the menu, the option is turned on, which is what you want. If not, click on the option to activate it. Turn off the other options in the menu, if they happen to be checked. (More about what you can do with those options in a bit.)

4. **Type the word or phrase that you want to replace in the Find option box.**

   Or click the arrow at the end of the box to select text for which you recently searched and replaced.

5. **Type the replacement word or phrase in the Replace With option box.**

   Or click the arrow at the end of the box to select replacement text that you recently used.

6. **Click the Find Next or Find Prev button.**

   Find Next finds the first occurrence of the incorrect text after the insertion marker. Find Prev searches for the first occurrence of the incorrect text before the insertion marker.

   After WordPerfect finds the incorrect text, it highlights the text in your document. If you click Replace, WordPerfect replaces that text and moves on to find the next occurrence. If you click Find Next or Find Prev, WordPerfect leaves the current text alone and starts hunting for another occurrence of the text.

   If you click Replace All, WordPerfect automatically replaces every occurrence of the text from the insertion marker through the end of the document. (You can change the extent of the search by changing the settings in the Options menu, which I describe in the bulleted list later in this section.)

If you want to edit the found text instead of replacing it, just click in your document and edit away. If you want to begin searching again, click inside the Find and Replace dialog box to make it active.

If WordPerfect can't find any more occurrences of the incorrect text, an alert box appears to tell you so. Click OK to get rid of the box.

7. Click Close to shut the Find and Replace dialog box.

If you prefer, you can leave the dialog box open and available for future searches. You can move the dialog box to a different spot, if necessary, by dragging its title bar.

If you replace a word by mistake, choose Edit⇨Undo or press Ctrl+Z to undo the replacement.

If you want to delete every occurrence of a word or phrase, leave the Replace With option box empty. WordPerfect then replaces each occurrence of the incorrect text with, uh, nothing, which is the same as deleting it. Nifty, huh?

Now that you know the basic steps involved in the Find and Replace dance, try out a few variations. The Find and Replace dialog box offers all sorts of options that enable you to customize your search:

✔ If you turn on the Word Forms option in the Type menu, you can search and replace all forms of a word. If you type **fish** in the Find text box, for example, WordPerfect finds the words *fish, fishing,* and *fishes.* WordPerfect also alters the Replace With text to match the form of the word it finds — for example, if you originally used **hare** as the Replace With text, and the search finds the word *fishes*, the Replace With text changes to *hares*. Sometimes, WordPerfect gives you a drop-down list offering several choices of Replace With text.

✔ Normally, WordPerfect finds any word that contains the characters you type in the Find text box. If you tell it to search for **bee**, for example, WordPerfect finds any words that contain those three letters, including *been*, *beer*, *beet*, and so on. If you turn on the Whole Word option in the Match menu, WordPerfect finds only the word *bee*. This option isn't available if the Word Forms option is turned on in the Type menu.

✔ Turn on the Case option in the Match menu to limit the search to text that uses the same case (uppercase or lowercase letters) as the text you type in the Find text box.

✔ The Match⇨Font command enables you to search for text that uses a specific font, type size, and type style. Type the text you want to find in the Find text box and then choose Match⇨Font. WordPerfect displays a Match Font dialog box in which you can specify the specific font characteristics that you want to use in the search.

✔ You can also replace just the font or case of the found text. If you want to make *ConsumerScam* boldface as well as italicized, for example, you can enter **ConsumerScam** in both the Find option box and the Replace With option box, choose Replace⇨Font, and turn on the bold and italic attributes in the Replace Font dialog box that appears. You can use the Replace and Match options together to find text with certain attributes and replace those attributes with other attributes — for example, to find all instances where *ConsumerScam* is italicized and make it bold-face instead.

✔ Notice that the Replace menu becomes available only if the Replace With option box is active; the Match menu is available only if the Find option box is active.

✔ The menu options stay active until you turn them off. If you turn on font matching for one search, for example, it's automatically turned on for the next search you do. So make sure that you check the options before you start each search to make sure that everything's the way you want it. Remember, a check mark next to an option means that the option is turned on. Click on the option to toggle it on and off.

✔ The options on the Action menu tell WordPerfect to select the text it finds or to position the insertion marker before or after the text. If you turn on Select Match, for example, WordPerfect selects the first text it finds in your document. You can then edit, delete, format, or move the text without needing to select it first. Just click in the document window to make it active; after you finish editing and are ready to continue your search, click inside the Find and Replace dialog box again.

✔ The commands on the Options menu control the direction and extent of the search. The first option on the menu tells WordPerfect to begin searching at the top of the document; the second option tells it to search from the insertion marker to the end of the document and then search from the beginning of the document to the insertion marker. If you don't turn on either option, WordPerfect searches from the insertion marker forward to the end of the document and then stops.

The Options menu contains two additional choices: The Limit Find Within Selection option searches selected text only; the Include Headers, Footers, etc. in Find option searches the main body of the document as well as in headers, footers, text boxes, and so on.

You also choose Options⇨Limit Number of Changes to display the Limit Number of Changes dialog box, which contains one option: Limit Changes To. As you can guess from the dialog box name, this option controls how many replacements WordPerfect makes after you choose the Replace All button. If you enter a value of 3 in the Limit Changes To option box, for example, WordPerfect replaces only the first three occurrences of the text that it finds. If you specify 0 as the limit, WordPerfect replaces all occurrences of the found text.

If all you want to do is find the next occurrence of a particular word or phrase, select the text and then click the Find Next button on the Property Bar or press Alt+Ctrl+N. WordPerfect locates the text and selects it. To find the preceding occurrence of the word or phrase, click the Find Previous button or press Alt+Ctrl+P.

Checking Your Spelling

Remember that kid in grade school who won all the spelling bees? Well, WordPerfect makes that kid's brain cells available to you through its Spell Checker. You can ask the Spell Checker — also known as Mr. Smarty Pants — to look over your document and point out any misspelled or duplicated words.

 The Spell Checker knows only whether the words you use are spelled correctly — it doesn't know whether you used the wrong word or the wrong form of a word. the Spell Checker doesn't notify you that you typed **your**, for example, if you meant to type *you're*. The moral of the story: Just like Mr. Smarty Pants in grade school, the Spell Checker isn't nearly as smart as you may have been led to believe. And running the Spell Checker is no substitute for proofreading your document.

Even so, running the Spell Checker before you print or save your finished copy is always a good idea. WordPerfect is likely to turn up some typos or misspellings that you missed.

If you want to be notified of incorrect spellings as you type, turn on the Spell-As-You-Go feature (by choosing Tools⇨Proofread⇨Spell-As-You-Go). WordPerfect underscores any misspelled word with a red, striped line after you type it. Right-click the word to display a QuickMenu of suggested spellings. Personally, I find the feature distracting, but you may like it. To turn Spell-As-You-Go off, choose Tools⇨Proofread⇨Off. Notice that, if Grammar-As-You-Go (which I discuss later in this section) is turned on, Spell-As-You-Go is automatically turned on as well.

 The far-right drop-down list on the Property Bar, known as the Prompt-As-You-Go list, displays suggested spellings after you click a misspelled word. If you click a correctly spelled word, the list offers synonyms for the word, acting like a mini-thesaurus. Click a word in the list to replace the original word in your text.

Here's how to give your document the spelling test by using the Spell Checker:

1. **Press Ctrl+F1 or click the Spell Checker toolbar button.**

   You can also choose Tools⇨Spell Check. The Spell Checker window opens, as shown in Figure 9-6. WordPerfect finds and highlights the first misspelled or duplicated word. The Replace With text box shows WordPerfect's suggested correction, and the Replacements list offers other possible corrections.

   If you want to check only a portion of your document, select it before opening the Spell Checker. Alternatively, tell WordPerfect which part of your document to check by choosing an option from the Check drop-down list in the Spell Checker window.

2. **Select the appropriate options to tell WordPerfect to replace, ignore, or add the word.**

   • To replace the misspelled word with the word in the Replace With text box, click the Replace button. If you want to replace the misspelled word with some other word, type it into the Replace With text box or choose it from the Replacements list box.

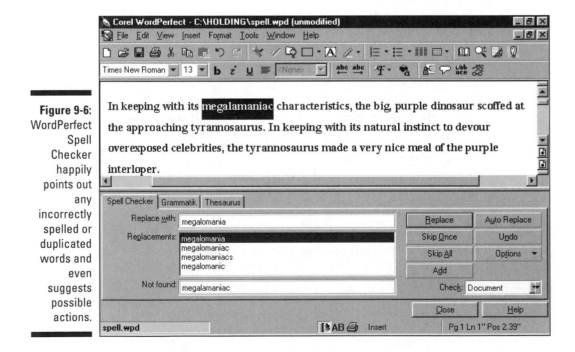

Figure 9-6:
WordPerfect
Spell
Checker
happily
points out
any
incorrectly
spelled or
duplicated
words and
even
suggests
possible
actions.

- Alternatively, you can click inside your document to make it active again and edit the word yourself. Click back inside the Spell Checker window and click Resume when you're ready to start checking more words.

- WordPerfect knows only the words that are included in its internal dictionary — which means that Spell Checker marks as incorrect many words that are really okay. To tell WordPerfect to ignore this particular word and move on to the next misspelled word, click Skip Once. To tell it to ignore this word throughout the rest of the document, click Skip All. To add the word to the WordPerfect dictionary, click Add.

- By default, WordPerfect checks words that contain numbers, checks for duplicate words, and checks for incorrect capitalization. If you don't want the Spell Checker to check any or all of these things, click the Options button and turn off these options in the drop-down list. (A check mark next to an option means that the option is turned on.)

- The Auto Replace button is, in my opinion, a dangerous little doodad. Click this button, and WordPerfect automatically replaces all occurrences of the misspelled word with the correct word. The misspelled word and its correction are also added to the QuickCorrect list. (I explain QuickCorrect in Chapter 6.)

The problem with the Auto Replace feature is that it's activated even if you never click the Auto Replace button. When you start the Spell Checker, WordPerfect consults the QuickCorrect list, and replaces *any* words on that list with their "correct" spelling and punctuation. Using the same example as I did in Chapter 6, say that you use the word *august* as an adjective, rather than as the month name. Because *August* is listed in the QuickCorrect dialog box as the appropriate replacement for *august,* the Spell Checker automatically makes the replacement in your document. I find this behavior frightening, because you have no way of knowing what words are being replaced. To be safe, I recommend that you click the Options button and turn on the Prompt Before Auto Replacement option. That way, the Spell Checker stops on every misspelled word and enables you to decide whether you want to replace the word.

If you replace a word by mistake, click on the Undo button.

After WordPerfect finishes grading your spelling, it asks whether you want to close the Spell Checker window. Click Yes to close the window or No to leave it open and available for your next spelling session. If you leave the window open, click the Start button to check more text.

You can resize the window by dragging its top edge up or down. You can also move it to another position on-screen by placing the cursor near the top of the window until the cursor becomes a four-headed arrow. After you see the arrow, you can drag the window.

A cousin of Spell Checker and Spell-As-You-Go, the Grammar-As-You-Go feature (which you access by choosing Tools⇨Proofread⇨Grammar-As-You-Go) is supposed to underline grammatical errors and offer suggestions for fixing those errors if you right-click the underlined phrase. But I don't find WordPerfect's grammar skills to be too hot. After I typed "Them there fools ain't no better than me," for example, Grammar-As-You-Go underlined only *fools* as a possible error. As a matter of fact, even the full-fledged WordPerfect grammar checker, Grammatik, didn't pick up the other obvious grammatical faux pas. Thank goodness we still have them there real-life copy editors to keep us on track, because ain't none of us would look too smart if we relied on Grammar-As-You-Go.

Using QuickWords

QuickWords is an expanded version of QuickCorrect. As with QuickCorrect, you can type a few characters to represent a long word or phrase and then have WordPerfect automatically replace those characters with the expanded version of the text. But QuickWords gives you a few more options than QuickCorrect.

To use QuickWords, follow these steps:

1. **Select the text you want to represent with the abbreviation.**

2. **Choose Tools⇨QuickWords to open the QuickCorrect dialog box, with the QuickWords tab at the forefront.**

3. **Type the abbreviation you want to use in the Abbreviated Form option box.**

4. **Set your expand options, as appropriate.**

   If you want WordPerfect to replace the abbreviation with the full text as you type the abbreviation, check the Expand QuickWords as You Type Them check box. If you don't choose the Expand QuickWords as You Type Them check box, WordPerfect waits until you issue the go-ahead to replace the abbreviations with the full text.

   If you want WordPerfect to use the same formatting as the original text every time it replaces the abbreviation with the expanded text, click the Options button and choose Expand as Text with Formatting. Otherwise, choose Expand as Plain Text.

5. **Click OK.**

If you didn't sign up for as-you-type replacements in Step 4, you can expand an abbreviation by clicking it and pressing Ctrl+Shift+A.

If you forget the abbreviation for a QuickWords phrase, click an abbreviation that looks familiar on the QuickWords tab of the QuickCorrect dialog box. A preview of the expanded text appears in the dialog box. Click the Insert in Text button to put the text in your document.

Using Corel Address Book

Corel Address Book was once part of the WordPerfect program but recently gained its independence and now operates as a separate utitlity in the Suite. Address Book gives you a convenient way to store and access the names, addresses, and phone numbers of all your friends, business contacts, and so-called friends. After entering names and addresses into Address Book, you can print mailing labels and envelopes, add a contact name and address to a letter or other WordPerfect document, and even get your computer to dial the contact's phone number, e-mail address, or Internet address for you.

I decided to cover this handy utility here because you're likely to use it most inside WordPerfect. WordPerfect is where you handle most of your correspondence, after all, and Address Book can help you get that correspondence done more quickly. Also, I couldn't figure out where else to cover this stray program, and this is as good a spot as any.

Now that I've rationalized my approach — hopefully to your satisfaction — you start Corel Address Book by clicking the Windows 95 Start button and then choosing Corel WordPerfect Suite 8⇨Accessories⇨Corel Address Book 8. Or, if you're already working in WordPerfect (or Quattro Pro or Presentations), you can choose Tools⇨Address Book. Whichever route you take, the Address Book window appears, as shown in Figure 9-7.

Each of the tabs in the dialog box represents a different address book. You can use just one of the books for all your contacts if you like, or you can separate your addresses into categories to make them easier to find. You can store the same contact on more than one tab, if you want, and you can create as many additional address books as you like by choosing Book⇨New. To open or close an address book, choose Book⇨Open and Book⇨Close, respectively.

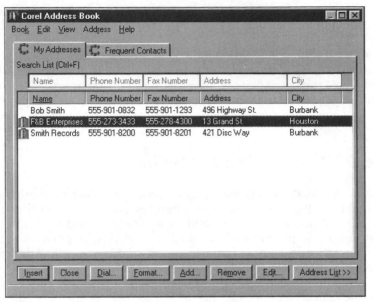

Figure 9-7:
The
Address
Book gives
you a way
to store
addresses
and other
contact
information
for use in
your
WordPerfect
documents.

Adding and deleting contacts

To add a name to an address book, choose Edit➪Add Name or click the Add button at the bottom of the window. A dialog box appears, asking you to specify whether you want to add an address for an organization or a person. Select the category you want and then click OK.

If you select the Person category, the Properties dialog box appears, as shown in Figure 9-8; a slightly different dialog box opens if you choose the Organization category. The different tabs of the dialog box contain option boxes in which you enter different types of information. Fill in the blanks that you want to store, and click OK to add the contact to the address book.

Here are a few other juicy bits of news about using Address Book:

- ✔ Organization entries appear with a little skyscraper icon in the address book, as you can see in Figure 9-7.

- ✔ If you fill in the Organization blank on the Business tab while adding a person to an address book, a separate entry automatically appears for the organization.

- ✔ To make changes to an entry, click it and then click the Edit button to redisplay its Properties dialog box. After you edit an entry in one address book, it's updated in all address books in which it's stored.

- While editing an individual's address information, you can edit the information for that person's organization by clicking the Edit button next to the Organization box (on the Business tab) to edit the organization information.

- You can copy entries from one address book to another by clicking the entry to select it and then choosing Edit➪Copy Names. A dialog box appears and asks you to choose the address book where you want to paste the names. You can also drag the names to the tab of the address book where you want to add them.

- To delete an entry, click it and press Delete or click the Remove button.

- To select more than one address to copy or delete, Ctrl+click each address you want to select.

Searching for a long-lost loved one

After you get many addresses entered into the Address Book, hunting down the one you want can be time-consuming. To track down an address quickly, use the Search List option boxes at the top of each address book tab. If you want to search by name, for example, click inside the Name box and begin typing the name of the contact you want to locate. If you want to search for a particular phone number, type it into the Phone Number box. Almost before you're finished typing, the Address Book finds the listing and highlights it for you in the Address Book window. Click outside the Search List box to end your search. If the search doesn't turn up the contact, the status bar displays a message saying that the search failed.

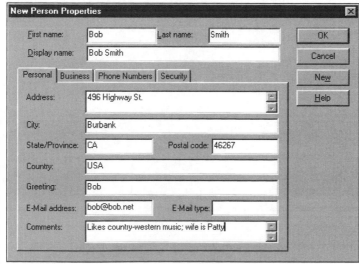

Figure 9-8:
Enter contact information for an individual in this dialog box.

The Address Book can search for names in the current address book only.

Changing the display of information

By default, the Address Book window displays the name, phone number, fax number, and e-mail addresses for a contact. If you want to display other items, choose Edit⇨Columns to display a submenu of available items. If you see a check mark next to an item, that item appears in the window. Click an item to turn the check mark on or off.

Drag the borders between the column headings in the Address Book window to change the width of the columns.

Inserting addresses into your documents

To insert a contact address into a WordPerfect document, open up the Address Book by choosing Tools⇨Address Book inside WordPerfect. A new button, Insert, appears at the bottom of the Address Book. Click the address you want to insert and then click Insert. You can also insert addresses onto envelopes that you create by using WordPerfect's Format⇨Envelope command. The Envelopes dialog box that appears contains icons that enable you to select both the return address and mailing address from the Address Book. (The icons look like little books.)

As I explain in Chapter 7, you can also create mailing labels by using the Address Book in conjunction with WordPerfect's Format⇨Labels command. See the section "Choosing a Page Size and Orientation" for details.

Part III
Crunching Numbers like a (Quattro) Pro

The 5th Wave   By Rich Tennant

"I SUPPOSE THIS ALL HAS SOMETHING TO DO WITH THE NEW MATH."

In this part . . .

In the interest of keeping everyone thoroughly confused, computer industry bigwigs like to give things obscure, meaningless names. Take Quattro Pro, for example. Loosely translated, *quattro* means *four* in some long-forgotten language. So it follows that Quattro Pro makes you a professional at . . . four?

The real story behind Quattro Pro's name has to do with a marketing ploy to unseat a rival program, Lotus 1-2-3. (Get it — 4 is one better than 3?) Well, at least that's the rumored reason, and it seems as plausible as any.

As you dive into this part of the book, don't waste another minute worrying about why Quattro Pro was given such a name. Concentrate instead on what this terrific program can do for you: build tables, do mathematical calculations, turn ordinary numbers into impressive charts, and generally help keep track of and calculate any kind of data, from your annual sales figures to your household budget. Come to think of it, that's four things that Quattro Pro does well . . . hmm.

Chapter 10

The Spreadsheet Solution

In This Chapter

▶ Avoiding math by using spreadsheets

▶ Starting and closing Quattro Pro

▶ Getting familiar with the spreadsheet window

▶ Moving around in your spreadsheet

▶ Customizing the on-screen display

▶ Working in the new Page View

▶ Creating, opening, and closing spreadsheets

▶ Saving your work

I hate math. If you want me to add, multiply, subtract, or divide, you darn well better give me a good reason — and a calculator. Numbers and I just don't get along. Never have, never will.

If you share my aversion to things mathematical, you're going to love Quattro Pro. "But," you ask, "isn't math one of the main things you do with Quattro Pro?" Yep. Sure is. And that's why I appreciate this program so much. Any time a project involving lots of calculations rears its ugly head, I just crank up Quattro Pro. I get the answers I need in no time, without needing to tax my numerically challenged brain.

Of course, if you're the sort who gets all giddy if presented with a fresh column of numbers to add — you sicko — you should like Quattro Pro even more. One of the top spreadsheet programs on the market, Quattro Pro gives you advanced mathematical features you've only dreamed about until now.

This chapter gets you started on the road to spreadsheet heaven by explaining the basics of the Quattro Pro spreadsheet window and showing you how to open, close, and save your work.

So What Can I Do with This Thing?

As I mention in Chapter 1, Quattro Pro is a whiz at figuring out the answers to any problem that involves numbers. This program is also a handy financial record-keeping tool. Here are some of the different types of projects you can manage with Quattro Pro:

- ✔ **Keep a household or business budget.** You can record your monthly expenses by category — rent, gas, utilities, and so on. You can then have Quattro Pro calculate your total monthly expenses, quarterly expenses, year-to-date expenses, and your actual expenses versus your annual budget forecast.

- ✔ **Perform a profit and loss analysis.** You can determine the net return on your company's latest product, given various pricing and manufacturing scenarios. You can easily try out different price points, for example, to determine which pricing structure nets you the most profit, considering your production, marketing, and distribution costs.

- ✔ **Track business sales and inventories.** You can record the monthly sales for each item you sell and then calculate the totals of all items in a certain category, figure out your net profit on different items, keep track of your remaining inventory, and even determine the top salesperson in your store for a particular month or quarter.

- ✔ **Create tables of information.** You can create a list of vendor names, phone numbers, addresses, and products. Quattro Pro makes entering and formatting table data easy.

- ✔ **Create charts to present financial information.** After you create an income and expense spreadsheet, for example, you can create a pie chart showing expenses by category so that you can easily see where your money goes each month. You can print your charts from Quattro Pro or put them in a WordPerfect document or Presentations slide show.

In other words, if your project involves many different pieces of data or lots of calculations, Quattro Pro can help you get the job done with less effort and in less time than if you were to attempt your calculations by using a piece of paper and a desktop calculator. Quattro Pro also gives you a painless way to turn on-screen spreadsheets into professional-looking printed reports. You look for all the world as if you really know what you're doing.

Don't get confused over the various terms used for *spreadsheet*. Quattro Pro calls spreadsheets *notebooks*, but they're spreadsheets just the same. You may also hear a spreadsheet referred to as a *worksheet*, *sheet*, *document*, or *file*.

Start It Up, Shut It Down

Starting Quattro Pro is just like starting any other program in the WordPerfect Suite: Click the Quattro Pro DAD icon or click the Windows 95 Start button, click the WordPerfect Suite 8 item, and choose Quattro Pro 8. The Quattro Pro screen comes to life, as shown in Figure 10-1.

To call it a day and send Quattro Pro packing, click the program window's Close button, press Alt+F4 or choose File⇨Exit. If you haven't saved your work yet, Quattro Pro prompts you to do so. (Saving is explained in the section "Open Me! Close Me! Save Me!" later in this chapter.)

Your Field Guide to a Spreadsheet

After you first start Quattro Pro, you get a brand new spreadsheet, contained in its very own spreadsheet window, as shown in Figure 10-1.

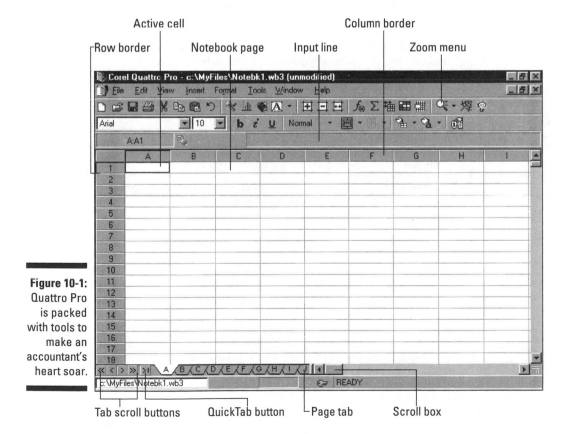

Figure 10-1: Quattro Pro is packed with tools to make an accountant's heart soar.

Most elements in the Quattro Pro program window and the spreadsheet window are standard Windows 95 program elements. (You can find more information about these gizmos in Chapter 2, in the section "Doing Windows.") But a few elements are unique to Quattro Pro and call for some explanation, as follows:

✔ That big, white, gridlike thing that consumes most of the spreadsheet window is a *notebook page*. Each spreadsheet contains 256 notebook pages, which are actually 256 individual spreadsheets. You probably never use all 256 pages, but knowing that you can if you want to sure is nice, isn't it?

✔ After the 256 notebook pages comes the *Objects page*, which is a special page you use for charts and other special objects you can create but probably won't (such as custom dialog boxes). The Objects page is discussed more fully in Chapter 14, in the section "Editing a Chart."

✔ A notebook page is divided into *columns* and *rows*. Columns are identified by the letters on the Column border, and rows are identified by the numbers on the Row border. Each notebook page has an incredible 8,192 rows and 256 columns. But you needn't feel compelled to use them all (and if you do feel so compelled, please seek psychiatric help immediately).

✔ The little boxes created by the intersection of a column and a row are called *cells*. Cells hold your actual spreadsheet data.

✔ Each cell has a unique *cell address* (name) that includes its notebook page followed by its column letter and row number. The cell in the top-left corner of the notebook in Figure 10-1, for example, is cell A:A1.

✔ The black border around a cell indicates the *active* cell — where the next piece of data you enter will appear. The active cell in Figure 10-1 is cell A:A1.

✔ The *input line* shows the data in the active cell. You can enter and edit data either in the input line or directly in a cell. The address of the active cell appears at the left end of the input line.

✔ To move from page to page in your notebook, you can click the *page tabs* or use the *tab scroll buttons*. From left to right, the buttons are Go Back Several Pages; Move Backward One Page; Move Forward One Page; and Move Forward Several Pages.

✔ The *QuickTab button* takes you to the Objects page. Click the button again to return to the last active spreadsheet page.

 ✔ You can zoom in or out on your work by clicking the *Zoom button* on the Property Bar and choosing a zoom ratio from the drop-down list.

If you want to focus on a particular area of your spreadsheet, select the area (as discussed in Chapter 13) and select the Selection option from the Zoom menu. Quattro Pro enlarges or reduces the selected cells to fill the available screen space.

✔ If you drag the *scroll box* on the vertical scroll bar, a little box displays row numbers as you move to tell you how far you're going. If you drag the horizontal scroll box, Quattro Pro displays column letters as you scroll.

Some buttons, keyboard shortcuts, and other Quattro Pro features don't work if you're in edit mode (in the process of entering data in a cell). So if you click a button or press a keyboard shortcut and nothing happens, click outside the cell and try again.

If you can't remember what a particular button does, just pause your mouse cursor on it for a few seconds. A little flag (QuickTip) appears to give you some helpful hints about what the button does.

I Don't Like What I See Here!

You can alter many aspects of the Quattro Pro display to suit your preferences. Display options are scattered about through several different dialog boxes, and some options have moved from their previous locations in Version 7, as the following list describes:

✔ Choose Tools⇨Settings or press Alt+F12 to open the Application dialog box. Click the Display tab to access options that hide or display the toolbar, Property Bar, Application Bar, input line, scroll indicators (the row and column position boxes that appear as you drag the scroll box), and QuickTips (the little boxes that appear as you pause your mouse over a button or other on-screen element).

✔ Choose Format⇨Notebook or press Shift+F12 to display the Active Notebook dialog box, which contains settings pertinent to the current notebook. On the Display tab of this dialog box, you can hide or display the scroll bars and page tabs and also control the display of objects such as charts and graphs. If you choose Show All, these objects appear in their entirety. If you choose Show Outline, you see only the outline of the object — this option can speed up screen displays if you use very complex objects. The Hide option, none too surprisingly, hides objects from view.

✔ Choose Format⇨Sheet or press Ctrl+F12 to open the Active Sheet dialog box, where you establish display preferences for the current worksheet. You can get to this same dialog box by right-clicking the page tab and choosing Sheet Properties from the QuickMenu.

However you get to the dialog box, click the Display tab to uncover the options shown in Figure 10-2. The Display Zeros options determine whether Quattro Pro displays a zero in a cell that has a value of zero or simply leaves the cell blank. The Border Options check boxes enable you to turn row and column borders on and off. And the Grid Lines check boxes are for hiding and displaying the horizontal and vertical grid lines that separate the cells in your spreadsheet.

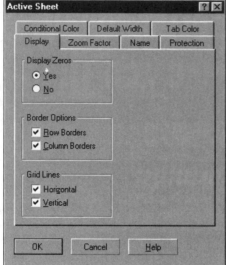

Figure 10-2: You can control whether zeros, borders, and grid lines appear on-screen by using this dialog box.

Want to add a little color to your view? Quattro Pro enables you to assign colors to your page tabs. Just click the Tab Color tab of the dialog box and deselect the Use System Color check box. Then click the drop-down list directly beneath the check box to display a palette of available colors. Click the color you want to use and then click OK.

✔ Version 8 offers a new Page View option, which enables you to see and manipulate margins and headers and footers right in the spreadsheet window. Previously, you had to switch to the Print Preview window to work with these elements. To switch to this view, as shown in Figure 10-3, choose View➪Page. The dotted lines represent the page and header/footer margins. If you place your cursor over a margin guideline, the cursor changes to a two-headed arrow, as shown in the figure. You can then drag the guideline to move the margin, just as you can in WordPerfect. (For more about margins and headers and footers, see Chapter 15.) To switch back to the regular view, choose View➪Draft.

See Chapter 2, in the section "Customizing Your View," for more information on fiddling with your screens in the WordPerfect Suite.

Margin guideline   Margin move cursor   Header

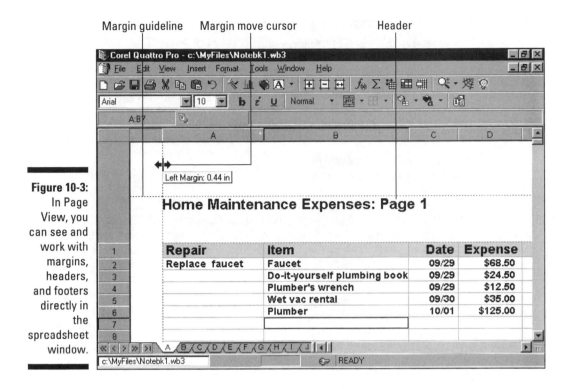

Figure 10-3:
In Page
View, you
can see and
work with
margins,
headers,
and footers
directly in
the
spreadsheet
window.

Naming Your Pages

After you open a new spreadsheet, Quattro Pro assigns a letter to each page in the notebook. The first page is page A, the second is page B, and so on. The page tabs at the bottom of the spreadsheet window reflect these page names.

You can, however, give a page a different name if you want. If you put your June sales data on page 1, for example, you can name that page *June* (or something more inventive, if you're in the mood). Naming your pages helps you remember what sort of data you're keeping on each page.

To name (or rename) a spreadsheet page, double-click the page tab, type the name, and press Enter. Or open up the Active Sheet dialog box (press Ctrl+F12 to get there quickly), click the Name tab, enter the new page name, and click OK or press Enter.

If you rename your pages, remember to use the new name in your cell addresses in entering formulas, as I discuss in Chapter 12, in the section, "Typing formulas using cell addresses."

My spreadsheet's in 3-D? Cool!

You may hear Quattro Pro and other advanced spreadsheet programs referred to as *3-D spreadsheets*. But this kind of 3-D is different from the kind you get if you wear those funky 3-D glasses at the movies.

Each spreadsheet you create in Quattro Pro is really 256 separate spreadsheets stacked like pages in a notebook. On any page, you can calculate in two dimensions — that is, you can calculate data in horizontal rows and in vertical columns. But you can also calculate in a third dimension, which in this case happens to be up and down through the stack of notebook pages.

Confused? Don't be. This 3-D business simply means that, in addition to calculating data you enter in one notebook page, you can calculate data entered in many different notebook pages. Say, for example, that page A of your notebook contains your monthly sales activity

for January: how many units you sold of each item, the price of each item, your cost for each item, the date of the sale, and the total sales for the month. Page B contains the same information for February, and page C contains the data for March. With Quattro Pro, you can create a fourth page that takes the data from pages A, B, and C and calculates all the sales information on a quarterly basis.

Before the days of 3-D spreadsheets, you could calculate only data contained in a single spreadsheet page, which meant that spreadsheets could quickly become very large and cumbersome. The real benefit of a 3-D spreadsheet is that you can segment your spreadsheet into more easily managed, easily updated, and easily viewed chunks of data.

And you don't even need to wear special glasses to see your results.

Ways to Move from Here to There

You can navigate your spreadsheet in numerous ways, including these:

- ✔ To make a cell active (so that you can enter data into it), click the cell.

- ✔ To scroll the screen display so that you can view another portion of the current notebook page, use the horizontal or vertical scroll bars.

- ✔ To move from page to page, use the page tabs or the tab scroll buttons, as discussed in the section "Your Field Guide to a Spreadsheet," earlier in this chapter.

- ✔ To move to a specific cell, press Ctrl+G or F5 (shortcuts for the Edit➪Go To command). Quattro Pro displays the Go To dialog box, as shown in Figure 10-4. Enter the cell address in the Reference option box and press Enter or click OK. Type the cell address in this order: notebook page, colon, column number, and row number — as in A:F238. You probably don't want to use this method of moving to a cell unless you need to find a cell that's buried deep in your spreadsheet or is way off-screen; otherwise, using the mouse and the scroll arrows is quicker.

✔ You can also navigate your spreadsheet by using the keyboard short-cuts outlined in Table 10-1. Notice that these keyboard shortcuts apply only if you're not in edit mode or inside a dialog box. Some key combinations do different things in those situations. Inside a dialog box, for example, Tab and Shift+Tab move you from one option box to the next.

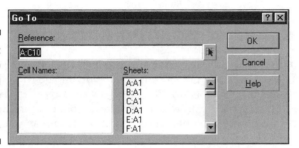

Figure 10-4:
Use the Go
To dialog
box to move
to a specific
cell.

Table 10-1	Keys That Really Move You
Press This	*To Do This*
→	Move up one cell.
↓	Move down one cell.
→ or Tab	Move right one cell.
← or Shift+Tab	Move left one cell.
Home	Go to the first cell on the current notebook page.
Ctrl+Home	Go to the first cell on the first page of the notebook.
Ctrl+←	Scroll left one screen.
Ctrl+→	Scroll right one screen.
PgDn	Scroll one screen down.
PgUp	Scroll one screen up.
End+Up Arrow	Go to the first cell in that column.
End+Down Arrow	Go to last cell in that column.
End+Left Arrow	Go to first cell in that row.
End+Right Arrow	Go to last cell in that row.

Open Me! Close Me! Save Me!

Opening, closing, and saving files in Quattro Pro is handled pretty much the same way as in any Windows 95 program. But here's the skinny on each job, just in case you need a refresher.

Opening a new or existing notebook

 To create a new notebook, choose File⇨New, press Ctrl+N, or click the New Notebook toolbar button. If you click the toolbar button, Quattro Pro gives you a new blank notebook. If you choose File⇨New or press Ctrl+N, Quattro Pro displays the New dialog box, in which you can choose to create a blank notebook or to create a notebook based on a template, just as you can in WordPerfect.

Templates produce spreadsheets you can use to handle some common tasks, such as household budgets and business forms. The templates contain preformatted data that you can edit as necessary. To use a template, click its name in the list on the Create New tab and click OK. To create a blank notebook, select the Quattro Pro Notebook item and click OK.

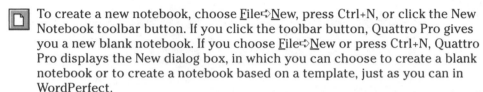 To open an existing notebook, choose File⇨Open, press Ctrl+O, or click the Open Notebook toolbar button. Quattro Pro answers your command by displaying the Open File dialog box, which looks and works the same as the WordPerfect Open dialog box that I discuss in Chapter 5.

 Files that you create and save in Quattro Pro end with the letters WB3. If you want to open a file that you created in an earlier version of Quattro Pro or in another spreadsheet program, select that program's file type from the File Type drop-down list. Quattro Pro can open many different types of files, including spreadsheets created in Microsoft Excel, and Lotus 1-2-3, as well as database files created in Paradox and dBASE.

 You can open the files you worked on most recently by choosing them from the bottom of the File menu or from the list on the Work On tab of the New dialog box (File⇨New).

Closing a spreadsheet

To close a spreadsheet, click the spreadsheet window's Close button, choose File⇨Close, or press Ctrl+F4. (You can also use the standard Windows shortcut, Ctrl+F4.) Quattro Pro gives you a gentle reminder to save your work if you haven't done so yet. Saving, in fact, is the subject of the very next section.

Saving your work

Saving early — and saving often — is essential. If you don't, your efforts can go up in electronic smoke after you shut down Quattro Pro, if the power goes out for some reason, or if your computer crashes just to see what kind of response it can get from you.

 To save your spreadsheet for the first time, choose File➪Save, press Ctrl+S, or click the Save Notebook toolbar button. Quattro Pro leaps to attention and shows you the Save File dialog box, which, conveniently enough, works just like the WordPerfect Save File dialog box. For all the ins and outs of this dialog box, see Chapter 5, in the section "Saving Your Work (and Your Sanity)."

 Quattro Pro can save your file in a variety of file formats, including those used by other, lesser spreadsheet programs. Be aware, however, that some of these file formats can save only the current page of your spreadsheet. Quattro Pro alerts you if the file format can't save multiple-page spreadsheets.

Remember, too, that saving a document once doesn't protect you forever. If you make any changes to your spreadsheet, those changes aren't saved until you choose the Save command again. The second time you save your spreadsheet, Quattro Pro doesn't bother you with the Save File dialog box.

If you want to save your spreadsheet under a different name, to a different folder or drive, or in a different file format, choose File➪Save As, as I explain in Chapter 5 in the section "Saving a document with a different name or format."

 To protect yourself even further, turn on Quattro Pro's Automatic Save feature. Choose Tools➪Settings or press Alt+F12 to display the Application dialog box. Click the File Options tab, select the Timed Document Backup Every check box, and set the interval for the automatic save in the neighboring option box. With automatic backup turned on, Quattro Pro can recover most of your spreadsheet if your computer happens to crash.

Chapter 11

Filling in the Blanks

• •

• •

After you first start Quattro Pro, the program graciously presents you with a sparkling new notebook filled with 256 pristine spreadsheet pages. What Quattro Pro doesn't do is give you any hints about what to do next. Where do you start? How do you get from these rows and rows of empty cells to a spreadsheet that actually does something?

Well, try pressing your forehead up to your computer screen, closing your eyes, and chanting, "Spreadsheet, spreadsheet, spreadsheet," in a loud falsetto voice. Rumor has it that, if you do this long and hard enough, Quattro Pro divines your problem and builds your spreadsheet for you.

Didn't work? Hmm, guess that rumor was off the mark. Fortunately, this chapter tells you everything you need to know to turn that blank notebook page into a working spreadsheet.

Building a Spreadsheet

Before you get into the nitty-gritty of entering data into your spreadsheet, you need a basic understanding of the process of building a spreadsheet. Take a look at Figure 11-1. It shows a spreadsheet that calculates the total sales and profits for one day — June 15, as indicated on the page tab. The approach I use to create this spreadsheet, sketched out in the following steps, is the same approach that you use to create any spreadsheet:

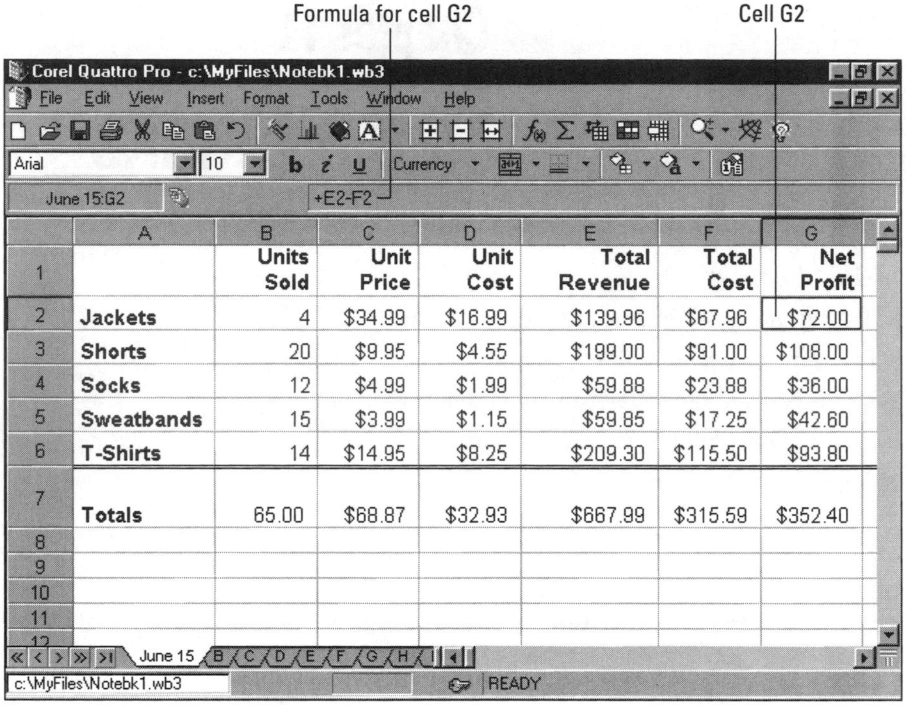

Formula for cell G2   Cell G2

	A	B	C	D	E	F	G
1		Units Sold	Unit Price	Unit Cost	Total Revenue	Total Cost	Net Profit
2	Jackets	4	$34.99	$16.99	$139.96	$67.96	$72.00
3	Shorts	20	$9.95	$4.55	$199.00	$91.00	$108.00
4	Socks	12	$4.99	$1.99	$59.88	$23.88	$36.00
5	Sweatbands	15	$3.99	$1.15	$59.85	$17.25	$42.60
6	T-Shirts	14	$14.95	$8.25	$209.30	$115.50	$93.80
7	Totals	65.00	$68.87	$32.93	$667.99	$315.59	$352.40

Corel Quattro Pro - c:\MyFiles\Notebk1.wb3

File Edit View Insert Format Tools Window Help

Arial 10 Currency

June 15:G2   +E2-F2

c:\MyFiles\Notebk1.wb3   READY

Figure 11-1:
Quattro Pro
makes
calculating
the day's
total sales
and profits
easy.

1. Enter the column and row labels.

I'm referring to the category names found at the top of each column and the beginning of each row. In Figure 11-1, the column labels are *Units Sold, Unit Price*, and so on, and the row labels are *Jackets, Shorts, Socks,* and so on.

2. Enter the known values.

Next, enter the known data — that is, the data that already exists and doesn't require any calculating by Quattro Pro. In Figure 11-1, for example, the known values are the units sold, the unit price, and the unit cost.

3. Enter the formulas for the values you want Quattro Pro to find.

In Chapter 10, I say that you don't need to do any math to use Quattro Pro. Well, that's not completely true. You don't need to do the actual calculations — the addition, the multiplication, and so on — but you do need to enter the basic mathematical formulas that you want Quattro Pro to solve. But cheer up — if I can do it, you can, too. Really. Just ask my accountant.

In Figure 11-1, I entered three different formulas: one to calculate the total revenue received from each item (Units Sold multiplied by Unit Price); one to calculate the total cost of each item (Units Sold multiplied by Unit Cost); and one to calculate the total profit of the day's sales (Total Revenue minus Total Cost). In Figure 11-1, the input line shows the actual formula used to calculate the value in cell G2, which holds the net profit from jacket sales. (Chapter 12 explains how to write and enter formulas, by the way.)

4. Edit and format your data.

After you enter your initial data, you no doubt find things that you want to fix. Chapter 13 shows you how to edit your data.

You find out how to do basic formatting, such as making your data boldface or italic, at the end of this chapter, in "Handling Basic Formatting Chores." Chapters 14 and 15 explain how to add graphs and put the finishing formatting touches on your data. Chapter 15 also shows you how to print your spreadsheet.

In reality, you don't always perform these steps in this order. You may find that formatting your data as you enter it, for example, is easier than formatting later. But the basic steps involved remain the same, whether you're creating a simple spreadsheet such as the one shown in Figure 11-1 or developing some mondo-complex thing that would turn Albert Einstein green with envy.

Entering Data

As I explain in Chapter 10, spreadsheet data goes into cells — those little squares created by the intersection of a row and a column. You can enter the following two types of data in Quattro Pro:

- ✔ A *label* is a text entry, such as a column title and a row title. Labels can actually contain numbers as well as letters (as in the label *1st Quarter*, for example).
- ✔ A *value* is a number or a formula.

I bring up this techno-nerd issue only because Quattro Pro treats labels a little differently than values, as you discover at the end of this section.

Basic data entry

To enter data — whether a label or a value — into a cell, just follow these steps:

1. **Click the cell in which you want to put the data.**

   You enter data into the active cell, which is the one surrounded by the little black box. Clicking a cell makes it active.

2. **Type the value or label.**

   As you begin typing, Quattro Pro displays an insertion marker that indicates where the next character you type appears, as shown in Figure 11-2. The mouse cursor also changes to the I-beam cursor. The data you type appears both in the cell and in the input line, as shown in the figure.

   If you make a mistake as you type, press the Backspace key to erase characters to the left of the insertion marker. Or use any of the other editing techniques that I discuss in Chapter 13. (I cover the specifics of entering formulas in Chapter 12.)

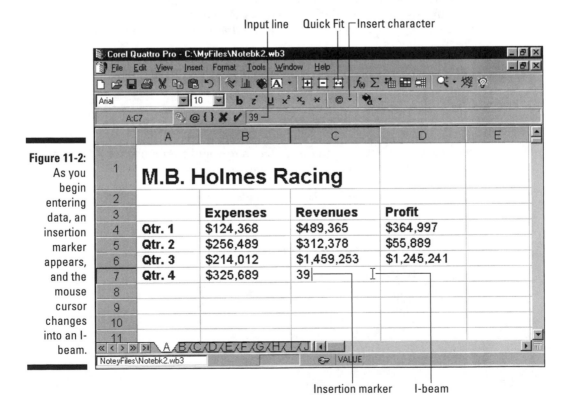

Figure 11-2:
As you begin entering data, an insertion marker appears, and the mouse cursor changes into an I-beam.

3. Press Enter, press Tab, or click another cell.

To complete your data entry, press Enter. By default, the cell directly below the current cell becomes active, ready for you to enter more data. (If you want to turn this feature off, press Alt+F12 to open the Application dialog box and deselect the Move Cell Selector on Enter Key check box on the General tab.)

Alternatively, you can move to another cell by clicking it or by using one of the other navigation keys listed in Chapter 10 (in Table 10-1). Press Tab, for example, to move one cell to the right.

If you enter a formula, as I cover in Chapter 12, Quattro Pro displays the results of its calculations in the cell and not the formula itself. The formula appears in the input line.

As you're entering data into a cell, the Property Bar offers an Insert Character button that displays all the available characters from the current font, giving you a quick way to insert special symbols such as foreign letters, copyright symbols, and the like (refer to Figure 11-2).

By default, the Insert Character button has a copyright symbol on it; after you select a different character from the menu, that character appears on the button instead. Click the character on the button face to insert that character again; click the downward-pointing arrow next to the button to display all the available characters and select a new character.

Basically, that's all you do to enter data. But the following things may trip you up:

✔ If you see a row of asterisks or some other weird characters in the cell after you press Enter, the cell is too small to hold the value you entered. Chapter 13 explains how to precisely resize cells, columns, and rows. But for a quick fix, click the cell and then click the QuickFit button on the toolbar.

You can now avoid this problem entirely by turning on the Fit-As-You-Go feature, found on the General tab of the Application dialog box. (Press Alt+F12 to open the dialog box.) If Fit-As-You-Go is active, Quattro Pro automatically enlarges a too-small-cell so that it can hold the value you typed.

You cannot use the Alt+F12 to access the Application dialog box while a cell is active (that is, when the Insertion marker is in a cell). I explain this issue in Chapter 10.

✔ If a label is too long to fit in a cell, it spills over into the neighboring cell. But if that neighboring cell contains an entry, Quattro Pro hides the part of the label that doesn't fit. The data's still in there — but it doesn't appear or print correctly until you fix things. Again, you can use the editing approaches that I explain in Chapter 13 or just click the QuickFit button. Fit-As-You-Go has no effect on too-long labels.

✔ After you enter a value or label, Quattro Pro automatically formats it according to the current style, which appears on the Style menu on the Property Bar. (I label this menu much later in the chapter, in Figure 11-5.) In some cases, the style can change what you enter into the cell. If the Normal style is active and you enter **9.00,** for example, Quattro Pro automatically changes your entry to just **9,** which complies with the numeric formatting used by the Normal style. For information on how to change the style or numeric formatting, see the section "Handling Basic Formatting Chores," later in this chapter.

✔ Version 8 brings another new data-entry feature, QuickType. If this feature is on, Quattro Pro tries to help you enter data. Type the word **Blech** into a cell, press Enter, and type a capital **B** into the cell directly below the first cell. Quattro Pro thinks, "Hey, you must want to enter *Blech* again, so I'm just going ahead and putting that label into the cell for you." If you didn't want to enter **Blech,** just keep typing the real label. Quattro Pro gets rid of the unwanted **lech** and slinks away in embarrassment. The same sort of thing happens if you enter a formula, except that Quattro Pro tries to intuit what formula you want to use.

On some occasions, you may find QuickType helpful, but my guess is that, more often than not, you'll just say *blech.* The check box that turns QuickType on and off is located on the General tab of the Application dialog box (press Alt+F12).

Data entry do's and don'ts

After you enter data into a cell and press Enter, Quattro Pro furrows its brow and tries to determine whether you entered a label or a value. Quattro Pro bases its guess on whether the cell contains any letters. If your entry contains any letters, Quattro Pro deems the entry a label. If the entry contains numbers only, Quattro Pro considers the entry a value. The difference is important because Quattro Pro applies different automatic formatting to labels than it does to values.

To make sure that your labels get treated as labels and values as values, be careful not to break any of the following taboos:

✔ Don't use any spaces or currency symbols in entering values. If you do, Quattro Pro treats the data as a label rather than a value. (The exception is the dollar sign, which you can use without problems.) If you're entering numbers that call for commas, Quattro Pro inserts the commas for you automatically.

✔ By Quattro Pro decree, labels can't start with the following punctuation marks: the plus sign (+), minus sign (-), dollar sign ($), left parentheses (( ), at symbol (@), period (.), pound sign (#), or equals sign (=). If you really, really want to start a label with one of these characters, enter one of the following label-prefix characters at the start of the label: apostrophe ('), quotation mark ("), or caret (^). The apostrophe aligns the label with the left edge of the cell; the quotation mark aligns it with the right edge of the cell; and the caret centers the label in the cell. The label prefix characters don't appear in the cell after you press Enter, but they do appear in the input line.

So what if you want to start out a label entry with a quotation mark? Enter one of the label-prefix characters first, according to the alignment you want. Then type your quotation mark.

✔ If you're not a fanatic about whether your stuff lines up perfectly in your spreadsheet, you can just enter a space before your label text instead of trying to remember that apostrophe, quotation mark, and caret stuff.

✔ If the first character in the cell is a backslash (\), Quattro Pro repeats the characters that follow over and over to fill up the cell. In other words, if you enter **\Hey!**, Quattro Pro fills your cell with Hey!Hey!Hey! I'm not sure whether you may ever find this feature helpful, but I thought you ought to know. (If you don't want the characters to repeat, enter a space before the backslash.)

QuickFilling Cells

Quattro Pro offers a neat feature called QuickFill that can speed up the entry of labels and values that fall in a sequence. Suppose that you want to fill the first 30 rows of Column A with the numbers 1 though 30 — to label the rows with the days of the month, for example. Instead of typing in each number, you can use the following technique and have Quattro Pro fill in the cells for you. Just follow these steps:

1. **Type the first label or value in the first cell that you want to fill and press Enter.**

2. Click and drag from the first cell over the rest of the cells that you want to fill.

The cells become highlighted (selected) as you drag, as shown in Column G of Figure 11-3. (If you see a little hand cursor rather than the highlighted cells, you're moving the cell contents instead of selecting the cells. Try again. This time, begin dragging a little quicker after you click the first cell.)

Notice that the cell you filled in Step 1 should still be the active cell — that is, the one surrounded by the black outline box.

 3. Click the QuickFill button.

Alternatively, you can right-click the selected cells and choose QuickFill from the QuickMenu that appears. Either way, Quattro Pro fills your rows with the remaining numbers or words in the sequence.

Figure 11-3 shows several rows and columns that I filled by using QuickFill. As you can see, you can QuickFill dates, months, and even a mixture of text and numbers.

Quick Fill

Corel Quattro Pro - c:\MyFiles\Notebk1.wb3

File   Edit   View   Insert   Format   Tools   Window   Help

Arial   12   **b** *i* <u>U</u>   Normal

A:G1   1996

	A	B	C	D	E	F	G
1	Client 1247	January	Monday	06/01	$10	Red	1996
2	Client 1248	February	Tuesday	06/02	$11	Green	
3	Client 1249	March	Wednesday	06/03	$12	Blue	
4	Client 1250	April	Thursday	06/04	$13	Yellow	
5	Client 1251	May	Friday	06/05	$14	Red	
6	Client 1252	June	Saturday	06/06	$15	Green	
7	Client 1253	July	Sunday	06/07	$16	Blue	
8	Client 1254	August	Monday	06/08	$17	Yellow	
9	Client 1255	September	Tuesday	06/09	$18	Red	
10	Client 1256	October	Wednesday	06/10	$19	Green	
11	Client 1257	November	Thursday	06/11	$20	Blue	
12	Client 1258	December	Friday	06/12	$21	Yellow	
13	Client 1259	January	Saturday	06/13	$22	Red	
14	Client 1260	February	Sunday	06/14	$23	Green	

A / B / C / D / E / F / G / H / I / J

c:\MyFiles\Notebk1.wb3   READY

Figure 11-3: QuickFill automates the entry of values and labels that fall in sequence.

You can create your own series, as I do in Column F in Figure 11-3, by typing all the elements of the series once. (I entered Red, Green, Blue, and Yellow in the first four cells.) After typing in the series once, click the first cell in the series, drag from that cell to the last cell you want to fill, and click the QuickFill button. Quattro Pro repeats the series as many times as necessary to fill the selected cells. You can also create number patterns, such as 1,3,5,7,9, by entering the first numbers in the pattern (1 and 3, in this case) and then using QuickFill to fill the following cells.

Another way to quickly fill cells is to copy the contents of one cell and paste the contents into other cells, as I explain in Chapter 13.

Handling Basic Formatting Chores

Like WordPerfect, Quattro Pro uses *styles,* which apply certain basic formatting attributes such as font, type size, and numeric format to your data. The default style is Normal, which uses 10-point Arial type and the General numeric format. If you click the Style menu on the Property Bar (which I label in Figure 11-5, in the section "Changing the font, type size, and type style), you display a drop-down list of other styles that you can apply to selected cells.

You can override the Normal style — or any style — by applying different formatting to selected cells. The following sections tell you how to change the font, type size, type style, alignment, and numeric format of your data.

Before you can apply formatting to data in a cell, you must select the cell. To select a single cell, just click that cell; to select a block of cells, drag over the cells or use one of the other techniques outlined in Chapter 13, in the section "Selecting Stuff."

Quattro Pro now enables you to apply some character formatting attributes, including type size and font, to individual characters within a cell. You can make one character in a cell bold, for example, and leave the rest plain. To apply formatting to specific characters in a cell, double-click the cell to enter the edit mode, drag across the characters you want to format, and apply the formatting.

To change the default formatting used by the Normal style or any other style, choose Format⇨Styles to open the Styles dialog box. Choose the style you want to change from the Define Style For drop-down list. Click the button for the formatting attribute you want to change — Font for font (duh!), type size, and style; Format for numeric format; and so on. Quattro Pro then displays the appropriate dialog box for changing the formatting you want to alter. After you finish setting all the default formatting attributes, click OK to make your changes official.

Changing the numeric format

The *numeric format* refers to how values are formatted. Numeric formatting controls such things as how many decimal places you can have and whether a dollar sign gets inserted before the number. Several of Quattro Pro's built-in styles, including Currency and Date, apply formatting designed to accommodate specific types of values. If one of these styles doesn't suit your fancy, click the cell you want to format (or select a range of cells) and press F12 or choose Format⇨Selection.

 For an even quicker solution, just click the Cell Properties button on the Property Bar.

Quattro Pro leaps to attention and displays the Active Cells dialog box, as shown in Figure 11-4. The Numeric Format panel of the dialog box offers a variety of formatting options for numbers, dates, and times. After you click some of the formatting radio buttons, additional options appear that enable you to get even more specific about the format. If you select the Currency option, for example, you can specify how many decimal places you want to include and select which country's currency standards you want to use. The little preview box in the bottom-right corner of the dialog box shows you how your data looks in the chosen format.

After you're satisfied with your choices, click OK or press Enter to apply the format.

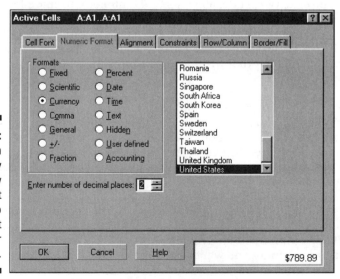

Figure 11-4:
You can specify exactly how you want Quattro Pro to format your numbers.

Changing the font, type size, and type style

To change the font, select the data you want to format and select a new font from the Font drop-down list on the Property Bar, as shown in Figure 11-5. To change the type size of selected data, select a size from the Type Size drop-down list.

As shown in Figure 11-5, the Property Bar also offers buttons for several type-style attributes, including boldface, italics, underline, superscript, subscript, and strikethrough. The last three buttons appear only if you're entering data or editing the contents of a cell. All these buttons act as toggles — that is, click once to apply the formatting; click again to remove it.

You can also access the font, type size, and type style formatting attributes on the Cell Font tab of the Active Cells dialog box, discussed in the preceding section. Press F12 or click the Cell Properties button on the Property Bar to open the dialog box.

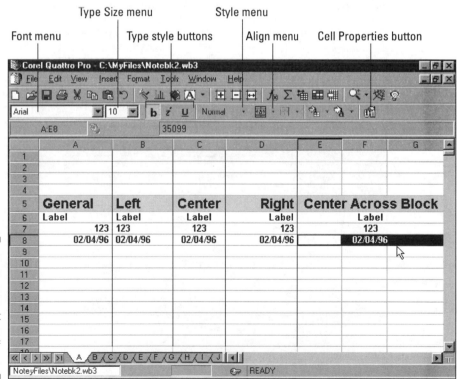

Figure 11-5:
You can align data within a cell or center it across a block of cells.

Changing text alignment

One of the many formatting attributes applied by Quattro Pro's built-in styles is the horizontal alignment of data within the cell. The Normal style uses the General alignment option, which aligns labels with the left edge of the cell and aligns numbers, formulas, and dates to the right edge of the cell.

 Click the down-pointing arrow on the Alignment button on the Property Bar to display a drop-down list of horizontal alignment options, which include General, Left, Right, Center, Center Across Block, and Indent. Figure 11-5 shows how labels and values are aligned using the first five options. The Indent option indents the first line of your data from the left edge of the cell, just as a first-line indent does in WordPerfect.

To apply any alignment but Center Across Block, select the cell or cells you want to format and then select the option from the drop-down list. The Center Across Block option, which centers the value or label within a specified number of cells, works a little differently. First, enter the data in the leftmost cell of the block of cells you want to center the data across. In the highlighted example in Figure 11-5, I entered the data in cell E8. Next, select the cell that contains the data, along with the rest of the block you want to center the data across. In Figure 11-5, I selected cells E8 through G8. Then select the Center Across Block option from the drop-down list.

To uncover still more alignment options, select the cell or cells you want to format and then press F12 or click the Cell Properties button on the Property Bar to open the Active Cells dialog box. Click the Alignment tab to display the alignment options, as shown in Figure 11-6.

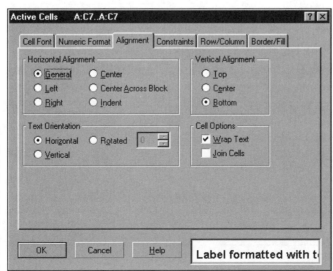

Figure 11-6: More alignment options reside in the Active Cells dialog box.

The Alignment tab contains the same horizontal alignment options found on the Property Bar drop-down list, plus these additional options:

- ✔ You have three vertical alignment options. Top aligns the data with the top of the cell, Center places the data smack-dab in the middle of the cell, and Bottom sinks the data to the bottom of the cell. The default is Bottom.

- ✔ If you turn on the Wrap Text option, Quattro Pro expands the cell vertically to accommodate any text that exceeds the width of the cell. It then wraps the overflow text to the next line in the cell. Figure 11-7 shows an example of this option in action.

- ✔ The Text Orientation options determine whether your text runs horizontally or vertically in the cell. You can also place your data diagonally in the cell by selecting the Rotated radio button and entering an angle of rotation in the corresponding option box.

- ✔ The new Join Cells option enables you to link two or more cells together and then align text within the entire block of cells as if it were contained in one cell. This option can be handy for creating titles or subtitles within your spreadsheet. You can also use it to create a "vertical" heading, as shown in Figure 11-7. To create the heading, I joined several cells in Column A, entered my text, and selected the Rotated option with a value of 90 degrees in the Active Cells dialog box. I chose the Center option for both Horizontal and Vertical alignment and, just to make things pretty, gave the cell a dark background and made the text white. (See the section "Applying color to text and backgrounds" in Chapter 15.)

To join cells and center the text horizontally within the cell block, you can simply click the Join and Center Cells button on the Property Bar.

This chapter covers just the basic formatting you can do in Quattro Pro. For information on how to add even more spice to your spreadsheets, see Chapters 14 and 15.

Figure 11-7:
Examples of
cells
formatted
with the
Join Cells
option
turned on
(Column A);
Wrap Text
turned on
(Column C,
top); and
Wrap Text
turned off
(Column C,
bottom).

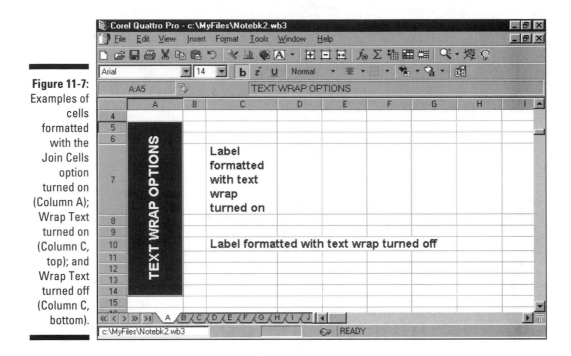

Chapter 12
The Formula for Success

*R*emember back in algebra class, when you had to solve lots of inane problems involving *x* and *y* and two trains headed for the same station at different speeds? Well, if you really got into that sort of thing, you're going to love this chapter, which shows you how to use those old algebra skills to write equations (aka *formulas*) for Quattro Pro to solve.

If, on the other hand, you spent most of your time in algebra class like I did, alternately wailing in frustration and complaining loudly that you didn't know why you needed to know this stuff anyway, you may be turned off by the fact that Quattro Pro requires you to create formulas before it does any work for you. Don't be.

First of all, most formulas you'll use are simple, involving basic addition, subtraction, multiplication, and division. Secondly, Quattro Pro offers some built-in formulas — called *functions* — that make creating more complex equations easy.

Creating a Basic Formula

Writing a formula is like being back in algebra class — only this time, you're the teacher. You give Quattro Pro a formula to solve, and it does the math for you.

You can enter formulas in two ways: You can type the formula directly into the cell, or you can use a combination type-and-click approach. The following sections give you the lowdown on both methods.

Typing formulas for simple calculations

You can use formulas to perform a simple calculation such as 45 + 87. To enter a formula such as this, follow these steps:

1. Click the cell in which you want the answer to the calculation to appear.

As you type a formula, it appears in that cell. But after you press Enter in Step 3, Quattro Pro displays the answer to the formula in the cell and hides the formula itself.

2. Type a plus sign followed by your formula.

The plus sign tells Quattro Pro that you're entering a formula. To calculate the value of 45 + 87, for example, you enter the following formula:

```
+45+87
```

Formulas can also start with a parentheses, as discussed in the upcoming section "Telling Quattro Pro What to Calculate First," or with the function symbol (@), as covered in the section "Working with Built-in Functions."

If you're used to starting formulas with an equal sign, as some other spreadsheet programs require, you can do that in Quattro Pro as well. Quattro Pro automatically converts the equal sign to a plus sign when you complete the formula.

3. Press Enter.

The answer to the formula appears in the cell. The formula itself appears in the input line.

In building formulas, you don't always use standard mathematical symbols, such as *x* for multiply and ÷ for division. Instead, you use the mathematical symbols listed in Table 12-1, which are known as *operators* in spreadsheet country.

To calculate simple numbers as in the preceding steps, you really don't need to enter the plus sign at the beginning of the formula. As long as your formula contains only numbers, Quattro Pro assumes that you want it to perform a calculation. In some cases, however, Quattro Pro can get mixed up. The formula for finding the result of 8 divided by 2, for example, is 8/2. Quattro Pro may think that you're entering the date August 2 instead of a mathematical formula. For this reason, I recommend that you always start your formulas with +, @, or (, which are the three symbols that Quattro Pro has established for starting formulas.

Table 12-1	Smooth Operators
Operator	*Function*
+	Addition
–	Subtraction
/	Division
*	Multiplication
%	Percentage
^	Exponentiation

Typing formulas using cell addresses

Although you can use Quattro Pro to perform simple calculations (such as the one I discuss in the preceding section), more often than not, you want to perform calculations on values that are stored in different cells in your spreadsheet. You can have Quattro Pro add the values in one row of cells, multiply that value by the value in another cell, and so on. You can even do calculations involving cells on different pages of your notebook.

Entering this kind of formula is no different than entering the formula described in the preceding steps. This time, however, you use cell addresses instead of actual numbers to identify the values you want to calculate.

Take a look at Figure 12-1. This simple spreadsheet calculates total book-store sales for each quarter. To find the total for Quarter 1, you can enter the following formula into cell B9, where you want the total to appear:

```
+B4+B5+B6+B7+B8
```

The formula tells Quattro Pro to add the values in cells B4, B5, B6, B7, and B8. The totals in columns C, D, and E use the same formula, except with different cell addresses — C4, C5, and so on for column C, for example.

If you don't enter the plus sign before the formula, Quattro Pro assumes that you're entering a label, not a formula.

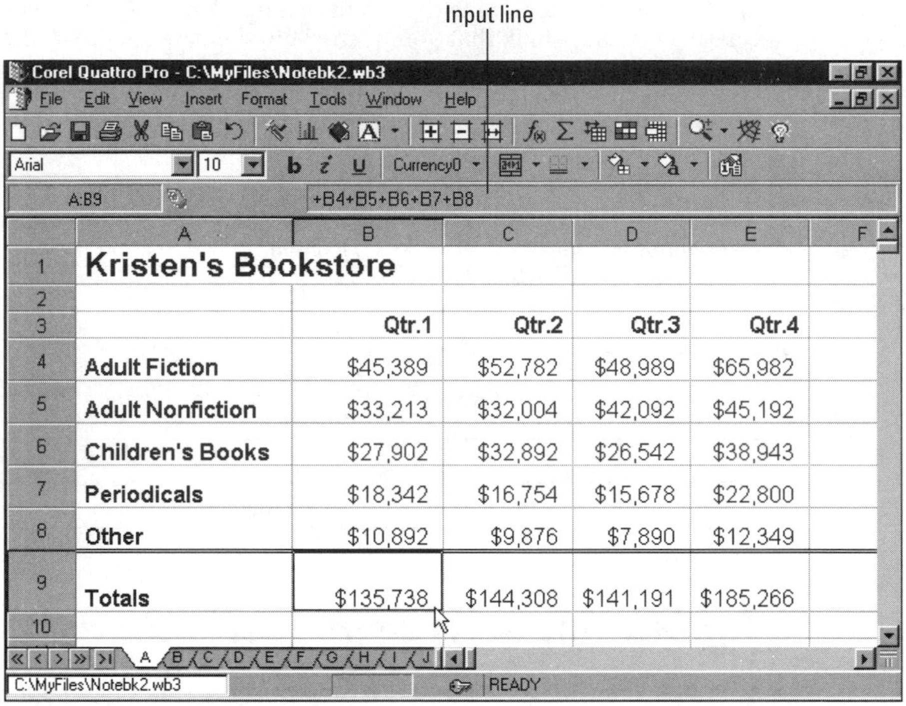

Input line

Figure 12-1:
Cell B9
displays the
results of
the formula
in the
input line.

	A	B	C	D	E	F
1	Kristen's Bookstore					
2						
3		Qtr.1	Qtr.2	Qtr.3	Qtr.4	
4	Adult Fiction	$45,389	$52,782	$48,989	$65,982	
5	Adult Nonfiction	$33,213	$32,004	$42,092	$45,192	
6	Children's Books	$27,902	$32,892	$26,542	$38,943	
7	Periodicals	$18,342	$16,754	$15,678	$22,800	
8	Other	$10,892	$9,876	$7,890	$12,349	
9	Totals	$135,738	$144,308	$141,191	$185,266	
10						

Corel Quattro Pro - C:\MyFiles\Notebk2.wb3

File Edit View Insert Format Tools Window Help

Arial 10 b i U Currency0

A:B9 +B4+B5+B6+B7+B8

C:\MyFiles\Notebk2.wb3 READY

If you add a long row or column of numbers, you really don't need to type each cell address in the row, as I did in the preceding formula. Instead, you can use the much quicker @SUM function or QuickSum button, as the section, "Adding Things Up by Using QuickSum," explains later in this chapter.

Suppose that, after finding the quarterly sales totals in Figure 12-1, you want to calculate the total sales for all four quarters and put the result in cell F9. You'd click cell F9 and enter the following formula:

```
+B9+C9+D9+E9
```

If you then wanted to find the average quarterly sales for the year, you'd enter this formula into another cell:

```
+F9/4
```

The formula tells Quattro Pro to divide the value in cell F9 (which contains the total sales for all four quarters) by 4.

If you want to perform a calculation on cells contained on different pages of your notebook, include the page name before the cell address in the formula. To add the value of cell B9 on Page A to the value of cell B9 on Page B, for example, you enter the following formula:

```
+A:B9+B:B9
```

If you named your page, as I explain in Chapter 10, in the section "Naming Your Pages," substitute that name in the cell address. If page A has the name *July* and page B has the name *August*, for example, you write the formula as follows:

```
+July:B9+August:B9
```

Quattro Pro sometimes tries to "help" you enter formulas (see Chapter 11 for more details). After you type a few characters, Quattro Pro inserts the formula that it thinks you're trying to create. If Quattro Pro guesses wrong, just keep entering your formula; the inserted formula disappears. And if you don't want Quattro Pro to intrude on your typing, turn off the QuickType option on the General tab of the Application dialog box. (Press Alt+F12 to open the dialog box.)

Entering cell addresses with the mouse

If you're creating a long formula and you're weary of typing in cell addresses — this computing business is such hard work, after all — you can use the mouse to enter the addresses instead. Just follow these steps:

1. **Click the cell in which you want the answer to the formula to appear.**

2. **Type a plus sign.**

3. **Click the cell you want to reference in the formula.**

   If you want to enter the formula +B3*52, for example, you click cell B3, as shown in Figure 12-2. The Application Bar displays the word `Point`, and the cell address appears in the input line and in the cell where you're entering the formula. In Figure 12-2, I entered the formula in cell C3.

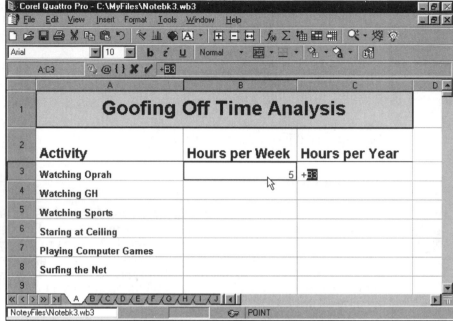

Figure 12-2:
To enter a
cell's
address
into a
formula,
just click
that cell.

4. **Type the next operator in the formula.**

   To continue the formula, type the next operator. In the example formula, I would type the * (multiplication operator). The cursor jumps back to the cell where you're entering the formula.

5. **Continue clicking cells and typing operators or known values until the formula is complete.**

   In the case of the formula shown in Figure 12-2, all I need to do to complete the formula is to type **52**.

6. **Press Enter.**

Would you like that address relative or absolute?

After you create a formula, you can copy it to other cells to save yourself the trouble of entering it again and again. (I present the how-to's in Chapter 13.) If you create formulas that you want to copy to other cells, an important point to consider is whether you want to use a *relative* or *absolute* cell address.

If you don't do anything special to your formulas, relative addressing is in force. Here's how a relative address works: Suppose that you have four columns of numbers — call them Column A through Column D. Each column contains three rows of numbers, and you want to find the total of each column. To do so, you enter the formula **+A1+A2+A3** in cell A4. Then you copy the formula to cells B4, C4, and D4. Quattro Pro is smart enough to realize that you don't want to calculate exactly the same thing as you did in the first column, and so it adjusts the formula to match each column. In cell B4, for example, it changes the formula to +B1+B2+B3. In other words, the formula always calculates the sum of the three cells directly above it.

What if you don't want Quattro Pro to tamper with your formulas in this way as you copy them? Just put a dollar sign before the column and the row name: **+$A$1+$A$2+$A$3**. The dollar sign tells Quattro Pro to use absolute addressing. The program then refers strictly to cells A1, A2, and A3 as it calculates your answer, no matter where you copy the formula.

You can mix absolute and relative cell addresses in the same formula, by the way. You can even make one part of the address absolute and the other part of the address relative, if you're so inclined. You could use the address $A1, for example, to make the column address absolute and the row address relative.

Telling Quattro Pro What to Calculate First

If you have a formula that contains more than one type of operator, you need to tell Quattro Pro the order in which you want to calculate the formula. Take a look at the following formula:

```
+B1+B2*B3
```

You may expect Quattro Pro to calculate this formula from left to right, adding B1 and B2 and then multiplying the sum by B3. But, in fact, Quattro Pro first multiplies B2 by B3 and then adds B1 to the result.

If you substitute numbers for the cell addresses, you can see that you get two different answers depending on which order you calculate the formula. Suppose that B1=4, B2=5, and B3=6. If you add 4 and 5 and then multiply the sum by 6, you get 54. If you multiply 5 times 6 and then add 4, you get 34.

So how does Quattro Pro decide which numbers to work on first? By following a set of mathematical rules called *order of precedence*. Translated into nonnerd terms, the rules assign a certain level of importance to each operator. A multiplication sign, for example, is more important than an addition sign, so the multiplying gets done first. If the formula contains several operators that are the same, Quattro Pro calculates the numbers separated by the leftmost operator first and then works its way to the right through the rest of the formula.

Table 12-2 shows the order of precedence for the most common operators. But the truth is, you really don't need to remember this stuff — unless you like filling your head with complex technical data, of course. You can tell Quattro Pro how to calculate your formulas by using another method you probably learned in algebra class — don't you wish you'd paid closer attention now? You can use parentheses to indicate which parts of your formula you want Quattro Pro to calculate first, second, third, and so on.

Table 12-2	Operator Order of Precedence
Operator	*Precedence*
^ (exponentiation)	1
* (multiplication)	2
/ (division)	2
+ (addition)	3
− (subtraction)	3

Suppose that you want to add B1 to B2 and then multiply the sum by B3. Enter the formula this way:

```
(B1+B2)*B3
```

If your formula begins with a left parenthesis, as here, you don't need to add the plus sign at the beginning as you do with other formulas. If you do add it, however, you don't hurt anything.

In long formulas, you may need to create several sets of parenthetical expressions (that's geek talk for equations inside parentheses), one inside of the other. Here, for example, is how you'd type in a formula that finds the sum of B1 and B2, multiplies the sum by B3, subtracts the result from B4, performs the same calculations on cells C1, C2, C3, and C4, adds the two results together, and divides the whole shooting match by 2:

```
((B4-((B1+B2)*B3)) + (C4-((C1+C2)*C3)))/2
```

To dissect this formula, Quattro Pro first calculates whatever parts of the formula are enclosed by the most sets of parentheses. In this case, that's B1+B2 and C1+C2, which are each enclosed by four sets of parentheses. The program then works its way outward, evaluating the expressions enclosed by three sets of parentheses and then those enclosed by two sets and then one set before moving on to divide the entire result by 2.

Now that I have your head completely spinning, let me just give you one more little nugget of information. After you type a left parenthesis, Quattro Pro initially displays it in red. After you type the corresponding right parenthesis, it displays both parentheses in neon green. This Christmas-tree color coding — or I guess you could consider it stoplight color coding — is Quattro Pro's way of helping you make sure that you always have a right parenthesis to match every left parenthesis.

If you leave out a parenthesis, Quattro Pro sometimes adds one at the end of your formula — which may or may not be okay, depending on the formula. Other times, you may get an error message or the formula may just sit there, doing nothing, after you press Enter. To track down the missing parenthesis, move the insertion marker through the cell. After you hit the parenthesis that doesn't have a matching open or close parenthesis, it turns red.

Well, now. I think that's just about enough of that, don't you?

Working with Built-in Functions

Quattro Pro wants to be your friend — it really does. And because it realizes that creating formulas can be a bit of a drag, your little math buddy thoughtfully provides some prefab formulas to make your life easier. These built-in formulas are formally called *@functions,* pronounced *at functions*. (Just because Quattro Pro wants to be your friend doesn't mean that it's willing to speak to you in plain English.)

To see a list of the available functions, choose Insert⇨Function. Or double-click a cell and click the @ symbol on the input line. Either approach displays the Functions dialog box, as shown in Figure 12-3. Click a category in the Function Category list, and the functions related to that category appear in the Function list box. At the bottom of the dialog box, Quattro Pro gives you some information about what the function does. The following sections introduce you to a few popular functions; see Chapter 20 for a look at a couple more.

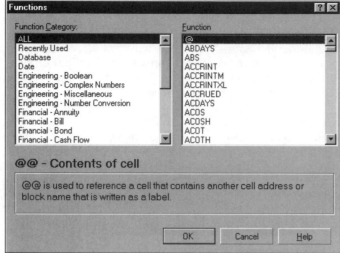

Figure 12-3:
Quattro
Pro's built-
in functions
range from
the simple
to the
extraordinarily
complex.

Writing formulas by using functions

One of the functions you're likely to use often is the @SUM function, which adds up the values in a range of cells. Say that you want to add the values in cells B1 through B20. You could type in **+B1+B2+B3+B4** and so on, entering the addresses of all the cells one by one. Or you could get the same results by entering the following formula:

```
@SUM(B1..B20)
```

The @ symbol tells Quattro Pro that you're about to enter a function; SUM is the name of the function. The parentheses contain the *argument* — that is, the data that you want to calculate by using the function. The two periods in the formula are Quattro Pro shorthand for *through*. So this formula tells Quattro Pro to find the sum of cell B1 through cell B20.

Functions always begin with the @ symbol. If your formula begins with a function, you don't need to put in the plus sign that you use to begin other formulas; the @ sign is enough. And Quattro Pro always displays function names in all caps. But you don't need to enter the names in all caps; lower-case letters are fine.

If you want to add values that aren't in a continuous block of cells, you separate the numbers by using commas instead of periods. If you want to find the sum of cells B1 though B20, C2, and C6, for example, you enter the following:

```
@SUM(B1..B20,C2,C6)
```

To have a function calculate data that's found on different pages of your spreadsheet, include the page names in the function argument. To find the sum of cells A1 through A3 on page A plus the sum of cells A1 through A3 on page B, for example, enter the page range and then the cell range as follows:

```
@SUM(A..B:A1..A3)
```

Or, if you don't want to include the same cells on both pages — for example, if you want to add the sum of cells A1 through A3 on page A with the sum of cells A4 through A6 on page B — enter both ranges and separate them with a comma, like this:

```
@SUM(A:A1..A3,B:A4..A6)
```

Notice that you can use functions as part of a longer formula. If you want to add the values in cells B1 though B20 and then divide the result by 4, you enter the following:

```
@SUM(B1..B20)/4
```

If you want to add a column or row of continuous cells, you can often do so more quickly by using the QuickSum button than by using the @SUM function. See the section "Adding Things Up by Using QuickSum," a little later in this chapter.

Finding the average and median values

Suppose that you run a flower shop and want to find your average daily sales for the month of May. The daily sales totals are stored in cells A1 through A30. To find the average daily sales, use the @AVG function by entering the following formula:

```
@AVG(A1..A30)
```

Now suppose that you're an eighth-grade teacher (you just do that flower-shop thing on the side) and you've stored all the scores for your final exams in cells A1 through A26. You can use the @MEDIAN function to find the median score. The median score is the score that's smack-dab in the middle of all the scores. Write the formula this way:

```
@MEDIAN(A1..A26)
```

Inserting current date

If you want a certain cell to always display the current date, you can enter the @ TODAY function into the cell. Quattro Pro initially displays the date as a serial number — but trust me; you don't even want to hear why. To display the date as a real date, you need to change the numeric format to Date, as Chapter 11 explains in the section, "Changing the numeric format."

Adding Things Up by Using QuickSum

 If you want to add up a bunch of numbers, you can use the @SUM function as I describe in the section, "Writing formulas by using functions," earlier in this chapter. But an even quicker way to add up a column of continuous cells is to click an empty cell at the bottom of the column and then click the QuickSum button (see Figure 12-4).

If any empty cells are in the row or column of cells that you want to sum, select all the cells you want to sum, plus an empty cell at the bottom of the column or end of the row to hold the sum. (To select a bunch of cells, you drag over them — see Chapter 13.) Then click the QuickSum button.

To find the sum for several columns and/or rows at a time, select the cells in those rows and/or columns that you want to sum, plus enough empty cells to hold the sums. In Figure 12-4, for example, the first three empty cells in row 11 are to hold the monthly sales totals for January, February, and March. The first five empty cells in column E are to hold the quarter sales totals for each category of goods. The empty cell at the bottom right corner of the block of cells (cell E11) is to hold the total sales for the entire quarter.

 Notice the Application Bar at the bottom of Figure 12-4. Thanks to a new feature called Calc-As-You-Go, the Application Bar displays five values after you select a row or column of cells. From left to right, you can see the sum of all the selected cells, the average of all values, the total number of cells containing values, and the maximum and minimum value in all the cells. If you don't see the values on your Application Bar, press Alt+F12 to open the Application dialog box, click the General tab, and select the Calc-As-You-Go check box.

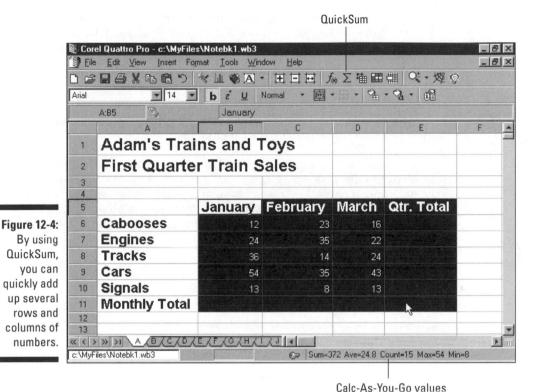

QuickSum

Calc-As-You-Go values

Figure 12-4:
By using
QuickSum,
you can
quickly add
up several
rows and
columns of
numbers.

Fighting the ERR Message and Other Snafus

Sometimes Quattro Pro displays the letters ERR or NA in a cell after you enter a formula and press Enter. This message is Quattro Pro's not-so-subtle way of telling you that you goofed. Something is wrong with your formula.

If, after checking things out, you can't figure out what went wrong, try clicking the cell containing the ERR or NA value. Then press F5 and press Enter. Quattro Pro activates the cell that's the source of the problem.

Of course, if the problem is how you entered the formula rather than a problem in some cell you referenced in the formula, the Go To trick just takes you right back to the cell that contains the formula. That's no help at all. If you're entering a function, check the Help system for information about the function (press F1 to open the Help window) and make sure that you structured the function argument correctly. If all else fails, beg your local Quattro Pro guru for assistance. Offering some sort of little math-related bribe is helpful — a slide rule or one of those tiny calculator keychains is always good.

Version 8 offers another tool to help you sort out formula problems: *Cell Reference Checker*, which alerts you if problems arise from copying or moving a formula. For details, see Chapter 14, in the section "Copying Data from Here to There."

If Quattro Pro displays a message about a syntax error or unknown function, you've left out a parenthesis, an argument, or some other vital portion of the function. Again, check the Help system for information about syntax rules for entering the specific function. (*Syntax*, by the way, is geekspeak for "little rules you must follow in entering data.")

Chapter 13

Editing Your Spreadsheet

● ●

In This Chapter

▶ Undoing mistakes

▶ Editing and deleting cell contents

▶ Selecting stuff before you format

▶ Inserting, deleting, and adjusting columns and rows

▶ Copying stuff from one cell to another

▶ Moving data around

▶ Transposing data

▶ Inserting little notes into cells

● ●

Don't you wish people would react to your mistakes the way they do whenever those celebrities on TV blooper shows muff their lines? Oh sure, it's funny if somebody *famous* goofs up, but if *you* make a mistake, nobody laughs hysterically and shouts, "That's a great one for the blooper reel!" Well, I'm sorry to say that the stuffy network brass who control our nation's TV viewing aren't likely to realize the appeal of *World's Funniest Quattro Pro Bloopers and Blunders* any time soon. So you may as well go ahead and fix those typos, faulty formulas, and other laughers that find their way into your spreadsheet.

This chapter shows you how to undo mistakes, edit data, and otherwise wipe all traces of comedy out of your spreadsheets. It also explains how to make other sorts of changes, such as inserting rows and columns and turning your spreadsheet on its ear.

Selecting Stuff

Before you can do much at all to your spreadsheet — whether you want to format or edit the data — you must select one or more cells. Selecting tells Quattro Pro exactly where to apply your next command or change.

If you select a single cell, Quattro Pro displays a black border (called the *cell selector)* around the cell. If you select only part of the data in a cell or select several cells, the selection appears highlighted on-screen, as shown in Figure 13-1. Notice that the active cell — the first (or sometimes the last) cell in a range of selected cells — does not appear highlighted, but is still part of the selection.

Here's a list of the most popular selection techniques known to man and Quattro Pro:

- ✔ To select a single cell, click it.

- ✔ To select part of the data in a cell, first get into edit mode by double-clicking the cell, clicking the cell and pressing F2, or clicking the cell and then the input line. Then drag across the data you want to select.

  If you double-click a cell that contains a formula, a blue border appears around the cells referenced by that formula. (If the cell contains the formula +A1+A2, for example, the border appears around cells A1 and A2.)

- ✔ To select a *block* (range) of cells, click the first cell in the range and drag to highlight the rest of the range.

Select All button

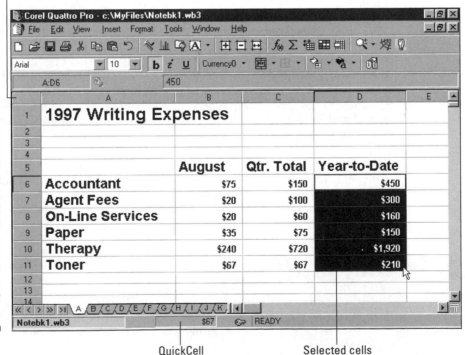

Figure 13-1:
Selected text appears highlighted — except for the first cell in the selection, which looks like an ordinary active cell.

QuickCell   Selected cells

✔ If you don't like dragging, click the first cell you want to select, press Shift, and use the arrow keys to add adjacent cells to the selection.

✔ Here's an even quicker way to select a large block of cells: Click the cell in one corner of the block you want to select. Then hold down the Shift key as you click the cell in the opposite corner of the block.

✔ To select all cells in the notebook, choose Edit➪Select All. Or click the Select All button (refer to Figure 13-1).

✔ To select an entire row of cells, click that row in the row border. (Your cursor changes into a right-pointing arrow as you move it onto the border.) To select several rows at once, drag across them in the row border.

✔ To select an entire column of cells, click the column name in the column border. To select several columns, drag across them in the column border.

✔ To select two or more noncontiguous cells — that is, cells that aren't touching — click the first cell you want to select. Then hold down the Ctrl key as you click the other cells you want to select. You can use this same technique to select noncontiguous blocks of cells.

✔ To "unselect" stuff, just click again.

Getting Rid of Bloopers

If the data you want to edit is short, the fastest method for fixing mistakes is to simply retype the data. Just click the cell, type the data again, and press Enter. Quattro Pro replaces the existing cell contents with the new data.

If you want to make a minor change to a long or complex piece of data (such as a formula), editing the data is probably easier than retyping it. You can make your edits either in the cell or in the input line. But you first must shift Quattro Pro into edit mode, which you can do in any of the following three ways:

✔ Click the cell and press F2.

✔ Double-click the cell.

✔ Click the cell and click the input line.

Whichever method you choose, the I-beam cursor and insertion marker appear, and the contents of the cell appear in the input line, just as they do when you enter data for the first time.

Editing data in Quattro Pro is pretty much the same as editing text in WordPerfect. Here's a recap of the basics:

✔ The insertion marker and I-beam play the same roles as they do when you enter text into a cell initially. The insertion marker shows where the next thing you type will appear. Click with the I-beam or press the left- and right-arrow keys to position the insertion marker. For a review of these and other data-entry techniques, see the Chapter 11 section "Entering Data."

✔ Press Delete to erase the character just to the right of the insertion marker; press Backspace to wipe out the character to the left of the insertion marker.

✔ If you want to keep an eye on how your edits affect the contents of a particular cell, click that cell, right-click the QuickCell button on the Application Bar (refer to Figure 13-1), and choose Display Current Cell in QuickCell from the QuickMenu. Or, place the cursor over the cell until you see the four-headed arrow cursor and then drag the cell to the QuickCell button. Now, whenever you change a value that's referenced by the formula in the QuickCell, the QuickCell displays the new result.

Okay, sorry, drifted off into chiphead-land for a moment. Here's an example that may clear things up: Suppose that, in cell A1, you enter the current price of chutney on the world market. In cell A2, you enter the number of vats of chutney you plan to order for your Chutney Delight restaurant. And in cell A3, you enter the formula **A1*A2**, which calculates how much cash you must fork over to lay in your chutney supply. Well, if you display cell A3 in the QuickCell, any time that you change either the market price in cell A1 or the number of vats in cell A2, the new total price of your order — which is simply the new result of the formula in cell A3 — appears in the QuickCell.

The QuickCell feature is especially helpful when the cell that contains the formula isn't visible at the same time as the cells referenced by the formula — for example, if your Chutney formula were on a different notebook page from the price and order quantity cells.

✔ Normally, Quattro Pro operates in insert mode. Any character you insert shoves the characters that follow to the right. If you press the Insert key, you switch to typeover mode, and new characters you type take the place of existing characters. When you're in typeover mode, a little pencil icon appears on the Application Bar. Press Insert again to get back to Insert mode. (Quattro Pro also returns you to Insert mode when you press Enter.)

✔ If you centered data across a block of cells (as I explain in the Chapter 11 section, "Changing text alignment"), select the leftmost cell in the block to edit the data. Although the data may appear to be contained in another cell, it's really stored in the leftmost cell. The same holds true for labels that are too long to fit inside a single cell and that spill over into adjoining cells.

> ✔ After you fix up the cell contents, press Enter to make your changes
> official. Or, if you want to put things back the way they were before you
> began editing, press Esc instead.

Deleting versus Clearing Cell Contents

If you want to get rid of the contents of a cell completely, click the cell and
press Delete. Simple enough, right?

Ah, but Quattro Pro throws in a little curve. The Delete key does wipe out
the contents of a cell, but any formatting you applied to the cell — such as
numeric style, type size, and so on — remains intact. So the next data you
enter into the cell uses that formatting, too.

To wipe out the formatting along with the cell contents, click the cell and
choose Edit⇨Clear⇨Cells. Or right-click the cell and choose Clear from the
QuickMenu. Quattro Pro zaps the data and returns all the formatting to the
default settings.

To clear just the formatting from a cell, choose Edit⇨Clear⇨Formats.
Edit⇨Clear⇨Values clears values and leaves formatting intact — the same as
pressing Delete.

To delete an entire row or column of cells, follow the steps in the section,
"Inserting and Deleting Columns and Rows," a little later in this chapter.
(Don't you just love these imaginative titles?)

Undoing Bad Moves

Like WordPerfect, Quattro Pro has an Undo command that can take you back
in time to the moment before you made that awful decision that you now
regret. Unfortunately, Quattro Pro's Undo command can reverse only your
last action — you can't undo several actions at once, as you can in
WordPerfect.

To undo your last action, choose Edit⇨Undo, press Ctrl+Z, or click the Undo
button on the toolbar. After you choose the Undo command, it changes to
the Redo command. If you change your mind about the undo, choose the
Redo command or click the Undo button again to undo your undo.

The names of the Undo and Redo commands change depending on what you
did last — for example, if your last action was to enter some data, the
command name is Undo Entry. If you're not sure what action you're undoing
or redoing, look at the command name before you proceed.

If Undo doesn't seem to be working, the feature may be turned off. You can undo some actions with Undo disabled, but not all. To turn Undo on, press Alt+F12 to open the Application dialog box, click the General tab, select the Undo Enabled check box, and press Enter.

Inserting and Deleting Columns and Rows

You can add an empty row or column of cells any time, any place, with just a few mouse clicks and drags. You can delete rows or columns from your spreadsheet just as easily.

Inserting an empty row or column

If you insert a row or column, Quattro Pro adjusts formulas in other cells as needed. If your spreadsheet contains the formula +A1+A2, for example, and you insert a row before row A1, Quattro Pro changes the formula to +A2+A3 to accommodate the new arrangement of the cells. This automatic adjustment is the result of Quattro Pro's relative addressing feature, which I explain in Chapter 12 (in the gray-shaded sidebar "Would you like that address relative or absolute?")

Here's how to insert a row or column of empty cells:

✔ To insert a row, click in the row border on the row immediately below where you want the new row to appear. Then click the Insert button on the toolbar.

✔ To insert several rows at once, select however many rows you want to insert in the row border. To insert three rows, for example, select three rows in the row border. Then click the Insert button. Quattro Pro inserts the new rows immediately above the top row in your selection.

✔ To insert a column, click the column border of the column immediately right of where you want the new column to appear and then click the Insert button. To insert several columns, select the number of columns you want to insert and then click the Insert button. Your new columns appear just to the left of the leftmost column in your selection.

✔ You can also insert rows and columns by using the Insert⇨Column or Insert⇨Row command, or by right-clicking and choosing the Insert and Delete commands on the QuickMenu. But really, simply using the Insert button on the toolbar is a heck of a lot easier.

Deleting rows and columns

Whenever you delete rows or columns, make sure that you aren't deleting cells that are referenced in formulas found elsewhere in your spreadsheet. If you do, you wind up with formulas that Quatto Pro either can't calculate or calculates incorrectly.

To delete a row or column, click it on the row or column border, as shown in Figure 13-2. Then click the Delete button on the toolbar or choose the Edit⇨Delete Column(s) or Edit⇨Delete Row(s) command. (The command name changes depending on whether you clicked a column border or row border before choosing the command.) Whichever approach you take, Quattro Pro tosses the column or row into the electronic wastebasket and shifts the remaining rows or columns over to fill up the empty space.

To delete several rows or columns at once, select them in the column or row border and then click the Delete button or choose Edit⇨Delete.

The Delete button on the toolbar doesn't do the same thing as the Delete key on your keyboard. The Delete button deletes the entire column or row, while the Delete key just deletes the contents of the cells in the column or row.

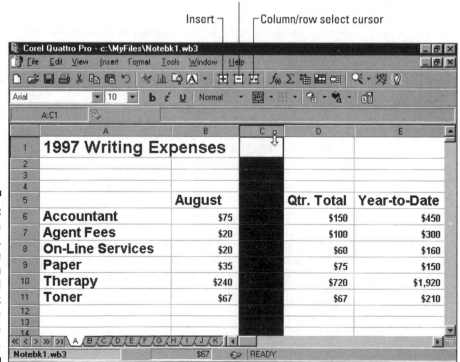

Figure 13-2: To delete a column, click on the column border and then click the Delete button on the toolbar.

Adding a Page

 If you need to insert a blank page between two pages in your notebook, click the page tab for the second of those two pages and choose Insert➪Sheet. Or, right-click the tab and choose Insert Sheet from the QuickMenu.

To delete a page, right-click its page tab and choose Delete Sheet from the QuickMenu.

Resizing Columns and Rows

After you first open a spreadsheet, Quattro Pro fills the page with columns that are about nine characters wide, given the default type size and font (10-point Arial). You can shrink or enlarge the columns to fit your data at any time, however. You can also change the height of any row in your spreadsheet. The following list tells all:

- The easiest way to change the column width is to place your cursor in the column border, directly over the line that separates the column you want to resize from its neighbor to the right. After you see the cursor change to a two-headed arrow, as shown in Figure 13-3, drag right or left to resize the column.

- You can change row height by dragging up or down on the line that separates the row you want to resize from the row directly beneath it.

 - To resize several rows or columns at once, select them in the row or column border and then drag the bottom or right border of any of the selected rows or columns.

 - To have Quattro Pro automatically fit the row or column size to fit the longest entry in the column or row, click the column or row border and then click the QuickFit button on the toolbar. Or, simpler yet, you can resize your column by double-clicking in the column border.

 - If you want Quattro Pro to enlarge rows and columns automatically as you type, turn on the Fit-As-You-Go feature, found on the General tab of the Application dialog box (which you access by pressing Alt+F12).

 If you want more precision over your column and row sizes — for example, if you want each column to be exactly $1^1/_2$ inches wide — click the column or row you want to adjust. Then choose Format➪Selection, press F12, or click the Cell Properties button on the Property Bar to open the Active Cells dialog box, as shown in Figure 13-4. Click the Row/Column tab. You can change row/column sizes as follows:

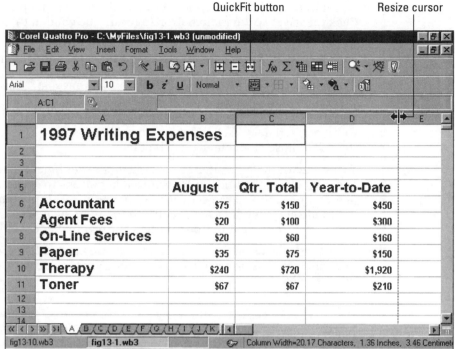

QuickFit button   Resize cursor

Figure 13-3: Drag the border between a column to resize the column.

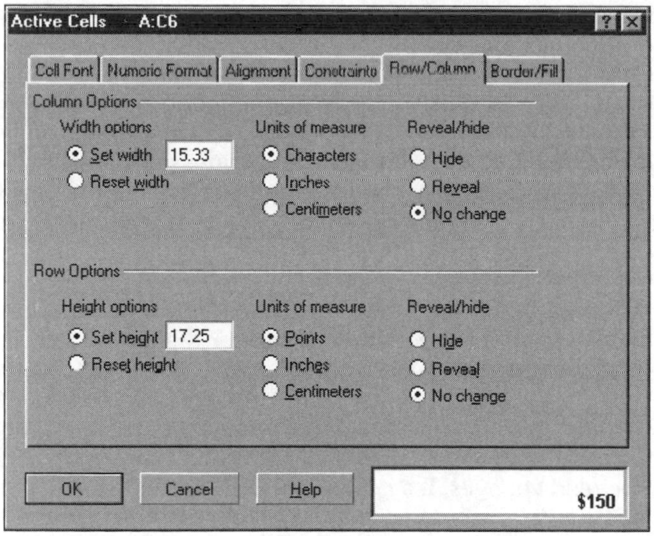

Figure 13-4: To make your columns or rows a precise size, press F12 to open this dialog box and then adjust the width and height values.

✔ To set the column width, enter a value in the Set Width option box. Click the Reset Width radio button to return the column to its original default size.

✔ You can choose from three measurement units for your columns: Characters, Inches, and Centimeters. I recommend that you avoid the Characters option, because it's pretty vague. The number of characters you can fit in the cell depends on the type size you use, the font, and the type style (bold or italic). In other words, you may set the column width at 15 characters, but you may be able to fit only 13 characters in the cell if those characters are in boldface.

✔ To set the row height, enter a new value in the Set Height option box and click one of the Units of Measure radio buttons to establish the unit of measurement. You can set your row height in terms of points (a point is a publishing unit of measure equal to $1/72$ inch), inches, or centimeters. The Reset Height button returns your row to its default size.

✔ The other options on the Row/Column tab are used to temporarily hide rows and columns, as I explain in Chapter 15 in the section "Hiding a Row or Column."

Copying Data from Here to There

If you have a label or formula that you need to use in more than one spot in your spreadsheet, don't keep entering it again and again — save yourself some time and effort and copy it.

Quattro Pro offers several methods for copying data, as outlined in the following sections. But before you begin your grand copying adventure, you need to be aware of an important piece of business: If you copy a formula, Quattro Pro automatically adjusts the formula relative to its new location, as I explain in Chapter 12 (in the gray-shaded sidebar, "Would you like that address relative or absolute?")

If you copy a formula that uses relative addressing, Quattro Pro may respond by displaying the Cell Reference Checker dialog box, as shown in Figure 13-5. This dialog box appears to warn you that a cell referenced by the copied formula is empty or that some other problem exists with the formula. Click the Details button to display the bottom half of the dialog box, as shown in the figure. Quattro Pro shows you the original formula and the recommended changes. If a cell referenced by the formula is empty, for example, Quattro Pro recommends that you change the formula to use absolute addressing. If you want Quattro Pro to make the change, click the Fix It button. Like the results? Click Close. If not, click Undo Fix to put things back to the way they were and then click Close.

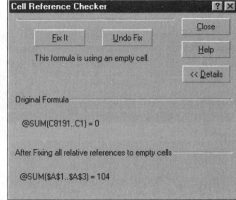

Figure 13-5:
The Cell
Reference
Checker
warns you
about
potential
problems
with a
copied
formula.

In addition to reading the following sections, make sure that read Chapter 19, which describes some additional copying techniques.

Dragging and dropping a copy

For simple copy jobs, the quickest method is to drag and drop the copy; to do so, just follow these steps:

1. Select the data you want to copy.

You can copy a single cell or a block of cells. (I outline selection techniques in the section "Selecting Stuff," earlier in this chapter.)

2. Place your cursor on a border of the cell until the four-headed arrow cursor appears.

3. Press and hold the Ctrl key as you drag the cell or block to its new location.

Your cursor should change to a little hand with a plus sign next to it, as shown in Figure 13-6. Be sure that you see a little plus sign next to the hand cursor — otherwise, you're moving the selected cells instead of copying them.

If you drag-and-drop data to cells that already contain data, Quattro Pro displays a dialog box to warn you that you're about to overwrite the existing data. If that's what you want to do, click Yes; otherwise, click No to cancel the copy.

After you copy data to one cell, you can copy it into other cells by clicking those cells and pressing Ctrl+V (which is the shortcut for the Paste command, as described in the following section).

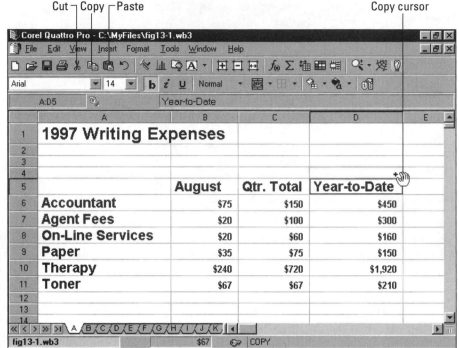

Figure 13-6:
To copy
data to
another
cell, just
Ctrl+drag it.

To copy cells to another open document, Ctrl+drag them to the Application Bar button for the second document. After that document appears on-screen, drag the cells to the spot where you want to place them and release the mouse button.

Using Copy and Paste to copy data

Another way to copy data is to use the Copy and Paste commands, as described in the following steps:

1. **Select the cell or block of cells you want to copy.**

2. **Press Ctrl+C or click the Copy button on the toolbar.**

   Alternatively, you can choose the Edit⇨Copy command from the menu bar or right-click and choose the command from the QuickMenu. Quattro Pro sends the data to the Windows Clipboard, where the copy stays until the next time you use the Copy or Cut command.

3. **Click the cell where you want to place the copy.**

   If you're copying a block of cells, click the upper-left cell of the block where you want to put the copy.

Make sure that you don't copy the data to cells that already contain data. If you do, Quattro Pro replaces the existing data with the data you're copying — and doesn't warn you first.

4. **Press Ctrl+V or click the Paste toolbar button.**

Or choose Edit⇨Paste or right-click and choose Paste from the QuickMenu. Quattro Pro pops your copy into its new home.

If you want to copy the data to yet another cell, just click the cell and use any of the methods described in Step 4 to paste the data again. You can paste the data as many times as you want.

You can paste the contents of a single cell into a whole block of cells at the same time. To do so, select the block of cells right before you choose the Edit⇨Paste command. Quattro Pro duplicates the data in every cell selected.

Getting more specific by using the Copy Block command

If you want to copy some parts of a block, but not all, the Edit⇨Copy Cells command in the menu bar is the ticket. By using this command, you can specify whether Quattro Pro copies formulas, numbers, labels, and cell formatting attributes used in the block. Here's how:

1. **Select the cell or block you want to copy.**

2. **Choose Edit⇨Copy Cells.**

The Copy Cells dialog box appears, as shown in Figure 13-7.

Figure 13-7: The Copy Cells dialog box enables you to specify which elements of the selected cells you want to copy.

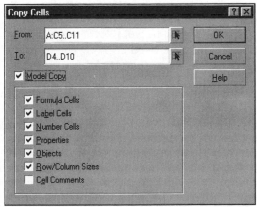

3. **Enter the address of the cell where you want to place the copy in the To option box.**

   If you're copying a block of cells, enter the address of the cell in the upper-left corner of the block where you want to place the copy.

   Quattro Pro doesn't warn you if you're about to copy data to cells that already contain data. So be careful when specifying a location for the copied data.

4. **Click the Model Copy check box to select it.**

5. **Select the check boxes for the elements you want to copy.**

   Formula Cells copies any formulas in the block; Label Cells copies labels in the block; Number Cells copies cells that contain plain old numbers; Properties copies the cell formatting; Objects copies any graphs or other objects in the block; and Row/Column Sizes copies, er, the row and column sizes. Cell Comments copies any hidden comments that you inserted into the cell, as I explain in the section "Inserting Juicy Remarks into Cells."

6. **Click OK or press Enter.**

   Quattro Pro copies just those elements of the block that you specified in the dialog box.

Moving Data Around

Moving the contents of a cell — or a block of cells — from one spot to another is a cinch. You can drag and drop the stuff you want to move or choose the Edit➪Cut and Edit➪Paste commands.

If you move cells that contain formulas, Quattro Pro does not adjust the cell addresses as it does when you copy cells that contain formulas. If you move the formula +A1/A2 from cell A3 to cell B3, the formula doesn't change to +B1/B2, for example, as it does when you copy it. The formula continues to refer to the same cells it did before you moved it.

If you move a cell that's referenced in a formula, however, Quattro Pro adjusts the formula so that it continues to reference that same cell. If, for example, you enter the formula +A1+A2 and then move cell A2 to cell A3, Quattro Pro adjusts the formula to read +A1+A3.

If you're moving cells just a short distance, using the drag-and-drop method is usually easiest. Use the same procedure outlined in the section "Dragging and dropping a copy," earlier in this chapter, but don't press the Ctrl key as you drag.

To move data from one document to another, drag the selected cells to the Application Bar button for the second document. Don't let up on the mouse button when you reach the Application Bar. When the second document appears on-screen, drag the cells to the spot where you want to place them and release the mouse button.

Alternatively, you can use the Cut and Paste commands to move data. To use Cut and Paste, follow the steps outlined in the section "Using Copy and Paste to copy data," earlier in this chapter — but choose the Cut command or click the Cut button in Step 2.

If you use Cut/Paste or Move Cells to move data, Quattro Pro doesn't warn you that you're about to move data into cells that already contain data. It simply overwrites the existing data with the moved data.

Check out Chapter 19 for more techniques you can use to move data between documents.

Transposing Cells

You're halfway through creating your spreadsheet, and you realize that you'd be better off if you oriented your data in a different way. You want to change your spreadsheet so that your columns become rows and vice versa — as I did with the data in Figure 13-8.

No problem; Quattro Pro is happy to transpose your data for you. Just select the block you want to flip and then choose Tools⇨Numeric Tools⇨Transpose. The Transpose Cells dialog box appears. In the To text box, enter the address of the upper-left cell of the block where you want to put the transposed data. Or just click the cell. Then click OK. Quattro Pro obediently turns your data on its ear.

Don't try to transpose blocks that contain formulas. Quattro Pro's brain simply isn't up to the task, and your formulas can get completely messed up. And if you tell Quattro Pro to put the transposed data into cells that already contain data, it overwrites the existing data without warning you. So be very careful whenever you set the upper-left corner of the block that's to hold the transposed data.

Did anyone but me notice that the hot keys for opening the Transpose Cells dialog box are TNT? Just thought I'd ask.

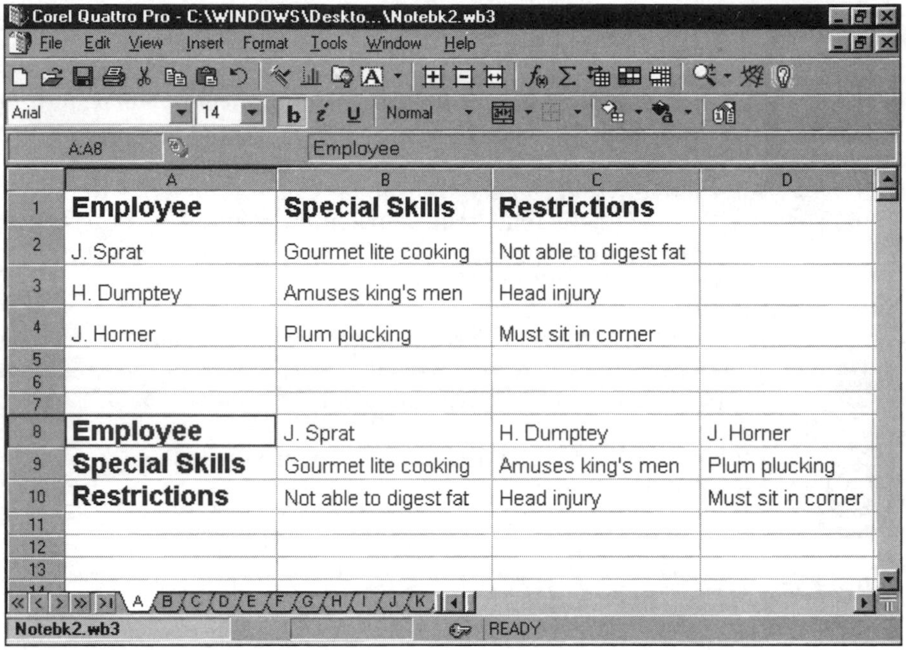

Figure 13-8: By using the Transpose command, you can turn your columns into rows and your rows into columns.

Inserting Juicy Remarks into Cells

Quattro Pro enables you to add little notes to your cells to remind yourself of important information, such as what a particular formula calculates. A little red triangle appears in the corner of cells that contain comments, and as you pass your cursor over the cell, the comment appears, as shown in Figure 13-9.

To add a comment, click the cell and choose Insert⇨Comment. Quattro Pro displays a little cartoonlike balloon to hold your text, as shown in the figure. (You wouldn't normally see both the balloon and a comment label on-screen at the same time; I took some creative liberties in creating this figure so that you could see both elements together.) Type your comment and then click outside the balloon. To remove a comment, choose Edit⇨Clear⇨Comments.

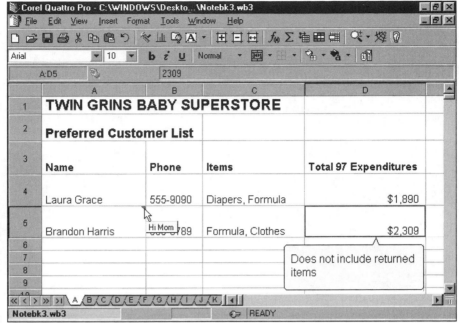

Figure 13-9:
Quattro
Pro's
Comments
feature
enables you
to insert a
note that
appears as
you pass
your cursor
over the
cell.

Chapter 14
Charting Your Course

· ·

In This Chapter

▶ Turning a boring block of numbers into a dazzling chart

▶ Uncovering the Chart menu and chart tools

▶ Choosing a chart type and layout

▶ Editing chart data and design

▶ Getting acquainted with the Objects page

▶ Naming your charts

▶ Printing charts by their lonesomes

· ·

*B*y using Quattro Pro's graphics capabilities, you can quickly turn a batch of boring numbers into an eye-catching chart that would make Ross Perot's heart pound. Charts not only add some flash to your spreadsheet, but they also help people make sense of your numbers.

Consider the chart shown in Figure 14-1, for example. The chart makes seeing which types of shows are more heavily watched much easier than does the table of numbers to the left.

This chapter gives you a lightning-fast tour of Quattro Pro's charting capabilities so that you, too, can captivate audiences by using pie charts, bar charts, and just about any other type of chart you can dream up.

QuickChart button

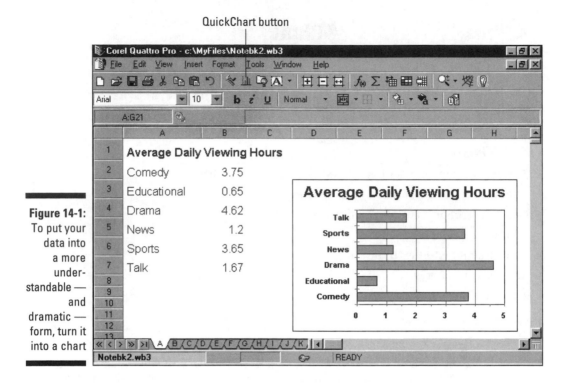

Figure 14-1:
To put your
data into
a more
under-
standable —
and
dramatic —
form, turn it
into a chart

Creating a New Chart

Quattro Pro gives you the following two quick ways to create a chart:

- ✔ **Use the Chart Expert.** The Expert walks you through the steps of
  selecting a chart type, adding labels, picking colors, and making other
  decisions regarding your chart. Using this method, you can put your
  chart right on a spreadsheet page or in a special chart-editing window,
  cleverly titled the Chart window. The chart then exists separately from
  the spreadsheet.

- ✔ **Use the QuickChart tool button.** When you use this tool, labeled in
  Figure 14-1, Quattro Pro makes the chart formatting decisions for you
  and creates the chart right on the spreadsheet page. You can change
  the formatting later if you want.

The following two sections explain each of these options in more detail.

Using the Chart Expert

The Chart Expert is supposed to be self-explanatory, but if you ask me, it's not. So here's how to use the Expert — just follow these steps:

1. **Select the data that you want to turn into a chart.**

   Select the column and row labels if you want them included in the chart — but don't select any titles or subtitles you may have given your spreadsheet. You add those to your chart later.

2. **Choose Insert⇨Chart from the menu bar.**

   The Chart Expert dialog box appears, as shown in Figure 14-2. A preview shows you the chart layout that Quattro Pro suggests; you get the chance to change the layout later. The two check boxes in the dialog box enable you to rearrange the order of the data in the graph. For more information about these two options, see the section "Exchanging rows, columns, and series," later in this chapter. You can also rearrange data after you create your chart.

3. **Click the Next button to advance through the remaining panels of the Chart Expert.**

   You advance first to a panel that asks you to select a general chart type. Click Next again, and you get to refine your chart type a little more. And with the third click of Next, you can select a color scheme for your chart. After you get to the fifth panel of the Expert, you can add a title, subtitle, and axis labels to your chart.

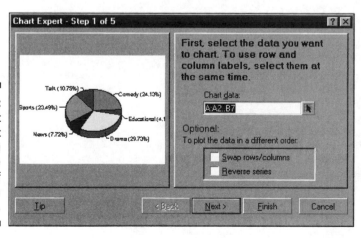

Figure 14-2: The Chart Expert walks you through the steps of creating a chart.

As you make selections, the preview provides updates to show how your chart is going to look. At any point, you can return to the previous panel and change a setting by clicking the Back button.

4. Select a Destination radio button and click Finish.

The last panel of the dialog box — titled Step 5 of 5 — contains two Destination radio buttons: Chart Window and Current Sheet.

Select Current Sheet and click Finish to place your chart on the current notebook page. Quattro Pro returns you to the spreadsheet page, and your cursor looks like a little chart. Place the cursor at the spot where you want to put the upper-left corner of the chart and drag to the opposite corner, as shown in Figure 14-3. After you release the mouse button, Quattro Pro draws your chart.

To keep your chart separate from the rest of the spreadsheet, select the Chart Window radio button and click Finish. Quattro Pro creates your chart and displays it the Chart window, as shown in Figure 14-4. To return to your spreadsheet, choose its name from the Window menu.

Figure 14-3:
Drag with the chart cursor to set the boundaries for your chart.

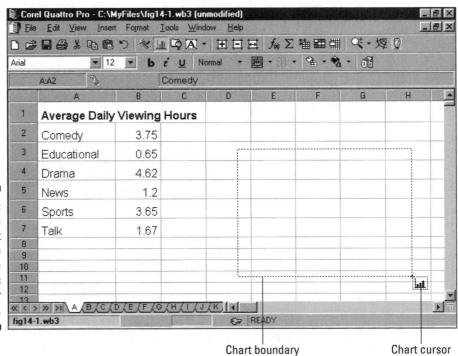

Chart boundary   Chart cursor

Creating charts by using the QuickChart tool

 To use the QuickChart tool, select the data you want to chart, click the QuickChart button on the toolbar, and drag with the chart cursor to set the boundaries for the chart (refer to Figure 14-3). After you release the mouse button, Quattro Pro draws the chart that it believes is most appropriate for your data. You can change the chart layout, titles, colors, and other features, as I explain in the following section.

Editing a Chart

 To change the data in a chart, change the original spreadsheet data you used to create the chart. Any changes to the spreadsheet are automatically reflected in your chart.

To change design-related aspects of your chart, such as the chart type, label font, titles, and so on, you edit the chart itself. You can edit your chart right on the spreadsheet page or inside the Chart window. For most edits, working in the Chart window is easier than working on the spreadsheet page because you can get a better view of your chart. But I can tell that you're the sort who likes to make up your own mind, so the following list provides a brief overview of your chart-editing options. Later sections provide more detail on specific editing tasks.

✔ To edit a chart that you created in the Chart window, as I explain in the section "Using the Chart Expert," a little earlier in this chapter, select the chart's name from the Window menu. Your chart appears in living color inside the Chart window, as shown in Figure 14-4.

Inside the chart window, click the element you want to change. Little black boxes called *selection handles* appear around the element, and the Property Bar changes to offer tools related to the item you clicked. The left end of the input line displays the name of the chart element that's selected. In Figure 14-4, the background pane of the chart is selected.

To switch from the chart window to your spreadsheet window, choose the spreadsheet window name from the Window menu.

Selection indicator

Selection handle

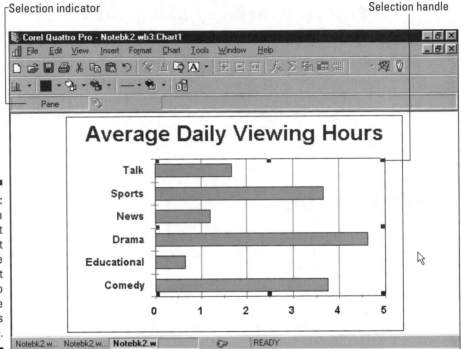

Figure 14-4:
Click a
chart
element
inside the
Chart
window to
change the
element's
appearance.

Average Daily Viewing Hours

✔ If your chart lives on a spreadsheet page and you want to edit it in the Chart window, click the chart border and then click the Chart Window button on the Property Bar. Or right-click the chart border and choose Open from the QuickMenu. The chart opens in the Chart window, ready for your edits. To return to your spreadsheet, choose the spreadsheet name from the Window menu. Any changes you made to your chart are automatically made in your spreadsheet as well.

After you edit a chart in the Chart window, simply click the chart on the spreadsheet page to reopen the chart in the Chart window.

✔ If you want to change the overall look of your chart without going to the Chart window, click the chart border. Selection handles appear around the perimeter of the chart, and the Property Bar changes to provide you with several chart-editing buttons.

To edit the fine details of the chart, such as the font of a particular label, click inside the chart boundary. The chart becomes surrounded by a dashed line, and the Chart menu replaces the Tools menu. Click the element you want to edit, and use the Property Bar buttons and Chart menu commands to make your changes.

✔ You can also edit any chart by clicking the QuickTab button to go to the Objects page. (See Figure 14-5, where the QuickTab button is labeled.) Click again on the button to return to your spreadsheet.

The Objects page contains a little icon representing each chart in your spreadsheet, as shown in Figure 14-5. Double-click the icon for the chart you want to edit. Quattro Pro opens the chart in the Chart window. To return to the spreadsheet window, choose its name from the Window menu. Or click the Application Bar button for the spreadsheet to return to the Objects page.

Unfortunately, the little icons on the Objects page don't look anything like the charts they represent, and Quattro Pro gives your charts vague names such as Chart 1, Chart 2, and so on. You can give a chart a more meaningful name by right-clicking its icon on the Objects page, choosing Icon Properties from the QuickMenu, and entering the name in the Name dialog box that appears, as shown in Figure 14-5. Quattro Pro limits you to a 15-character name.

✔ To get a really good look at your chart, click the View Chart button or choose Chart➪View Chart. Quattro Pro fills the entire screen with your chart. Click to return to the regular Chart or spreadsheet window.

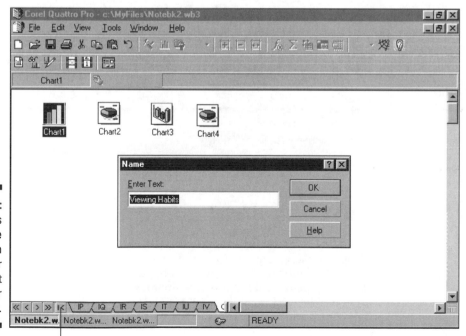

Figure 14-5:
The Objects page contains an icon for every chart in your spreadsheet.

QuickTab button

Changing the chart type and color scheme

 If you want to change the color scheme, chart type, or layout of your chart, click the Chart Gallery button on the Property Bar or choose Chart⇨Gallery to display the Chart Gallery dialog box, as shown in Figure 14-6. (If you're editing your chart in the spreadsheet window, click inside the chart border to switch to the Chart window or make the Chart Type button and Chart menu available inside the spreadsheet window.)

Select the color arrangement you want to use from the Color Scheme drop-down list. You can also change the chart type and layout in this dialog box. Select a chart type from the Category drop-down list and click a chart style in the scrolling Style list. The preview box shows how your chart looks with the selected changes. Click OK to apply your changes.

 If all you want to do is change the chart type, you can click the Chart Type button on the Property Bar and choose a new type from the drop-down menu.

Figure 14-6:
Inside the
Chart
Gallery
dialog box,
you can
change the
chart type,
layout, and
color
scheme.

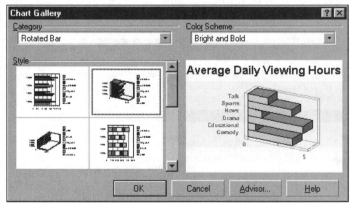

Giving your chart a title and a border

 To add a title, subtitle, or axis title to your chart, click the Title button on the Property Bar or choose Chart⇨Titles. (Click inside the chart boundary to display the button and menu if you're editing in the spreadsheet window.) Quattro Pro opens a dialog box that enables you to enter a main title, a subtitle, and labels for the X and Y axes, if your chart has them. (The *X axis* is the horizontal one; the *Y axis* is the vertical one.) Click OK to apply your titles.

The process for changing the chart border depends on whether you're working in the Chart window or the spreadsheet window:

✔ In the Chart window, choose Chart⇨Background. Or click outside the chart to deselect everything and then press F12 or click the Chart Properties button. Whichever method you choose, the Background dialog box appears. On the Box Settings tab, you can select a color and line style for your border. If you don't want a border at all, choose the first line-style button — the one with the X through it.

Borders that you create in the Chart window are *not* applied to your chart in the spreadsheet window. The specialized borders available in the Chart window can be created, displayed, and printed inside the Chart window only.

✔ In the spreadsheet window, click the border and choose Format⇨Selection, click the Chart Properties button, or press F12. The Chart dialog box appears, with the border options available on the Box Type and Border Color tabs. Your options are more limited than they were in editing the border in the Chart window. Alternatively, you can click the chart border and choose a new border style and color from the drop-down lists that appear on the Property Bar. Borders that you apply in the spreadsheet window affect the chart when it is printed with the spreadsheet.

Editing individual chart elements

In Version 8, editing the individual elements of a chart is easier than ever — for example, changing the font used for the titles or the color used for a bar in a bar chart.

If you're doing your editing in the Chart window, click the element you want to change. In the spreadsheet window, double-click the element. Either way, you can then use the Property Bar buttons and drop-down lists to change the element's color and other formatting attributes. (Pause your cursor over each button to discover your options.) To display all your formatting controls in one dialog box, click the Chart Properties button, press F12, or choose Format⇨Selected Object.

Adding lines and callouts

Quattro Pro offers a small selection of drawing tools that you can use to add lines, arrowhead lines, and callouts (text) to your chart. To select a drawing tool, choose Insert⇨Shape and then click in the Shape submenu the name of the shape you want to create.

You can also select some of the shape tools from the drop-down list that appears after you click the down-pointing arrow on the Shape button, which is on the toolbar. If you want to be able to access all the drawing tools easily, however, right-click the toolbar and select the Chart and Drawing Tools option. Quattro Pro then displays a toolbar full of drawing tools.

Notice that, as you're working in the spreadsheet window, the available drawing tools change depending on whether you click the border of your chart or an element inside the border.

The drawing tools in Quattro Pro work just as their counterparts in Presentations do, as I discuss in Chapter 16. For the most part, you simply drag with the tool to create your shape. You can then click the shape to select it and change its color and other formatting attributes, just as you do any other chart element.

 To add a box filled with text, choose the Text Box option from the Shape submenu or Shape drop-down list on the Property Bar. Drag to create the box and then type the text that you want to appear in the box. To edit text in a text box, click the box. You get the standard insertion marker that appears while you're editing text in a regular cell.

Exchanging Rows, Columns, and Series

Take a gander at Figure 14-7. I got this arrangement of data as I first created my chart. Obviously, this layout is not the best way to present this particular data; the arrangement shown in Figure 14-8 makes comparing how each gender reacts to the various life irritants much easier.

 To change the arrangement of the data in your chart, you can go back and re-enter the data in the spreadsheet, changing your rows into columns and vice versa. Or you can take the easy way out: Click the Row/Series button on the Property Bar. (In the spreadsheet window, click the chart border to make the button appear.) Alternatively, choose Chart⇨Series. Either way, the Series dialog box appears. Ignore the top half of the dialog box; the option you want is the Row/Column Swap check box at the bottom of the dialog box. Click the check box and click OK to make the swap official.

The other check box in the Series dialog box, Reverse Series, changes the order of the data series in your chart. If I applied the option to the chart in Figure 14-8, the bars representing the female point of view would move to the left of the bars representing the male perspective.

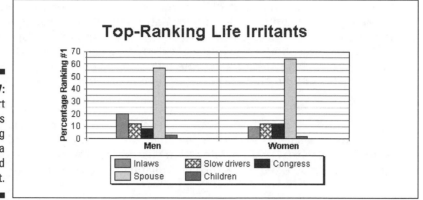

Figure 14-7:
This chart
makes
absorbing
the data
presented
difficult.

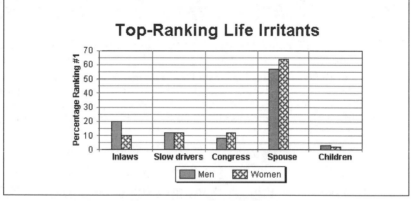

Figure 14-8:
With the
rows and
columns
swapped,
the data
takes on
a more
meaningful
appearance.

Moving, Resizing, and Deleting Charts

Want to move that chart from one place in your spreadsheet to another? Place your cursor over the chart border until you see the four-headed arrow cursor. Then drag your chart to its new home. If you want to clone the chart and move the clone, press Ctrl as you drag. You can also move and copy charts by using the Cut, Copy, and Paste commands, just as you do in using Cut, Copy, and Paste to move and copy cells.

To copy a chart from the Chart window into a spreadsheet, choose Edit⇨Select All and then choose Edit⇨Copy or press Ctrl+C. Or right-click the chart icon on the Objects page and choose Copy from the QuickMenu. Then return to your spreadsheet page, click at the spot where you want to place the chart, and choose the Paste command (Ctrl+V).

To resize a chart in the spreadsheet window, click its border to display the chart selection handles. Drag a top or bottom handle to change the height of the chart only; drag a side handle to change the width only; drag a corner handle to change both the width and height. You can't resize a chart in a chart window, but you can reduce or enlarge it for printing by using the print-scaling options that I describe in Chapter 15, in the section "Changing the page setup."

Finally, to delete a chart from your spreadsheet, click the chart border and press Delete. Quattro Pro deletes the chart both from your spreadsheet and from the Objects page. To delete a chart in the Chart window, choose Chart⇨Delete Chart. Or click the chart's icon on the Objects page and press Delete.

Printing a Chart without Its Spreadsheet

Chapter 15 spells out the steps for printing a spreadsheet. If you created your chart on your spreadsheet page and want to print both the spreadsheet data and chart, follow the instructions in that chapter. If you want to print your chart without the spreadsheet data, however, click your way through the following steps. These steps work like a charm, whether you're printing a chart from the spreadsheet window or Chart window.

1. **Click the chart border to select the chart.**

   If you created the chart in its own window, you can skip this step.

2. **Choose File⇨Print, click the Print button, or press Ctrl+P.**

   The Chart Print dialog box appears, with the Selected Chart radio button selected, which is exactly what you want.

3. **Adjust other print settings as needed.**

   The options in the Chart Print dialog box are the same as their cousins in the regular Spreadsheet Print dialog box, as Chapter 15 explains.

4. **Click Print or press Enter.**

If you want to print several charts at once, click the first chart and Shift+click the others. Then choose the Print command.

You can also print charts from the Objects page. Click the QuickTab button to go to the Objects page. (The QuickTab button's labeled back in Figure 14-4.) Then click and Shift+click the icons of the charts you want to print and choose the Print command.

Chapter 15
The Finishing Touches

● ●

In This Chapter

▶ Formatting in a flash with SpeedFormat

▶ Adding lines, borders, and colors

▶ Adding headers and footers

▶ Adjusting margins by dragging guidelines

▶ Hiding columns or rows temporarily

▶ Inserting a page break

▶ Printing your spreadsheet

● ●

*P*ackaging is everything. Think about it: Would you rather open a present that's encased in shiny, colorful wrapping paper or one that's stuffed in a dirty, wrinkled bag that smells suspiciously like last night's Chinese carryout? Why, given the right presentation, even a cheap gift can convey the impression that somebody really cares about you.

The same is true with spreadsheets. You make a much better impression on the folks who see your spreadsheet if you fancy up the page with charts, borders, headers, and the like. In fact, a nicely formatted spreadsheet can help divert everyone's attention from the actual information you're presenting, which can be really helpful on occasion.

Of course, you don't always want to dress up your spreadsheets in their Sunday best. For everyday number-crunching, you just want to enter your formulas, run your calculations, and print the results. For those times, skip to the end of this chapter, which tells you how to print your spreadsheet.

But if you want your spreadsheets to really wow your audience — whatever your motives — play around with the advanced formatting options discussed in the rest of this chapter. (I cover chart-making techniques in Chapter 14.) With a little effort on your part, you can make even the most horrible spreadsheet data look as delightful as a gift-wrapped box from Tiffany's.

Using SpeedFormat

Don't want to spend much time formatting your spreadsheet? Afraid of making some awful formatting faux pas? Let SpeedFormat take care of everything for you. The SpeedFormat command enables you to apply a predesigned set of formatting attributes to your data — font, shading, alignment, and more — with a wave of your hand (or rather with a few clicks of the old mouse).

 To use this handy feature, select the cells you want to format, as I explain back in Chapter 13, in the section "Selecting Stuff." Then click the SpeedFormat button or choose Format⇨SpeedFormat. The SpeedFormat dialog box appears, as shown in Figure 15-1.

Figure 15-1: To quickly turn your spreadsheet from dull to dazzling, use one of the formatting templates available through the SpeedFormat command.

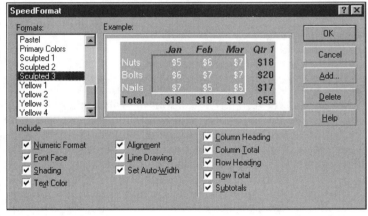

You can select from a variety of different spreadsheet designs, which are listed in the Formats list box. Click a design name to display a preview of that format in the Example box.

At the bottom of the dialog box are check boxes that enable you to select which parts of the design you want to incorporate into your spreadsheet. If you don't want to use the font that the design applies, for example, deselect the Font Face check box.

After you're satisfied with your selections, click OK or press Enter. If you don't like what you see, choose Edit⇨Undo or press Ctrl+Z.

 You can add your own design to the SpeedFormat dialog box. Just format a block of cells, open the SpeedFormat dialog box, click the Add button, and give your design a name. Any time you want to use that same design again, you can apply it from the SpeedFormat dialog box.

Adding Lines, Borders, and Colors

Quattro Pro enables you to draw lines around cells, surround blocks with borders, and even paint your spreadsheet with color. To whet your artistic appetite a little, the spreadsheet in Figure 15-2 shows an example that incorporates all these formatting options. You can see that even a spreadsheet printed in black-and-white can benefit from a little color and border action.

Notice anything different about the spreadsheet in Figure 15-2? The cell gridlines that normally appear on-screen are missing. When you're adding lines, borders, and color to your spreadsheet, turn the gridlines off so that you can get a better idea of how your printed spreadsheet is going to look. (Gridlines normally don't print; see "Choosing print options," later in this chapter, for more details.)

To turn off gridlines, press Ctrl+F12 or choose Format⇨Sheet to display the Active Sheet dialog box. Then deselect the gridlines check boxes on the Display tab and press Enter.

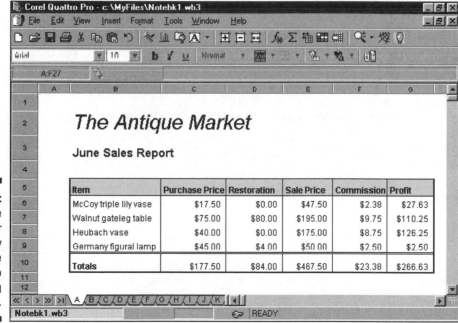

Figure 15-2:
Exercise your creativity by using the Quattro Pro formatting options.

Corel Quattro Pro - c:\MyFiles\Notebk1.wb3

The Antique Market

June Sales Report

Item	Purchase Price	Restoration	Sale Price	Commission	Profit
McCoy triple lily vase	$17.50	$0.00	$47.50	$2.38	$27.63
Walnut gateleg table	$75.00	$80.00	$195.00	$9.75	$110.25
Heubach vase	$40.00	$0.00	$175.00	$8.75	$126.25
Germany figural lamp	$45.00	$4.00	$50.00	$2.50	$2.50
Totals	$177.50	$84.00	$467.50	$23.38	$266.63

Notebk1.wb3   READY

Drawing lines and borders around cells

The process of drawing lines and borders has been greatly simplified in Version 8. Just select the cell (or cells) you want to format and click the arrow on the Lines button on the Property Bar. A drop-down list of line style options appears. Click the one you want to use. The selected line style then appears on the face of the Lines button. If you want to apply that same line style to other selected cells, click the button face itself instead of the arrow. To remove all lines from around a cell, choose the first option in the drop-down list.

If none of the options on the drop-down list suits you, press F12 or click the Properties button to open the Active Cells dialog box and click the Border/ Fill tab, as shown in Figure 15-3. This dialog box has improved in Version 8, but it's still a little less-than-intuitive. Here's how to get the job done:

Figure 15-3:
The process of drawing borders around cells isn't really as complicated as the Active Cells dialog box makes it seem.

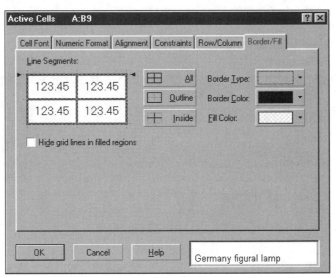

- ✔ The Line Segments area of the dialog box shows where your lines appear. If you click the All button, you get lines around each and every selected cell. If you click the Outline button, Quattro Pro draws a line around the perimeter of the selected block of cells. And if you click the Inside button, you get lines between the cells but not around the perimeter of the block.

- ✔ You aren't limited to the All, Outline, or Inside options, however. You can select whatever lines you want by clicking in the example grid. If you click at the intersection of two lines — on a corner, for example — both intersecting lines are selected. To select a line by itself, click anywhere on the line except at the point where it intersects with another line.

The little black arrows in the example grid indicate which lines are selected. In Figure 15-3, the arrows indicate that the line at the top of the block is selected.

✔ You can add a line to the selection by Shift+clicking it. To delete a line from the selection, Shift+click it again.

✔ Click the Border Type button to display a drop-down list of line styles. You can select a thin, thick, or double line. If you want to remove a previously drawn line, select the No Line option, which is the one with an X through it. If you want to cancel your changes to the line, click the empty spot at the top of the drop-down list, which represents the No Change option.

✔ The default line color is black. If you want to select another color, click the Border Color button and click the color that tickles your fancy.

✔ You can specify as many different types of lines in the dialog box as you want. You can add a thick line to the top and bottom of the block, for example, and put a thin line on the right and left sides of the block. For each line type, just select the lines you want to format in the Line Segments grid and then select a line type and color.

✔ After you finish applying your lines, press Enter or click OK to see the results. If you don't like what you see, go back to the Line Drawing panel to make some changes or just press Ctrl+Z to get rid of all the lines you just applied.

Applying color to text and backgrounds

If you have a color printer or if you're creating an on-screen presentation, you may want to add some color to your spreadsheet. Even if you plan to print your spreadsheet on a black-and-white printer, you can get some nice effects by coloring the background of some cells with shades of gray or by reversing your text (putting white text on a dark background).

To change the color of spreadsheet text, select the text you want to format and click the arrow of the Text Color button on the Property Bar. A palette of color swatches appears. Click the color you want to use. That color then appears on the Text Color button face. If you want to apply the same color to other text, select the text and click the button face instead of the arrow. Alternatively, you can apply a new color via the Active Cells dialog box. (Press F12 or click the Cell Properties button on the Property Bar to access the dialog box.) The Text Color drop-down list appears on the Cell Font tab of the dialog box.

If you select the cell(s) and then choose a color, the color is painted onto all text in the cell(s). But remember that, in Version 8, you don't need to apply the same color to all text in a cell; you can select individual characters and apply color to those characters only. For details on how to select text, see Chapter 13.

To change the background color of a cell, click the cell and click the Fill Color button on the Property Bar. This button works like the Text Color button that was just explained. You can also choose a background color by using the Fill Color button on the Border/Fill tab of the Active Cells dialog box (accessed by pressing F12). To remove shading from a selected cell, choose the first color swatch (the one with the X through it) from the Fill Color drop-down list on the Property Bar or in the dialog box.

Don't find any of the available background colors to your liking? You can create one that better suits your artistic sensibilities by clicking the More option in the Fill Color drop-down list. Quattro Pro displays the Shading dialog box, as shown in Figure 15-4. Here you can mix two colors together to create that just-right shade of salmon or ecru. Click one color in the Color 1 palette and one in the Color 2 palette. Quattro Pro fills the Blend palette with swatches that start with the Color 1 color and gradually blend into the Color 2 color. Click the mixture that you want to use and click OK.

Figure 15-4:
If you really want to goof off, mix your own custom colors in the Blend dialog box.

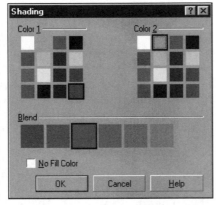

Inserting Page Breaks

As you enter spreadsheet data, Quattro Pro automatically inserts a page break at the bottom of the page. If you want to insert a page break at some other spot, select the leftmost cell in the row where you want the break to occur. If you want the break to be at row 30, for example, click cell A30. Then choose Insert➪Page Break➪Create.

If the cell where you want to enter the page break is empty, you can enter the characters |:: into the cell instead of using the menu commands (thus adding some spice to your life). That's a vertical bar — which you get by pressing Shift and the backslash key (\) — followed by two colons. Either way, Quattro Pro displays a thin black line across your spreadsheet to indicate the page break.

To remove a page break, click the cell that contains the break and choose Insert⇨Page Break⇨Delete.

Quattro Pro determines where to break your pages by looking at the paper size you selected in the Spreadsheet Page Setup dialog box (more about that in the next section). If you change the page size, your page breaks are likely to change as well.

Changing the Page Setup

If you want to change the paper size, change the page orientation (the direction it prints), set new margins, or add a header or footer to your spreadsheet, choose File⇨Page Setup to open the Spreadsheet Page Setup dialog box, as shown in Figure 15-5. You can also access this dialog box by clicking the Page Setup button inside the Print dialog box or in the Print Preview window (both discussed later in this chapter, in "Going from Screen to Printer").

Figure 15-5:
Choose your paper size, orientation, and other layout options inside the Spreadsheet Page Setup dialog box.

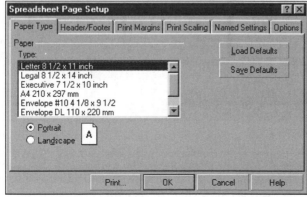

This dialog box contains six tabs, two of which — Print Options and Print Scaling — are related specifically to printing and are covered in the section "Choosing print options," later in this chapter. The page setup options on the remaining tabs are discussed in the following two sections.

Any settings you make in the dialog box are stored with your spreadsheet and remain in effect until you change them again.

If you want to return all the settings to their default values, click the Load Defaults button. To save your current page setup values as the new default values, click the Save Defaults button.

The Named Settings tab enables you to save all your page setup settings under a specific name so that you can easily reuse those same settings when you print another spreadsheet. To save your settings, enter a name in the New Set option box and click the Add button. To reuse a setting, select it from the settings list box and click the Use button.

Changing margins, paper size, and page orientation

The options on the Paper Type tab and Print Margins tab control . . . uh, I think you're clever enough to figure out the end of that sentence. But just in case. . . .

- ✔ Select your paper size from the Type list box on the Paper Type tab of the dialog box.

- ✔ Select the paper orientation by clicking either the Portrait or Landscape radio button. In Portrait orientation, the rows of your spreadsheet run parallel to the short edge of the paper. In Landscape orientation, things print out sideways so that the rows print parallel to the long edge of the paper.

- ✔ Set your page margins and header/footer margins on the Print Margins tab. Alternatively, you can drag the margin guidelines that appear after you choose View⇨Page (see Figure 15-6 for a look at the guidelines). Place your cursor over a guideline until you see the double-headed arrow and then drag the guideline to the spot where you want to place the margin, just as you do in WordPerfect. You can also drag the margin guides in the Print Preview window, as explained in the section "Previewing before you print," later in this chapter.

- ✔ The Break Pages check box on the Print Margins tab determines whether your pages print with or without any automatic page breaks that Quattro Pro inserted. (You may want to turn the option off to print on continuous-feed printer paper, for example.) If the check box is turned off, the spreadsheet prints without the page breaks. Any page breaks that you inserted on your own do print, however. (For more information on page breaks, see "Inserting Page Breaks," earlier in this chapter.)

Adding headers and footers

The Header/Footer tab of the Spreadsheet Page Setup dialog box enables you to add a header (text that appears at the top of every page) and a footer (text that appears at the bottom of every page). You may, for example, want your name to appear on the bottom of every printed page.

To create a header or footer, click the Create check box and then type your text into the adjacent text box. Click the Font button to pick a font, size, and style for your text. The Height value sets the amount of distance between the header or footer and the data in your spreadsheet.

In Page view, you can see your header and footer on-screen along with the rest of your spreadsheet, as shown in Figure 15-6. And you can edit the header or footer text by double-clicking the header or footer area. Click in the main spreadsheet page or press Enter to exit the header/footer zone and resume work on your spreadsheet.

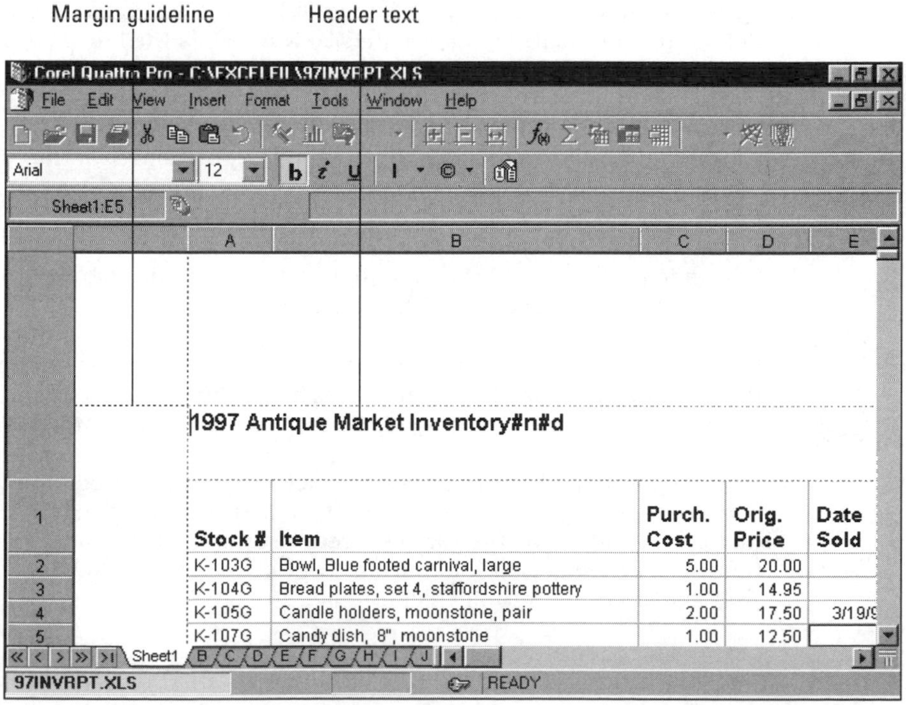

Margin guideline   Header text

Figure 15-6:
In Version 8, you can edit headers and footers on the spreadsheet page by switching to Page view.

	A	B	C	D	E
	1997 Antique Market Inventory#n#d				
1	Stock #	Item	Purch. Cost	Orig. Price	Date Sold
2	K-103G	Bowl, Blue footed carnival, large	5.00	20.00	
3	K-104G	Bread plates, set 4, staffordshire pottery	1.00	14.95	
4	K-105G	Candle holders, moonstone, pair	2.00	17.50	3/19/9
5	K-107G	Candy dish, 8", moonstone	1.00	12.50	

Corel Quattro Pro - C:\EXCEL FIL\97INVRPT.XLS

File Edit View Insert Format Tools Window Help

Arial   12   **b** *i* <u>u</u>

Sheet1:E5

Sheet1

97INVRPT.XLS   READY

Quattro Pro uses special codes for inserting line breaks, setting text alignment, and inserting dates, page numbers, and other stuff into headers and footers. To see a list of the available codes, choose the Headers and Footers item in the Help index. (See Chapter 3 for more about using Help.)

 If you're editing a header or footer in Page view, the Property Bar displays a Header/Footer Codes button you can click to display a drop-down list of some popular header/footer codes. Pause your cursor over the different codes to see what each one does. In Figure 15-6, the #n code inserts a line break, and #d inserts the current date. After you press Enter to exit the header/footer editing area, Quattro Pro formats your text according to the codes.

To remove a header or footer, switch to Page view, right-click the header or footer, and choose Remove Header or Remove Footer from the QuickMenu. Or go back to the Header/Footer tab of the Page Setup dialog box and deselect the Create check box for the offending header or footer.

Hiding a Row or Column

Suppose that you created a bang-up spreadsheet that lists each of your employees' names, titles, phone numbers, years at the company, and salaries. Someone asks you for an employee information list, and the spreadsheet immediately pops into your head. It would be a quick way to deliver the information, but the person who needs the information isn't supposed to know how much money everybody makes.

Here's the solution: You can temporarily hide the salary information for printing or on-screen viewing. Just right-click the border of the row or column you want to hide and choose Hide from the QuickMenu. Or, select the border, press F12 or choose Format➪Selection to display the Active Cells dialog box. Then click the Row/Column tab, select the Hide radio button in the Column Options or Row Options section (depending on what you want to hide), and click OK or press Enter.

 If you hide a row or column, the following rows or columns shift over to fill the empty space. But the row numbers and column letters don't change — which gives you one easy way to see that you hid some data.

To redisplay a hidden row or column, select the rows or columns on both sides of the hidden row or column. Then press F12 to open the Active Cells dialog box and follow the same procedure outlined for hiding data, but this time select the Reveal radio button. (Unfortunately, the Reveal command isn't available on the QuickMenu.)

You can also use the mouse to hide and reveal rows and columns, as follows:

- ✔ To hide a column, drag its border to the left until you reach the right border of the preceding column. To reveal a hidden column, put your cursor slightly to the right of the border of the column that lies to the right of the hidden column and then drag. If you hide Column A, for example, place your cursor just to the right of the left border of Column B. (Try it; this stuff all makes more sense if you see it on-screen.)

- ✔ To hide a row, drag up on the bottom row border until you reach the bottom border of the preceding row. To redisplay the hidden row, put your cursor slightly below the top border of the row that falls after the hidden row. To redisplay the hidden Row 1, for example, place your cursor slightly below the top border of Row 2 and drag.

Going from Screen to Printer

Ready to make the leap from digital spreadsheet to printed page? The following steps give you the basic how-to:

1. **Choose File⇨Print, press Ctrl+P, or click the Print button.**

   The Spreadsheet Print dialog box appears from out of nowhere, as shown in Figure 15-7.

2. **Choose a printer from the Name drop-down list.**

   If you're hooked into a network and have access to several printers, you may need to select a printer. Otherwise, you can probably skip this step.

3. **Tell Quattro Pro what you want to print.**

   Select the Current Sheet radio button to print just the current notebook page. Select Notebook to print more than one page in the notebook. Enter the starting page number in the From option box and enter the last page number in the To option box.

   Entering the page numbers in the From and To option boxes does not automatically select the Notebook radio button, as you may expect. Be sure both to click the button and to enter the appropriate page numbers.

   You can also print specific cells or a chart by selecting them before you choose the Print command and then selecting the Selection radio button. (For more about printing charts, see the last section in Chapter 14.)

If you forget to select the area you want to print before you open the dialog box, click the Selection button and then select the cells you want to print. (If necessary, move the dialog box out of the way by dragging its title bar.) The Spreadsheet Print dialog box momentarily shrinks itself but springs back into full view after you release the mouse button.

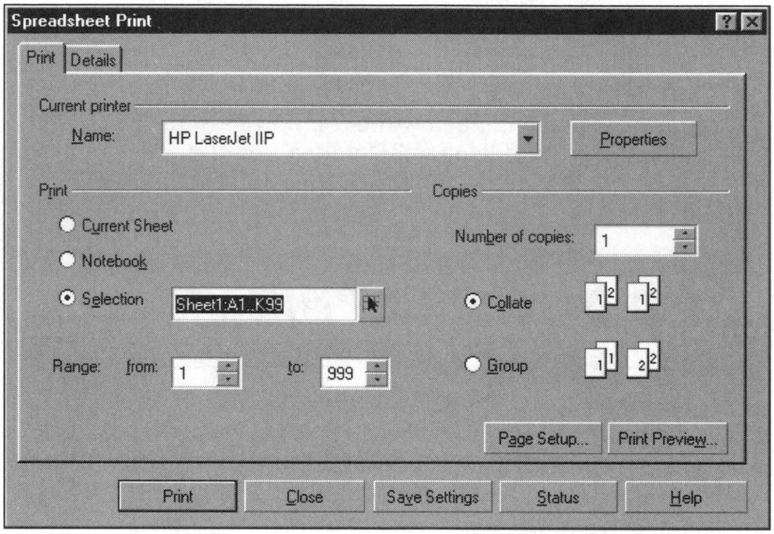

Figure 15-7:
Use the
Spreadsheet
Print dialog
box to
shove your
work out
of the
computer
and onto
paper.

4. **Enter the number of copies you want to print in the Number of Copies option box.**

   If you're printing more than one copy, you can have Quattro Pro collate your pages by selecting the Collate button. If you choose the Group radio button, all copies of page 1 print first, followed by all copies of page 2, and so on.

5. **Click Print or press Enter.**

   Assuming that your printer is correctly set up and configured to work with your computer, your spreadsheet should come sliding out of your printer any minute now.

Previewing before you print

Before you print, you may want to take a look at what the printed piece is going to look like. You may decide that you want to shrink or enlarge the margins, adjust the type size or font, or make other formatting changes before you actually transfer your spreadsheet to paper.

To preview your spreadsheet, choose File⇨Print Preview to open the Preview window, as shown in Figure 15-8. Or click the Print Preview button in the Spreadsheet Print dialog box. The figure shows the preview of a budget spreadsheet I created to track everyday expenses. I've zoomed way out on the page so that no one can see how much I spend per week on sugar-free Fudgsicles and *Soap Opera Digest*.

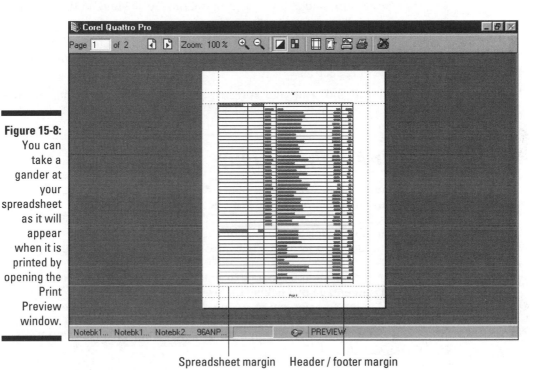

Figure 15-8: You can take a gander at your spreadsheet as it will appear when it is printed by opening the Print Preview window.

Spreadsheet margin   Header / footer margin

The Preview window offers a number of helpful tools and options, as follows:

 ✔ After you first open the preview window, it shows you a full-page view of the first page in your notebook. Click the page to zoom in; right-click to zoom out. Keep clicking or right-clicking until you reach the magnification you want to use. Alternatively, you can zoom in and out by clicking the Zoom buttons.

 ✔ To see a different page of your notebook, enter the page number in the Page option box or click the Next Page or Previous Page button.

 ✔ Use the Color Preview and Black-and-White Preview buttons to switch between a preview that shows your spreadsheet in glorious living color or stark black and white.

✔ To display or hide margin guidelines (refer to Figure 15-8), click the Margins button. You can drag the guidelines to change the page margins (see "Changing margins, paper size, and page orientation," earlier in this chapter).

 ✔ Click the Page Setup button to open the Spreadsheet Page Setup dialog box. I describe this dialog box in witty and insightful detail in "Changing the Page Setup" and "Choosing print options," elsewhere in this chapter.

 ✔ Click the Print Options button to display the Options tab of the Spreadsheet Page Setup dialog box, where you can make still more adjustments to the way your spreadsheet prints. For more information, see the following section.

 ✔ To go ahead and print your spreadsheet, click the Print button. To close the Preview window, click the Close Preview button or press Esc.

Choosing print options

As if you hadn't already had your fill of printing options, still more adventures in printing await you on the Print Scaling and Options tabs of the Spreadsheet Page Setup dialog box. To get to the dialog box, choose File⇔Page Setup or click the Page Setup button in the Print Preview window or the Print dialog box. Look at the control you can wield on these two tabs:

✔ You can *scale* — that is, reduce or enlarge — your spreadsheet by a certain percentage by clicking the first radio button on the Print Scaling tab and entering a percentage value. A value of exactly 100 percent prints the spreadsheet at its actual size; a value lower than 100 percent reduces the spreadsheet; and a value higher than 100 percent enlarges the spreadsheet.

 If you want Quattro Pro to scale your spreadsheet so that it fits on a certain number of pages, click the second radio button and specify how many pages wide and how many pages tall you want your spreadsheet to be.

 ✔ If you have a long spreadsheet that can't print entirely on a single page, you may want to print the top row and/or left column of the spreadsheet on every page. Why? Because the top row and left column usually contain the titles of the rows and columns of data in your spreadsheet, and without those titles, you can easily forget what type of information each row and column holds.

To print the column and row titles, click the Options tab, as shown in Figure 15-9. Enter the name of the row (or rows) you want to appear in the Top Heading option box; enter the name of the column (or columns) you want to print on each page in the Left Heading option box.

If you use these options, you need to print your document in a special way. Select everything except the top row or left column that you specified as the Top Heading or Left Heading. Then print by using the Selection option in the Spreadsheet Print dialog box. Otherwise, the top row and left column print twice on the first page of your printout.

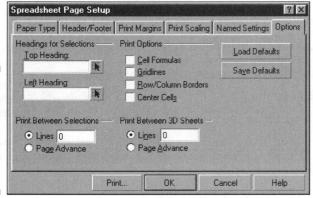

Figure 15-9:
The Options tab gives you precise control over your printouts.

- ✔ Normally, Quattro Pro prints the answers to formulas and not the formulas themselves. But if you want to print the formulas rather than the answers, select the Cell Formulas check box. One reason you may want to do so is if you're having trouble making your spreadsheet work and you want to have a Quattro Pro guru review the formulas you're using.

- ✔ Normally, the gridlines marking the boundaries of each cell on-screen don't print. If you want these gridlines to print, select the Gridlines check box. But be forewarned that including the gridlines increases the amount of printer memory you need to print your spreadsheet.

If your printer memory isn't sufficient to handle gridlines, you can create "fake" gridlines by drawing them as explained in the section "Drawing lines and borders around cells," earlier in this chapter. Select the part of your spreadsheet that needs gridlines, and then choose the All line segments button and the thin Border Type option on the Border/Fill tab of the Active Cells dialog box.

- ✔ If you want to print row and column borders, check the Row/Column Borders option box. You may want to do so if you want to know the exact cell address of each cell in the printed spreadsheet so that you can go back and edit specific cells easily.

- ✔ To center the spreadsheet on the page, check the Center Cells check box. Otherwise, the spreadsheet aligns to the left margin.

✔ If you chose the Selection printing option and are printing more than one block of selected cells, select the Page Advance radio button in the Print Between Selections area of the dialog box to print each block on a separate page. If you select the Lines option, the different blocks are printed on the same sheet of paper but are separated by the number of lines you enter in the Lines option box. (To find out how to select multiple blocks to print, see "Selecting Stuff" in Chapter 13.)

✔ If you want each page of your notebook to start on a new sheet of paper, select the Page Advance radio button in the Print Between 3D Sheets area of the dialog box. If you just want to separate the different pages with a few lines of space, select the Lines radio button and enter the number of line spaces you want in the option box.

✔ To reset the print options to Quattro Pro's defaults, click Load Defaults. To make your settings the new default settings, click Save Defaults.

You now know more than you ever wanted about printing spreadsheets in Quattro Pro. That headache you have is a sure sign that your brain is growing by leaps and bounds.

Part IV
Those Other Programs

"THE FUNNY THING IS, I NEVER KNEW THEY HAD DESKTOP PUBLISHING SOFTWARE FOR PAPER SHREDDERS."

In this part . . .

This part of the book is a heaping smorgasbord of information about the programs not covered in Parts I, II, and III. In this part, I dish up tasty servings of techniques and tips for using Presentations, Netscape Navigator, and Photo House. For dessert, I offer valuable insights on how to use all the programs in the Suite together to save yourself some time and effort.

Dig in, and bring a hearty appetite. As they say, there's something here to satisfy every taste. And at this buffet, you can fill your plate as many times as you want without winding up with that uncomfortable bloated feeling or without adding any extra pounds.

Chapter 16

Let's All Get Together and Put on a Show!

Hoo, boy. You really stepped in it this time, didn't you? When they asked if you'd give a presentation to the big brass at the annual company meeting, you didn't even hesitate before saying yes. Okay, maybe you hesitated just a little, but you didn't want to look uncooperative, so you acted as if the idea was a good one. Or maybe you out and out refused, but they said that if you didn't agree to their evil plan, you'd be looking for another employer.

Well, however you got yourself into this predicament, Presentations can help get you out of it. By using Presentations, you can create a multimedia slide show that you can play back on any computer running Microsoft Windows — even one that doesn't have Presentations installed. You can also create regular 35mm slides and printed drawings.

This chapter shows you how to use Presentations to create a show that not only entertains and informs your audience, but also draws attention away from the fact that you spilled salad dressing on your shirt during lunch.

Starting and Stopping

To start Presentations, click the Presentations DAD icon or click the Start button on the Windows 95 taskbar, choose the Corel WordPerfect Suite 8 item from the Start menu, and then choose Corel Presentations 8 from the submenu. Presentations pops to life and presents you with the New dialog box, which works just like the one in WordPerfect and Quattro Pro:

➤ Click the Create New tab to create a new slide show or drawing. Like WordPerfect and Quattro Pro, Presentations offers a variety of templates for different types of slide shows. You can either select one of these templates and then replace the template text and graphics with your own as needed, or you can start entirely from scratch by choosing the Presentations Drawing or Presentations Slide Show item.

➤ The Work On tab lists the Presentations documents you've edited most recently. If you want to do more work on one of these documents, select it from the list and press Enter.

You can also open existing documents by pressing Ctrl+O or choosing File➪Open and selecting your document in the Open File dialog box, which I discuss in Chapter 5. To create another new drawing or slide show, press Ctrl+N or choose File➪New. By default, the New dialog box also appears any time you close all your open Presentations documents.

If you choose the Presentations Slide Show item in the New dialog box, Presentations takes you next to the Startup Master Gallery dialog box, which I explain in "Building a Really Big Shew," later in this chapter. If you're creating a new drawing, a shiny new drawing page appears, where you can use the tools described in "Adding Pretty Pictures," also later in this chapter, to create simple drawings. And if you're editing an existing show or drawing, the show or drawing appears on-screen.

The Presentations window contains many of the same elements as other programs in the WordPerfect Suite, including a toolbar, Property Bar, Application Bar, and menu bar. For more information on using the different window elements, see "Basic Stuff You Need to Know," in Chapter 2.

To close a drawing or presentation, choose File➪Close, press Ctrl+F4, or click the document window Close button. To shut down Presentations, choose File➪Exit, press Alt+F4, or click the program window Close button.

Navigating Your Slide Show

Figure 16-1 gives you a look at a slide show that's in the works. If you're upgrading from Version 7, notice that things look very different in Version 8. The drawing and slide navigation tools that used to live on the left side of the Presentations window now reside on the toolbar and Property Bar. Version 8 also is heavy on tabs: Tabs on the right side of the window enable you to switch between slide views and play your show, for example, and each slide appears on its own tab as well.

The Property Bar buttons shown in Figure 16-1 control things related to the overall slide show — playing the show, choosing transition effects and backgrounds, and so on. If you have a text box or graphic selected on the slide, these buttons are replaced by buttons that apply effects to the selected object. So if I refer you to a button related to the slide show and you don't see that button on your screen, press Esc to deselect everything on your slide and reveal the buttons.

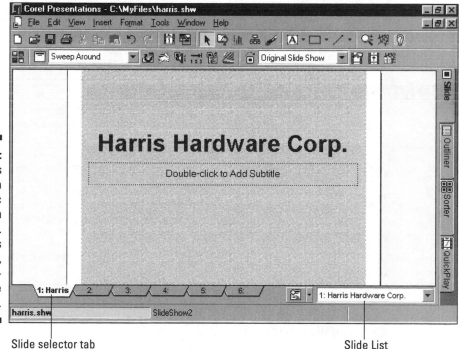

Figure 16-1: Presentations got a dramatic makeover in Version 8. The result is a cleaner, easier-to-use interface.

Slide selector tab   Slide List

Among the many changes to Version 8 are new ways to move from slide to slide and view your work:

✔ To switch to a different slide, click its slide tab or select the slide from the Slide List drop-down menu (refer to Figure 16-1).

 ✔ Zoom in and out on your work by clicking the Zoom button on the toolbar and choosing a view size from the drop-down list.

✔ Click the Slide tab on the right side of the program window to see your slides as they appear in your presentation. To see your slide text in outline form, click the Outliner tab. You can edit text, add slides, and delete slides in this view, as you can in Slide view.

✔ Click the Sorter tab to display thumbnail views of your slides, along with information about the transition and advance modes selected for each slide. (You can read more about transition and advance modes in "Adding Transitions and Other Special Effects," later in this chapter.) In this view, you can see several slides on-screen at once, and you can rearrange slides by dragging them.

✔ A view available in Version 7, Slide List view, bit the dust in Version 8. Its functions were absorbed by the new Sorter tab and the Slide List drop-down menu.

Building a Really Big Shew

To understand how Presentations works, you need to understand that each slide has three layers:

✔ The *Background layer* contains a picture or design that appears behind the text and graphics on your slides.

✔ The *Layout layer* is a template that contains preformatted areas to hold your slide text. You select a layout for each type of slide you create — such as title slide, bullet chart, and so on.

✔ The *Slide layer* holds the actual text and graphics that you put on the slide.

The following sections show you how to combine these three layers to create your slides. Later sections explain how to edit your slides and save, print, and play your show.

Choosing a Master

After you tell Presentations that you want to create a slide show, it presents you with the Startup Master Gallery dialog box, as shown in Figure 16-2. The *Master* determines the overall look of your show. The Master includes the background for your slides, plus layouts to hold different types of slide text. Although the purpose of the Master is to give your show a consistent design, you can override the background and layout for any slide.

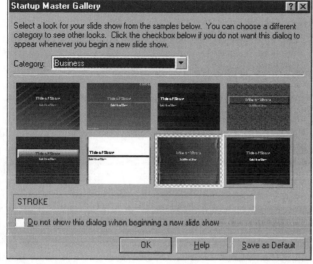

Figure 16-2:
The first
step in
creating a
slide show
is to choose
a Master.

The available Masters are organized into seven different categories. You can display a different category by choosing it from the Category drop-down list. Click the picture of the Master you want to use and press Enter to make your choice official. Presentations displays the first slide in the program window and assigns the Title layout, as I discuss in the following section.

You can use any Master that tickles your fancy, but you may want to keep these tips in mind:

✔ Masters in the Color category are especially suited for presentations that you show on a color monitor.

✔ Select the 35mm slide category if you plan to convert your presentation to 35mm slides for use in a slide projector.

✔ Select the Printout category if you're going to print your show as black-and-white transparencies or print black-and-white copies of your slides to use as handouts.

You can apply a different Master to your slide show at any time. Just choose Format⇨Master Gallery to display the Master Gallery dialog box — which is different from the one shown in Figure 16-1 in name only.

 If you don't want to be bothered with the Startup Master Gallery dialog box after you start a new slide show, select the Do Not Show This Dialog check box at the bottom of the dialog box.

Choosing a slide layout

 Although Masters control the overall appearance of your slides, *layouts* — called templates in Version 7 — aid you in placing text on the slides in your show. The layouts position and format your text in a way that meshes with the Master you selected. You can choose from the following layouts:

- ✔ **Title:** The background from the Master Gallery, plus text boxes formatted to hold a title and subtitle.

- ✔ **Bulleted List:** The background and formatted text boxes to hold a title, subtitle, and bulleted list of information.

- ✔ **Text:** The background, plus areas formatted for a title, subtitle, and paragraph text.

- ✔ **Org Chart:** The background and areas formatted to hold a title, subtitle, and organizational chart.

- ✔ **Data Chart:** The background, plus areas formatted for a title, subtitle, and data chart (such as a bar chart or pie chart).

- ✔ **Combination:** The background and formatted areas for a title, subtitle, paragraph text, and data chart.

- ✔ **None:** The background and nothing else.

 After you start a new show and select a Master, Presentations displays the first slide. Presentations assumes that you want your first slide to contain the title and subtitle of your show, so it selects the Title layout for you. To change to a different layout, click the Layout button on the Property Bar and choose the layout you want from the drop-down list.

 To change the layout for several slides in your show, click the Slide Properties button on the toolbar or choose Format⇨Layout Gallery to display the Appearance tab of the Slide Properties dialog box, as shown in Figure 16-3. The seven layout options are presented as icons at the top of the dialog box. By using the arrows and the drop-down list at the bottom of the dialog box, you can move from slide to slide and change the layout for each slide. Click OK to apply the new templates in one grand, sweeping gesture.

Another option for changing layouts is to switch to Sorter view (click the Sorter tab on the right side of the Presentations window). Click the first slide you want to change and Ctrl+click the others. Then choose a new layout from the Property Bar. Presentations applies the layout to all selected slides.

Don't fret too much about this layout business. The layouts just give you some guidance in placing stuff on your slides. But you can rearrange, delete, and add text boxes at whim, regardless of which layout you use.

You can edit the layout itself to make changes to all slides by using that template. If you want to delete the subtitle text box from all slides that use the title layout, for example, go to a slide that uses the layout. Choose Edit⇨ Layout Layer. Click the subtitle text box to select it and press Delete. Then choose Edit⇨Slide Layer to return to your normal slide view.

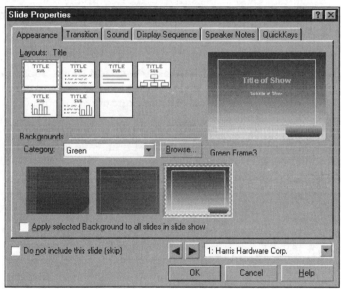

Figure 16-3:
You can choose a new Layout and Background for your slides in this dialog box.

Playing with backgrounds

The curious (or very bored) in the crowd may have noticed that the Slide Properties dialog box in Figure 16-3 also has options related to the slide background. You can open the dialog box by clicking the Slide Properties button on the toolbar, choosing either Format⇨Background Gallery or Format⇨Layout Gallery; choosing Format⇨Slide Properties⇨Appearance; or right-clicking and choosing Appearance from the QuickMenu. If I figure out why Presentations gives you so many options for opening this same dialog box, I'll let you know. For now, just revel in the possibilities. Have it your way, as they say.

To change the background for a slide, first select that slide by using the arrows or the drop-down list in the bottom-right corner of the dialog box. The dialog box contains previews of the backgrounds currently available — by default, you get the background that comes with the slide show Master and a blank white background. But you can choose from a mess of other backgrounds by selecting an option from the Category drop-down list, as I did in Figure 16-3.

If you stumble across a background that sets your heart racing, click it. To apply the background to the selected slide only, press Enter. To apply the new background to all slides, select the oddly named Apply Selected Background to All Slides in Slide Show check box. Notice that the Do Not Include This Slide check box, although visible while you're working on the Appearance tab, is related to playing slide shows and has no effect on applying backgrounds and layouts.

If you have a certain element — say, a logo or company name — that you want to appear on every slide in your show, place it on the background layer. (You can read about adding text and graphics in "Adding Tantalizing Text and Dynamic Data" and "Adding Pretty Pictures," later in this chapter.) Choose Edit⇨Background Layer to display your background by itself. Place your logo or other element on the background and then choose Edit⇨Slide Layer to return to the standard slide-editing mode. Your logo appears automatically on all slides that use the background you edited.

What if you want to put that logo on some slides, but not on all? Create an entirely new background by pressing Ctrl+Enter. Give your background a name and then proceed as just discussed. You can then apply the background to selected slides inside the Slide Properties dialog box as you do any other background.

Adding and Deleting Slides

To add a slide to your show, click the tab of the slide that falls immediately before the spot where you want to insert the new slide. Then click the arrow on the Add Slide button at the bottom of the Presentations window. A menu appears, listing the seven layout choices available for your slide (Title, Bulleted List, and so on). Click the layout you want to use. After you choose a layout, Presentations inserts the new slide after the current slide.

You can add several slides at once by choosing Insert⇨New Slide to open the New Slide dialog box. Click the icon for the layout you want to use and then enter the number of slides you want to insert in the Number to Add option box. Press Enter to insert the slides after the current slide. Keep in mind that you can always change the layout later, so the New Slide dialog box is a good choice for adding multiple slides even if you don't want to use the same layout on all of them. Pick one layout and then change the layout for selected slides as described earlier in this chapter.

To chuck a slide from your show, click its tab and choose Edit⇨Delete Slides. Presentations asks for reassurance that you really want to lose the slide. Click Yes or No, depending on your feelings.

For an easy way to delete several slides at once, click the Sorter tab to switch to Sorter view, click the first slide you want to delete, and Ctrl+click the others. If you select a slide by mistake, Ctrl+click it again. After you select all the slides you want to delete, choose the Delete Slides command.

Adding Tantalizing Text and Dynamic Data

Whew, here we are already several pages into this chapter, and all you've discovered so far is how to establish the look of your slides and add and delete slides. You're no doubt squirming with impatience, wondering when I'm going to tell you how to actually put some information on your slides. Or . . . is something else causing that pained look on your face? No, that's okay — really, I don't want to know.

Regardless, the time to add text to your slides has arrived. You add all your pithy thoughts and other data to slides by entering them into text boxes, such as the one shown in Figure 16-4. You use the same techniques to create text in a Presentations drawing, as the following list describes.You can use the text boxes provided by the slide layout or draw your own, as outlined in the following list.

- ✔ To enter text into an existing text box, double-click the box. The text box border changes and selection handles appear to show that the box is selected, as you can see in the figure. You also see the standard blinking insertion marker and I-beam cursor used for entering text in WordPerfect, Quattro Pro, and almost every other Windows program.

- ✔ The insertion marker indicates where the next character you type will appear. To reposition the insertion marker, click at the spot where you want it to appear. Or use the arrow keys to move the insertion marker.

- ✔ As soon as a text box is selected, the Property Bar displays tools and drop-down menus for formatting text, including controls that change the font, text color, alignment, and so forth. Pause your cursor over the buttons and menus to see what decorative touches you can apply.

Selection handle   Text box   Insertion marker   I-beam cursor

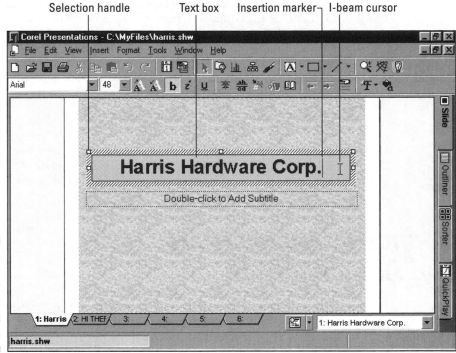

Figure 16-4:
Double-click a text box to enter or edit your text.

✔ If the characters you type fill up the text box, the box enlarges and text wraps to the next line. You can also press Enter to start a new line of text. After entering your text, click outside the text box to deselect it, or press Esc to deselect the text but leave the text box selected.

✔ Text boxes in which you don't enter text don't appear on your finished slide.

✔ To create an additional text area, click the arrow button (which is the Text Object Tool button) near the top of the window and choose one of the text tools from the resulting drop-down menu. As shown in Figure 16-5, your menu options are: the Text Area tool, which creates a regular text box; the Text Line tool, which creates a text box for a single line of text; the Bulleted List tool, which creates a text box formatted to hold a bulleted list; and the Text Art tool, which opens up the Text Art dialog box, where you can apply special effects to your text. (See Chapter 20, in the section "Twist and Stretch Your Words," for more information on this last option.)

After you choose a text tool, your cursor changes to a little hand, as noted in Figure 16-5. Drag with the Text Area or Bullet Chart tool to create your text box; just click with the Text Line tool to create a one-line text box.

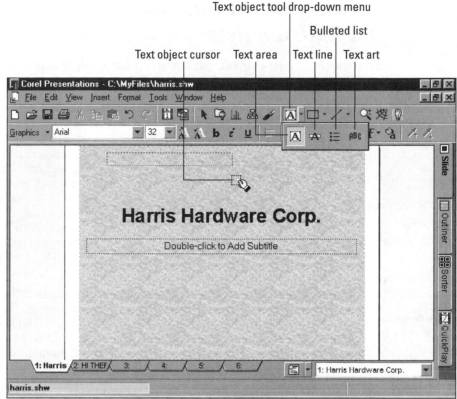

Figure 16-5:
Draw with
one of the
Text Object
tools to
create a
new text
box.

Notice that, after you select a Text Object tool, that tool appears on the Text Object Tool button face. To use the same tool again, click the button instead of the arrow.

✔ If you select a text tool and then change your mind about creating a text box, click the Selection tool (the one that looks like an arrow) to return to the regular arrow cursor.

To edit your text, just double-click the text box to make the insertion marker and I-beam reappear. You can then use most of the standard text-editing techniques you use to edit text in WordPerfect (see Chapter 6).

After you double-click the first text box to select it, you can press the down-arrow key (↓) to select and edit the text box below the first box. Press the up-arrow key (↑) to move up one text box.

That sums up the process for entering and editing text in regular text boxes. Entering and editing text in data charts, bulleted lists, and organization charts involves some special tricks, as I explain in the next section.

Creating and editing charts and bulleted lists

Certain slide layouts contain text boxes formatted for charts and bulleted lists (the Org chart layout contains organization chart text boxes, for example). But you can also create your own boxes for these elements. Here's what you need to know to create and edit your chart and bullet text:

✔ After you double-click a text box for a data chart, Presentations displays the Data Chart Gallery dialog box, where you select a chart type and layout. Presentations then creates a sample chart on your slide and displays a separate window containing a data sheet — which looks like a Quattro Pro spreadsheet — prefilled with sample data. You replace the sample data in the data sheet with your data. (Drag a corner of the data sheet window to enlarge it, if necessary.) If you don't want Presentations to display sample data, deselect the Use Sample Data check box in the Data Chart Gallery dialog box. Close the data sheet window after you finish entering data. Click outside the data chart to deselect it.

Along with the data sheet, Version 8 displays a little dialog box called Range Highlighter. The three drop-down color palettes enable you to change the background color of your row and column labels and data cells — but only inside the data sheet, not in your actual chart. The Range Highlighter is a mighty fine presentation of minimally helpful options. I say close the dialog box and unclutter your screen.

You can add a chart created in Quattro Pro to your Presentations slide. For information about bringing items created in one program into another program, see Chapter 19.

✔ To create a data chart text box, click the Data Chart button and then drag to draw the boundaries of the text box. After you release the mouse button, the Data Chart Gallery appears and you can proceed as just described.

✔ Need to change some data in your chart? Double-click the chart and choose View➪Datasheet. Presentations redisplays the data sheet window, where you can edit the data as needed.

✔ To enter text into an organization chart, double-click the text box. Then double-click a box in the chart to enter a person's name and title into the box. Click outside the box to deselect it. Click outside the organization chart to deselect the entire chart.

✔ If you don't like any of the chart styles created by the Org Chart template, create your chart this way instead: Choose Insert➪Organization Chart or click the Organization Chart button and then drag to create a text box. If you use either method, Presentations displays the Layout dialog box, in which you can choose a new chart style.

✔ To edit the contents of a box in the organization chart, double-click the chart and then double-click the box. Click outside the chart boundary after you're through promoting and demoting people.

✔ To enter text into a bulleted list text box, double-click the text box. A bullet appears for the first item in your list. Type the item and then press Enter to create a bullet for the second item in the list. If you want to put a second-level item underneath a bulleted item, press Tab. To change an item from a second-level item to a first-level item, click at the beginning of the line and press Shift+Tab; press Tab to change a first-level item to a second-level item. You can create as many levels of bulleted text as you want by pressing Tab to move to a lower level and Shift+Tab to move up a level.

✔ To create a new bulleted list text box, choose Insert⇨Bulleted List. Or select the Bulleted List tool from the Text Object tool menu (refer to Figure 16-5) and drag to create your text box.

Playing with colors, fonts, and other fun stuff

You can use various formatting commands to add artistic touches to your text, as shown in Figure 16-6. You can use these same techniques to format text in a Presentations drawing.

Before you can format text, you must select it. To apply the formatting to the entire text box, click the box once to display the square selection handles. To apply the formatting only to certain characters, double-click the text box and then drag across those characters.

Here are just some of the different ways to make your text stand out:

✔ If text is selected, the Property Bar displays all kinds of menus and buttons for jazzing up your text. But to get total control over formatting, choose Format⇨Font or press F9 to display the Font Properties dialog box. In this dialog box, you can not only choose text basics — font, type size, and type style — but also give your text a border, a colored or patterned fill, and add a shadow behind the text. Notice that you can't apply a shadow and some other effects to selected characters; you must format the entire text box. Also, you can't apply some effects (including shadows) to Title or Subtitle text boxes created by a slide layout; several effects are available only for text boxes you draw yourself using one of the Text Object tools. After you're done fooling around, click OK or press Enter.

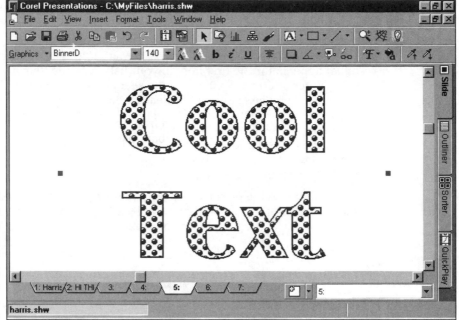

Figure 16-6:
You can
create all
kinds of
cool text
effects in
Presentations.

✔ Want to spin your text around? Click the text box to select it, click the arrow on the Rotate button and choose a rotation angle from the drop-down menu. (Or choose Rotate from the Graphics menu on the Property Bar.) If you choose Manual Rotation, little curved arrows appear around your text box. Drag on the arrows to rotate your text to any angle you please. Notice that you can rotate only text boxes that you create by using the Text Area and Text Line tools; evidently, the prefab text boxes that come with the Presentations layouts get queasy on the Rotator ride.

✔ See how the letters *x* and *t* are sort of bumping into each other in Figure 16-6? To fix this sort of unattractive character co-mingling, select the two letters you want to pry apart and choose Format⇨Manual Kerning. (*Kerning* is the technical name for shoving characters closer together or farther apart.) In the Manual Kern dialog box that appears, enter a positive value in the option box and click OK. If you need to spread the characters even farther apart, select them and press Ctrl+Shift+plus. Presentations kerns the characters by the amount specified in the Manual Kerning dialog box.

To kern characters closer together, enter a negative value in the Manual Kerning dialog box. Press Ctrl+– (hyphen) to mash the characters together even more after you leave the dialog box.

- ✔ If it looks like nothing is happening as you make changes to your text, zoom in for a closer look. Some effects aren't visible if you've zoomed out.

- ✔ You can adjust the alignment, line spacing, indents, and other formatting of your selected text by using the Property Bar buttons and commands on the Format menu.

- ✔ If you want to change the formatting of a bulleted list — including the character used for your bullets — click the list text box and choose the Bulleted List Properties command from the Format menu or click the corresponding button on the toolbar. Also see the section "Jazzing up your bulleted lists," later in this chapter.

If you want to format the nontext parts of the text box — for example, to change the thickness of the border around the text box or change the color of the boxes in an organization chart — click or double-click the element to display the square selection handles. Then use the myriad formatting tools on the Property Bar and toolbar or choose one of the commands on the Format menu. The formatting you apply depends on the type of text box or object that you select.

Adding Pretty Pictures

Nothing's as dull as a presentation that includes screen after screen of plain text. To liven up your show — and help keep audience snoring to a minimum — you can add clip art, photographic images, and even your own homemade artwork to your slides.

In addition to creating artwork inside your slide show, you can create stand-alone drawings in the Presentations drawing window. To create a drawing on its own page, choose File➪New and select Presentations Drawing from the New dialog box. You can access the same tools in either window, but the toolbars and Property Bars in the drawing window are set up to offer more convenient access to the drawing tools, as shown a few pages from now, in Figure 16-9.

All the techniques presented in this section are presented from the perspective of creating graphics inside a slide show, but they work similarly inside the drawing window. If you want to create a complex drawing, you may want to do so in the drawing window and then copy and paste the drawing onto your slide.

As I explain in "Saving Slide Shows and Drawings," later in this chapter, you can save a drawing that you create on a slide as a stand-alone drawing, if you want.

Using ready-made art

The WordPerfect Suite ships with scads of clip art. To add one of the clip art images to your slide, you use the new Scrapbook, as the following steps describe:

 1. Click the Scrapbook button or choose Insert⇨Graphics⇨Clip Art.

The Scrapbook appears, as shown in Figure 16-7. The Scrapbook has two tabs: The Clipart tab contains thumbnail views of the clip art that's installed after you install the WordPerfect suite. The CD Clipart tab contains the kazillion other graphics stored on the Suite CD-ROM.

Up One Level—

Figure 16-7:
The new Scrapbook enables you to drag and drop the Suite clip art onto a slide.

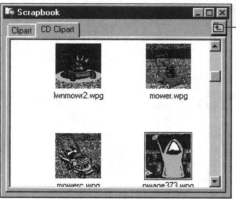

The Scrapbook is really an independent utility that lives in its own window. You can keep the Scrapbook open while you work and even after you shut down Presentations. The Minimize, Maximize, and Close buttons work as they do in any other program window. To resize the Scrapbook, drag one of its corners.

2. Find the image you want to use.

On the CD Clipart tab, double-click a folder to view the images in the folder. To go back to the previous level of folders, click the Up One Level button (refer to Figure 16-7).

3. Drag the image to your slide or drawing page.

Or right-click the image, choose Copy from the QuickMenu, place your cursor at the spot where you want to paste the image, right-click, and choose Paste from the QuickMenu.

The graphic appears on your slide, selected and ready to resize, move, or otherwise edit, as shown in Figure 16-8. (The four-headed arrow is the move cursor. Drag to move the graphic, as I discuss in the section "Moving, Deleting, Resizing, and Copying Stuff," later in this chapter.)

You're not limited to using the graphics in the Scrapbook, however. You can add graphics stored on disk or CD by choosing Insert⇨Graphics⇨From File. This command displays the Insert File dialog box, which looks and works just like the Open File dialog box that I discuss in Chapter 5. Make sure that you turn on the dialog box preview so that you can get a look at your graphics before you place them in your document. After you find the graphic you want, double-click it or click once and then click Insert.

Make sure that you change the File Type option to All Files or the specific file format for the graphic you want to use.

Move cursor   Selection handle

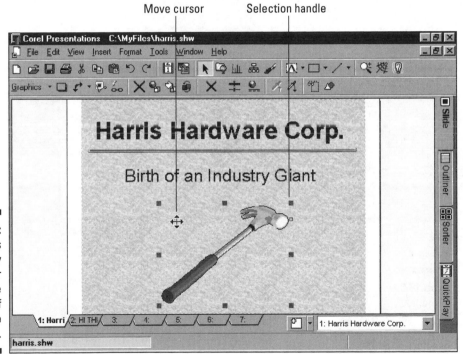

Figure 16-8:
Graphics
can really
hammer
home the
message of
your slide
(yuk, yuk).

Creating simple graphics

Presentations offers some tools that you can use to create basic drawings, such as the one shown in Figure 16-9. I'm not sure what that big white circular thing is, but I think it's a giant tennis ball descending on a spoiled tennis star who's shouting at a line judge.

To create a drawing on a slide, just select the drawing tool you want to use and sketch away. To create a new drawing in the drawing window, as in Figure 16-9, choose File⇨New to open the New dialog box and then select the Presentations Drawing option from the scrolling list.

The drawing tools, arranged on flyout menus and positioned along the left side of the drawing window in Version 7, now appear on two drop-down lists on the toolbar. One drop-down menu offers tools for creating closed shapes, such as circles, squares, and polygons. The other offers tools for drawing various kinds of lines.

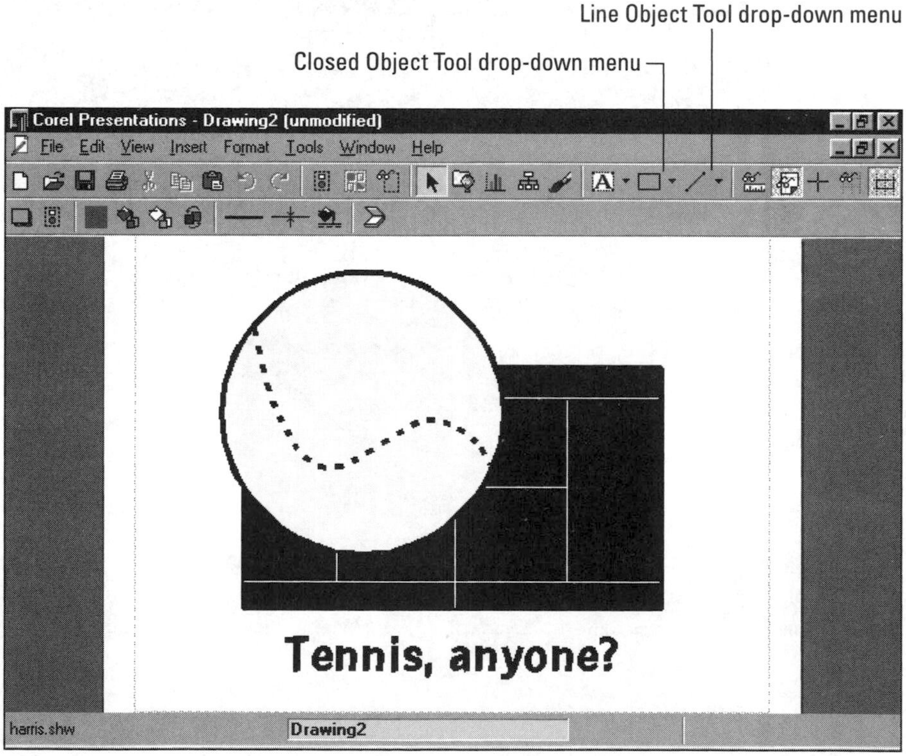

Line Object Tool drop-down menu

Closed Object Tool drop-down menu

Figure 16-9:
You, too, can create museum-quality art such as this in Presentations.

Tennis, anyone?

To display all the tools in a drop-down menu, click the down-pointing arrow on the button face. Click the tool that you want to use. That tool then appears on the button face. If you want to draw again with that tool, click the button face itself and not the arrow. Table 16-1 gives you more information on what each tool does and how you use it. For the most part, you click a tool and then drag to draw a line or shape.

If you're upgrading from Version 7, you may think, "Hey! What happened to the Line Attributes, Fill Attributes, Line Color, and Fill Colors buttons that were on the drawing toolbar?" (Or, if you're a person of fewer words, you're thinking "What the . . . ?") Anyway, in Version 8, the Property Bar displays buttons and drop-down lists that perform the functions of those buttons. The Property Bar controls change depending on what type of object or shape you select. Pause your cursor over the controls to see what options are available. For more information on changing the fill, line width, and other attributes of drawing objects, see the section "Editing graphics," later in this chapter.

Table 16-1	Presentations Drawing Tools	
Icon	*Tool*	*How You Use It*
Selection	↖	Click an object to select it; Shift+click to select a second object; drag around several objects to select them all.
Bitmap	🖌	Drag to create a bitmap image.
Rectangle	▢	Drag to create a rectangle. Shift+drag to create a square.
Rounded Rectangle	▢	Drag to draw a rectangle with rounded corners; Shift+drag to create a square with round corners.
Circle	○	Drag to draw a circle.
Ellipse	○	Drag to draw an ellipse; Shift+drag to draw a circle.
Polygon	◁	Drag to create the first segment in a polygon; click and drag again to start another segment. Double-click to end the shape.

(continued)

Table 16-1 *(continued)*

Icon	Tool	How You Use It
Closed Curve		Drag to create the first segment of the curved shape; release the mouse button and drag again to start another segment. Double-click to end the shape.
Arrow		Click to position the head of the arrow and then click to set the end of the arrow. To create a curved arrow, drag to start the arrow, release the mouse button, move the mouse to shape the arrow, and click to end the shape.
Regular Polygon		Draws a polygon with sides that are all the same length. Click the tool, set the number of sides in the Regular Polygon dialog box that appears, and drag to create the shape.
Line		Drag to create a straight line. Shift+drag to draw a perfectly vertical, horizontal, or diagonal line.
Curved Line		Drag to create the first segment in a curved line, release the mouse button to set the curve, and drag to create the next segment. Double-click to end the line.
Elliptical Arc		Drag to create an elliptical arc (section of an ellipse); Shift+drag to create a circular arc.
Freehand		Drag to create a freehand line.
Polygon Line		Drag to create a line that has several angles. Drag to create the first segment, release the mouse button, and drag to start the second segment. Double-click to end the line.

Icon	Tool	How You Use It
Bezier Curve		Drag to create a line by using Bezier curve theory. (If you don't know what that means, stay away from this tool.)
Circular Arc		Drag to set the size of the arc, release the mouse button, move the cursor to shape the arc, and click.

Working with bitmap images

The main Presentations drawing tools create *vector drawings,* which are graphics that the computer creates by using mathematical formulas to generate lines, arcs, and other shapes. Presentations also offers some tools that enable you to create and edit *bitmap images,* which are composed of tiny squares called *pixels* that work sort of like tiles in a mosaic. Scanned photographs and graphics created in a painting program such as Corel Photo-Paint or Corel Photo House are bitmap images.

Creating and editing bitmap images requires some expertise and experience, however. And if you have that kind of knowledge, you probably also have full-fledged image editing software — in which case, you're better off doing your bitmap work in that program. The Presentations bitmap editing tools are okay for small repairs to images, but you don't get the kind of sophisticated controls offered by a program such as Photo-Paint or Adobe Photoshop.

To insert an existing bitmap image onto your slide, use Insert➪Graphics➪ From File, as I explain in "Using ready-made art" earlier in this chapter. Double-click the image to edit it in the Bitmap Editor window, which contains tools specifically for painting and editing bitmap images. (See Chap-ter 20, in the section "Play with Special Effects in Photo House and Presentations," for a look at one of these tools in action.) To create a bitmap image from scratch, choose Insert➪Bitmap or click the Bitmap tool on the Property Bar. Drag the cursor to create a frame for the graphic. Presentations takes you to the Bitmap Editor, where you can use the paint tools to create your image.

After you're done fooling around, choose File➪Close Bitmap Editor to put your bitmap image on your slide or drawing page. Or choose File➪Cancel Bitmap to close the Bitmap Editor without adding your image to the slide or drawing.

Editing graphics

Before you edit a graphic, first determine whether it's a bitmap image or a vector drawing. The distinction is important because the two types of graphics have different editing rules. To find out whether you're staring at a bitmap image, double-click the graphic. If the graphic is a bitmap, the Bitmap Editor window opens, full of tools for playing with the graphic. You can read more about bitmaps in the preceding section.

If you double-click the graphic and you aren't whisked away to the Bitmap Editing window, you're working with a vector drawing, and the following editing techniques apply:

- ✔ To change a drawing's fill, border, pattern, and other characteristics, click it to select it and then click the Object Properties button on the Property Bar. Or choose one of the commands from the Format⇨Object Properties submenu. Presentations displays the Object Properties dialog box, which is full of options related to the graphic.

- ✔ To edit an individual element in a drawing, double-click the graphic to select it. Then click the element you want to edit. Any drawing commands or tools you use then affect only the selected element.

- ✔ You can stack shapes, lines, and other objects on top of each other to create a lovely country scene or some other work of art, such as the masterful tennis scene in Figure 16-9. To shuffle the order of the objects in the stack, select the object you want to move and then use one of the first four commands on the Graphics menu at the left end of the Property Bar.

- ✔ Many of the clip-art images provided with the WordPerfect Suite are actually comprised of dozens of small shapes and lines. In this case, you don't need to double-click to edit an individual element of the graphic. Just click to select it.

- ✔ If you want to meld all the individual pieces of a clip-art graphic or drawing together, drag with the Selection tool around the whole shebang. Then choose the Group command from the Graphics menu on the Property Bar. Presentations now treats all the bits and pieces of the drawing as a single entity. You can move, copy, and resize your graphic without fear of mucking up the image.

  Even though a graphic is grouped, you can still edit the individual elements. Double-click the graphic and then click the component you want to edit. To separate a grouped graphic into its individual elements again, choose the Separate Objects command from the Graphics menu.

Moving, Deleting, Resizing, and Copying Stuff

Want to move that tennis ball drawing to the top of your slide? Enlarge a text box so that it fills the entire screen? Copy a fabulous bulleted list from one slide show to the other? You're in luck: Moving, deleting, resizing, and copying things in your drawing or slide show is painless in Presentations — well, at least as painless as you can expect if you're working on a computer. Here's the skinny:

✔ To move a text box or graphic, click it to select it and then drag it to a new position. The four-headed arrow cursor is your cue that the object is ready to move.

✔ To resize a graphic, select it and then drag one of its selection handles. To maintain the original proportions of the graphic or text as you resize, drag a corner handle.

✔ Drag a side handle of a text box to alter the margin between the text and the sides of the text box. Drag a corner handle to resize the text box and text together.

✔ Don't enlarge or reduce a bitmap image by more than 10 or 15 percent. The image becomes all blurry and yucky.

✔ To delete a text block or graphic, select it and press Delete. To delete the text inside a text block but leave the text block intact, select the individual characters inside the block and press Delete.

✔ To undo your last action, press Ctrl+Z or choose Edit⇨Undo.

✔ You can copy a graphic or text block by selecting it and choosing Edit⇨Copy or by pressing Ctrl+C. Click the spot where you want to put the copy and choose Edit⇨Paste or press Ctrl+V. To delete the graphic or text block from one spot and paste it in another spot, choose Edit⇨Cut (Ctrl+X) instead of the Copy command.

✔ As in WordPerfect and Quattro Pro, you can copy and move stuff from one slide show or drawing to another by using the Application Bar. To move an item, select it and drag it to the Application Bar button for the destination document (the one into which you want to place the copy). After the destination document appears on-screen, drag the item into place and release the mouse button. To copy something instead of move it, press Ctrl at any time before you release the mouse button.

✔ Before you move, resize, or copy a clip-art graphic or a drawing composed of many objects, group all the components by using the technique that I describe in the preceding section.

Adding Transitions and Other Special Effects

Back in the days before interactive multimedia, people didn't expect a whole lot from a presentation. But if you want to captivate an audience today, you need to add a little sizzle to your show. This section explains how to add transitions, sound clips, and other effects that create the kind of pizzazz that makes a presentation memorable.

Be careful not to overload your show with too many effects — you want to enhance the messages on your slides, not detract from them.

Choosing a transition

A *transition* determines what the viewer sees as you switch from one slide to the next. You can have the two slides dissolve seamlessly into each other so that the viewer hardly notices the transition, or you can use a more dramatic effect.

You apply a transition to each slide in your show. You can choose a different transition effect for each slide or apply the same transition throughout all slides. To apply a transition to a single slide, click the slide's tab to select the slide. Then choose a transition from the drop-down list on the Property Bar, as shown in Figure 16-10. As you move your cursor over the different effects, Presentations gives you a preview of the effect in a small box next to the drop-down list, also shown in Figure 16-10.

You can change the direction and speed of the transition by using the two buttons to the right of the drop-down list. The first button, the Direction button, displays a drop-down list of four direction options — left to right, top to bottom, and so on. (If you don't see the button, the selected transition doesn't come with a choice of directions.)

The second button, the Speed button, displays a drop-down list of three speeds: Fast, represented by a rabbit icon; Medium, represented by a walking man; and Slow, represented by a turtle. (These icons get my vote for the most entertaining ones in the entire WordPerfect Suite. I only wonder who came up with "man walking" to represent medium.)

To apply the same transition to several slides at the same time, switch to Sorter view (by clicking the Sorter tab). Click the first slide you want to select, Ctrl+click the others, and then choose your transition options.

Transition drop-down menu

Direction

Speed

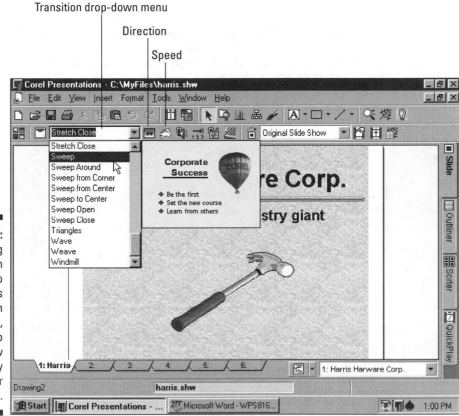

Figure 16-10:
Adding
transition
effects to
slides is
easier in
Version 8,
thanks to
new
Property
Bar
controls.

If you want to apply the same transition to all slides in your show, the
quickest route is to choose Format⇨Slide Properties⇨Transition to open the
Slide Properties dialog box. (You can also click the Properties button on the
toolbar and then click the Transition tab of the dialog box.) Choose your
transition options, check the Apply to All Slides in Slide Show option box,
and click OK.

The Skip Slide option, contrary to what you may expect, doesn't really have
anything to do with transitions. This option tells Presentations to skip the
slide altogether when you play your show.

Choosing an advance mode

You can choose whether each slide advances on its own after a specified
period of time or advances only after you click the mouse button or press
the spacebar. As with transitions, you can apply an advance mode to
selected slides only or to all slides in your show.

To get to the advance options, choose Format⇨Slide Properties⇨Display Sequence or click the Display Sequence button on the Property Bar. The Display Sequence tab of the Slide Properties dialog box comes to life, as shown in Figure 16-11. To set the advance for a specific slide, select the slide by clicking the right- or left-pointing arrows at the bottom of the dialog box or by using the neighboring drop-down list.

 If you want to apply the same advance option to several slides in your show, switch to Sorter view and select the slides (by clicking and Ctrl+clicking) before heading to the Display Sequence tab. You can apply the same advance option throughout your show by selecting the Apply to All Slides in Slide Show check box.

If you want to advance the slides via a mouse click or by pressing the spacebar, select the Manually radio button. (This option is the default setting.) If you want the slides to advance automatically, select the After a Delay radio button and set in the adjacent option box the amount of time that you want each slide to appear.

You can also control how animated objects and bulleted list items appear. (See the section "Animating an object," later in this chapter.) If you choose the manual option for display of bulleted lists, you need to click or press the spacebar during the slide show playback to display each item in a bulleted list.

Figure 16-11:
You can control whether your slides advance automatically or on your signal.

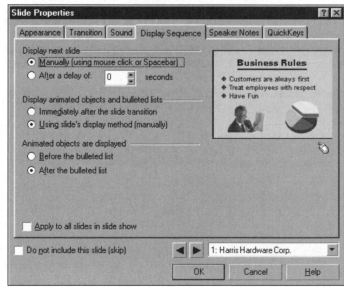

Adding sounds

Remember the days of filmstrips? (Come on, I'm not that much older than you!) Anyway, a little bell inside the projector dinged to signal the teacher that it was time to advance the filmstrip to the next frame. Presentations enables you to add a similar sound effect between your slides — only these sounds are much cooler than your average filmstrip-projector ding. You can even have a music clip play through your entire show. (All depending, of course, on whether the computer you're using to play the show has a sound card that can play the sound files you use.)

 To add a sound to a slide, choose Insert⇨Sound or click the Sound button on the Property Bar. The now-famous Slide Properties dialog box opens with the Sound tab selected, as shown in Figure 16-12. Use the arrows or drop-down list at the bottom of the dialog box to select which slide gets the sound effect. The sound plays whenever the selected slide appears on-screen during playback.

 As you can do with transitions and advance modes, you can apply the same sound to several slides by selecting them in Sorter view before opening the dialog box. To play the same sound to all slides in the show, check the Big Blue Aliens Land in Vegas check box. Whoops, no, that's not right, my *National Enquirer* distracted me for a moment. The check box you want is Apply to All Slides in Slide Show.

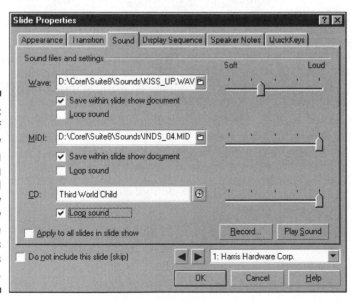

Figure 16-12: Kicking off my show with a big kissing sound followed by a Johnny Clegg tune really gets people's attention.

Among the types of sounds that you can add to your slides are WAV and MIDI files. For your amusement, WordPerfect Suite 8 provides some WAV and MIDI sound files; select the Wave or MIDI option and then click the little white file folder at the end of the neighboring option box to locate the files. The sound clips are stored on the CD in the Corel\Suite 8\Sounds folder. (I'm personally quite taken with KISS_UP.WAV, which makes a smooching sound similar to the ones that corporate managers often make while discussing important issues with their vice presidents.)

If you insert a Wave or MIDI sound file, the dialog box changes to offer two related check boxes. One enables you to specify whether you want to save the sound as part of the slide show file. If you don't select this option, make sure that you take the disk or CD that contains the sound whenever you play your slide show on another computer. And make sure that you change the file location in the Slide Properties dialog box so that Presentations knows where to find the sound clip. The other check box controls whether the sound *loops* — that is, continues or repeats until Presentations encounters a slide that has a different sound attached.

If you can't get a CD sound file to play when you run your show, make sure that you don't have another CD player open (for example, the Windows CD Player utility). Having another CD program running can mess with Presentation's mind.

You can set the volume for your sounds in the dialog box. But in Version 8, you can also control the volume during the slide show playback by pressing the plus key (louder) or minus key (softer) on the numeric keypad.

In Figure 16-12, I assigned three sounds to the same slide so that I could show you the controls for each type of sound. In reality, you probably don't want to double up on sounds as I do here. Although, I must admit that playing a slide show with a track from my favorite Johnny Clegg CD entertained me for a good hour, if not more. (*Major note:* Recording artists expect to protect their originality through minor details called copyrights. If your thoughts wander to setting your presentation to the words or music of a commercial CD, make sure that you ask for written permission. Otherwise, you risk being tagged with a heavy copyright infringement lawsuit.)

To remove a sound clip from a slide, double-click the option box for the sound and press Delete.

Animating an object

Okay, here's a cool effect you simply must try, if only to enjoy a laugh on a rainy day. You can bring a graphic or text box to life. To try the animation effect, click a graphic to select it. Then choose Format⇨Object Properties⇨Animation or click the Object Animation button to display the dialog box shown in Figure 16-13. (By the way, you can animate only text boxes that you draw by using the Text Area or Text Line tool.)

Version 8 gives you two animation options: You can animate an object in place, which really means that the object is hidden after the slide first appears and then is revealed bit by bit according to the pattern you choose. Or you can make an object bounce or fly across the screen. After choosing the radio button for the option you want, click an effect in the Effects list to see a preview inside the dialog box. Other options enable you to adjust the direction and speed of the animation. Click OK to apply the animation to the object.

If you assign animation effects to more than one object on a slide, you can specify which one moves first by using the Object Display Sequence option box. Assign number 1 to the object you want to move first, number 2 to the second object, and so on. Click OK or press Enter after you're done.

Figure 16-13:
You can
make
graphics
and text
boxes fly
across the
screen by
applying an
animation
effect in
this dialog
box.

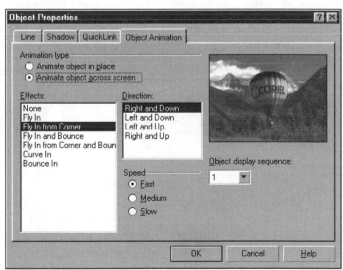

Jazzing up bulleted lists

 One more fun effect before we get back to serious business: You can add special effects to bulleted lists on your slides. Click the text box that holds your bulleted list and click the Bulleted List Properties button or choose Format⇨Bulleted List Properties. Click the Bullet Animation tab to display the panel shown in Figure 16-14.

 As you can do with graphic objects, you can animate a bulleted list in place, so that the bullet items fade into view, one by one. Or you can make the list items bounce or fly across the screen. Play around with the different options until you find a combination that strikes your fancy; the Sample box shows you a preview of the effect as you select different options.

These effects are available only for bulleted lists created by applying the bulleted list layout, though. You can't animate the individual items in a list created using the Bulleted List tool. For those lists, you can only animate those lists as a whole, as if they were graphics. (You get the same animation options shown in Figure 16-13.)

While you're in the Bulleted List Properties dialog box, you can change the color and shape of the bullets (by going to the Bullets tab), adjust the spacing between list items (on the Spacing tab), and change the font, border, and other aspects of the list's appearance. Click OK to apply your changes.

Figure 16-14:
If you really want to get fancy, add animation effects to your bulleted lists via this dialog box.

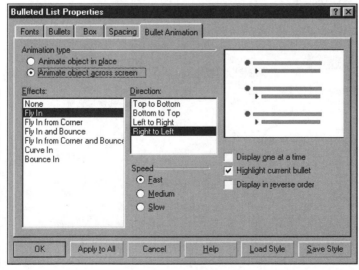

Playing Your Show

Ready to view the results of your creative genius? Version 8 gives you a multitude of ways to fire up your slide show, as the following list describes:

- ✔ Click the QuickPlay tab to play your slide show from the current slide forward.

- ✔ Click the Play Show button on the toolbar to play your entire slide show, starting with slide 1.

- ✔ Click the Play Slide Show button on the Property Bar or choose View➪Play Slide Show to set up playback options for your show before you play it. The Play Slide Show dialog box appears, as shown in Figure 16-15.

Figure 16-15:
The Play Slide Show dialog box is where you set playback options for your show.

- ✔ Use the Beginning Slide drop-down list to indicate where you want the show to begin — at the first slide, second slide, or some other slide. If you want the show to repeat continuously, select the Repeat Slide Show check box.

- ✔ The Highlighter enables you to draw on-screen as the show plays by using the mouse — sort of like how TV sports commentators draw little Xs and Os over slow-motion replays. You set the color and width of the highlighter pen by using the controls at the bottom of the Play Slide Show dialog box.

- ✔ The Create QuickShow option creates a version of your show that advances the slides faster than usual — which you may want to do while checking out how a certain editing choice works, for example. QuickShow files are very large, however, and take up much more of your computer's resources than does a regular file. To play the QuickShow version, select the Use QuickShow option.

Click Play to set your show in motion.

No matter what option you pick to play your show, your computer screen turns black for a few seconds and then your show begins. If you're using the manual advance option (as I explain in the section "Choosing an advance mode," earlier in this chapter), click the left mouse button or press the spacebar to advance to the next slide or animation effect. Right-click or press PgUp to go back one slide. Press the plus key on the numeric keypad to increase sound volume; press minus to lower the volume.

Drag with the mouse to use the highlighter. Using the highlighter temporarily halts the show; click or press the spacebar to advance the show.

To bail out and stop the show at any point, press Esc. You return to the Presentations window after you stop the show or it finishes playing.

Creating custom versions of your show

Suppose that you're a marketing manager in a pharmaceutical company, and you're creating a presentation to promote your company's latest miracle drug. You're going to show the presentation to two distinct audiences: a group of would-be investors and a group of doctors. You want to present a bunch of technical data to the physician crowd, but you know that stuff would make the investor group fall asleep faster than you can say, "Goodbye, investment capital."

Happily, Version 8 offers an easy way to create customized versions of your show. You can create one version that includes those deadly boring technical slides and one that skips right to the fun stuff.

Here's how to go about the process of creating a customized version that skips selected slides:

1. **Open the slide show that you want to use as the basis for your custom show.**

2. **Choose Tools**⇨**Custom Audiences or choose Custom Audiences from the drop-down list at the right end of the Property Bar.**

   The Custom Audiences dialog box appears, as shown in Figure 16-16.

3. **Click New and give your custom show a nice name.**

   After you click New, a Copy of Original Presentation item appears in the Names list. Click inside the box and give the presentation a more meaningful name, as I did in the figure.

4. **Click OK and click the Sorter tab.**

Figure 16-16:
The new
Custom
Audiences
feature
enables you
to create
different
versions of
your show
for different
audiences.

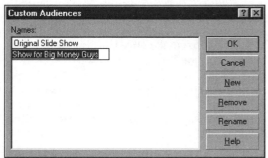

5. Select the slides that you want to skip.

Click the first slide and Ctrl+click the others.

6. Click the Skip Slide button.

The selected slides are dimmed on-screen to indicate that they don't appear if you play this version of the show.

To play the customized version of the show, just choose its name from the Audience drop-down list in the Play Slide Show dialog box (which I discuss in the preceding section).

Any changes you make to either your original slide show or your customized version appear in *both* versions of the show. You see, you're really just creating a separate playback list, not two separate, free-standing shows.

If you want to create two independent shows, use File➪Save As to save a copy of the original show under a new name, as I explain in the section "Saving Slide Shows and Drawings," later in this chapter. You can then edit either the copy or original without affecting the other.

Playing your show on someone else's computer

Playing your slide show on your own computer is fine and dandy, but chances are that you won't want to lug your system with you whenever you need to show a presentation. That's why Presentations offers an option that makes your show portable.

You can save your show to a floppy disk or other portable storage device (such as a Zip drive) as a *Runtime file*. A Runtime file contains the show files plus the Presentations program files needed to play the show. You can then play the show on any computer that uses Windows — without needing to install Presentations. (You need to make sure that the computer can accept your type of floppy disk or storage device, of course.)

To create a Runtime file, follow these steps:

1. **Open your show and choose File⇨Show on the Go or click the Show on the Go button.**

   The Show on the Go dialog box appears, as shown in Figure 16-17. Presentations tells you where the file is saved, what name the show is saved under, and what display options are in force. Most likely, none of these specifications are what you want, but if they are, skip to Step 3.

2. **Click Change.**

   Presentations displays a Wizardlike dialog box that contains several panels for setting your file options, which I explain in the following list. Click Next to work your way through the panels, and click Finish after you're done.

3. **Click Create.**

   Presentations saves your show as a Runtime file and compresses the file so that it takes up less space on disk.

Figure 16-17:
With Show on the Go, you can save a copy of your show that you can play on any Windows computer.

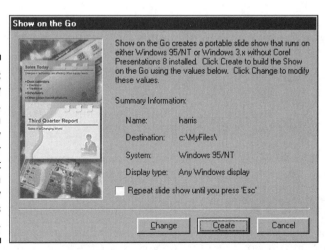

Not sure which of the cryptic options in the Show on the Go dialog box to choose? Here's a simplified look at your choices:

✔ You can save your file to another location on your computer's hard drive; to a floppy drive (Drive A or B); or as an e-mail attachment.

If you choose the e-mail option, Presentations asks you to select the e-mail program you want to use. After you click Create, Presentations opens up your e-mail program and presents you with a new message that includes the show as a file attachment.

✔ If the computer that you're using to view the show uses Windows 95 or Windows NT, select the Windows 95/NT radio button. If you choose the Windows 3.*x* and Windows 95/NT radio button, you can play the show on computers that use Windows 3.*x* (3.1, 3.11, and so on), but some special transitions and animation effects, however, won't work.

✔ If you select the Any Windows Display button, the show plays on any computer capable of displaying 256 colors at a 640 x 480 resolution (which includes most computers running Windows today). If you select the other display option, the Runtime show uses the display settings that are in force on your monitor only. This restriction can cause display problems if the computer that you play the show on doesn't use the same monitor settings.

To play your slide show in Windows 95, click the Start button and choose Run from the Start menu. Type the name of the drive and the name of the Runtime file. (Runtime files have the file extension EXE.) To play a show named WOWTHEM.EXE, for example, type **A:\Wowthem.exe**. Press Enter or click OK.

After you save a Runtime file, don't rename it. If you do, the Runtime program files don't work correctly. Also, be aware that video and sound drivers (the files that run the computer's sound card and video card) aren't copied with the Runtime file. The computer you use to play the show must have a sound card that's capable of playing the type of sound files used in your show, and the video display depends on the computer's video capabilities.

Remember, too, that if your show includes sound from a music or audio CD, you need to have the CD in the computer's CD-ROM drive. Ditto for any other sound files that you didn't save with the show, as I discuss in the section "Adding sounds," earlier in this chapter.

Saving Slide Shows and Drawings

Saving a drawing or slide show in Presentations is the same as saving a file in WordPerfect or Quattro Pro. For detailed information, see Chapter 5, in the section "Saving Your Work (and Your Sanity)." But here's a brief reminder of the process: Choose File⇨Save or press Ctrl+S to open the Save dialog box. Enter a name for your work in the File Name option box and specify where you want the file to be saved (drive and folder). Click OK or press Enter to save the file.

Presentations assigns the file extension SHW to slide shows and WPG to drawings (WPG is the WordPerfect graphics format). After you save a file for the first time, just press Ctrl+S or choose File⇨Save to resave it without opening the Save dialog box. To save the file under a different name or in a different location, choose File⇨Save As or press F3.

You can save a single slide as an independent drawing in the WPG format. Simply select the slide, choose File⇨Save As, give the drawing a name, and select the WordPerfect 7/8 Graphics format from the File Type drop-down list.

Printing Your Masterpieces

To print your drawing or slide show, choose File⇨Print, press Ctrl+P, or click the Print button on the toolbar. The Print dialog box appears, as shown in Figure 16-18. You can print handouts that have a specified number of slides printed on each page, print each slide on its own page, or select from a variety of other printing options. The Print Details tab of the dialog box offers more printing choices, including one that enables you to print the slide number on each page.

Unless you have a color printer, select the Adjust Image to Print Black and White check box on the Details tab. Presentations automatically adjusts the colors in your slides and drawings to appropriate shades of gray. However, if graphics print too light, try turning the check box off. Some graphics may print better without being converted to black and white.

If you have a film recorder hooked up to your computer, you can print your show as 35mm slides by selecting the film recorder from the Current Printer drop-down list. If not, you can save your show to disk and take it to a service bureau for conversion to 35mm slides. Make sure that you ask the service bureau what format you should use in saving the show to disk.

To change the margins, page size, and page orientation, choose File⇨Page Setup. To get a preview of how your pages are going to look after you print them, click the Print Preview button inside the Print dialog box.

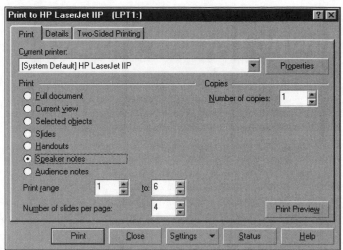

Figure 16-18:
The Print
dialog box
lets you
print your
slide shows
and draw-
ings in a
number
of ways.

Chapter 17

Internet Adventures

• •

In This Chapter

▶ Getting acquainted with Netscape Navigator

▶ Exploring the World Wide Web

▶ Marking your favorite Web pages so that you can find them again

▶ Sending e-mail over the Internet

▶ Participating in newsgroups

▶ Printing and saving pages and messages

• •

Not too long ago, Netscape Communications sent Wall Street into a tizzy with the initial public offering of its stock, which soared to unbeliev-able heights minutes after its debut. The enthusiasm for Netscape seems to have been well-founded. On the strength of its Navigator Web browser and companion products, the company is now a leader in the battle for Internet software dominance, holding its own against all comers, even Mighty Microsoft.

If you were lucky enough to grab some Netscape shares at a decent price, I'd like to congratulate you (and get the name of your broker, please). If not, well, at least you can take some satisfaction in owning Netscape Navigator, which is included in the WordPerfect Suite. Okay, I know that's a lame substitute for making a killing on Wall Street. But the software undoubtedly is going to entertain and inform you long after the market bulls move on to some other hot stock.

This chapter shows you how to explore the Internet and World Wide Web by using Netscape Navigator — which, by the way, is commonly referred to as simply Netscape. You find out how to move between pages, send e-mail, post messages to newsgroups, and do all those other things you hear everyone talking about these days.

If you want to know more about the Internet and Netscape — and there's much more to explore than I can cover in this book, check out *Netscape and the World Wide Web For Dummies*, 2nd Edition, by Paul Hoffman (published by IDG Books Worldwide, Inc.). And if you're itching to create your own Web pages, keep an eye out for *WordPerfect Suite 8 Web Publishing For Dummies,* by David Kay, soon to be published by IDG Books. The WordPerfect Suite contains many tools for creating and editing Web pages, and Kay's book does a good job of helping you take advantage of those tools.

A Crash Course in Internet Lingo

As with most things related to computers, the Internet has its own vocabulary. Here are just a few basic terms to make your Internet exploration easier (and help you avoid sounding like a rube at parties):

- ✔ The *Internet* — also called the *Net* — is nothing more than a big group of computers located all around the world and tied together via modems and other communication devices. The Internet is not unlike the computer network you may have in your office, except that it's much bigger and offers you access to cooler stuff. On the Internet, you can find information about every topic under the sun, buy products from local and international vendors, carry on conversations with other computer users, and send and receive electronic mail.

- ✔ Individuals and corporations who want to distribute information, products, and services create and maintain Internet *sites*. Computer users around the world can "visit" those sites by *logging in* (connecting via a modem) to the Internet.

- ✔ The *World Wide Web* is only one part — albeit the flashiest part — of the Internet. If you visit many sites on the Internet, all you see are *pages* (screens) full of plain-looking text. Web sites, on the other hand, incorporate stylish text formatting, full-color graphics, and sometimes even sound and video clips.

- ✔ Web pages also contain *hypertext links*. A hypertext link is a graphic, button, or piece of text that you click to move from one Web page to another page that offers related information.

- ✔ A Web *browser* is a software program designed for finding and accessing information on the World Wide Web. Netscape Navigator is a Web browser. Netscape not only enables you to find and view Web pages, but also provides access to other Internet services, such as e-mail and newsgroups.

- ✔ A *newsgroup* is a group of people who carry on conversations with each other by sending messages back and forth through an Internet service called Usenet. Different newsgroups focus on different topics. When people send messages to a newsgroup, they say that they're *posting* an article or *posting news.*

✔ HTML is short for *HyperText Markup Language*. This language is the most popular language for creating Web pages.

✔ URL stands for *Uniform Resource Locator*. A URL is, in essence, an address on the Web.

✔ ISP is short for *Internet Service Provider*. An ISP is sort of like the phone company — a middleman you need to go through to connect to all those other computers on the Internet. Of course, the middleman's service isn't free; typically, $19.95 a month buys you unlimited *connect time* (the time you spend connected to the Internet by modem).

Leaping onto the Net

Before you can access the Internet by using Netscape or any other browser, you must sign up with an Internet Service Provider (and have a modem, of course). You also need to establish some settings in Netscape so that your modem can communicate with the service provider's computers. Your service provider should help you do this setup work.

After you get set up with an Internet service provider, you can start Netscape by double-clicking the shortcut icon on your desktop. (It's placed there as you install the software.) Or choose Start⇨Programs⇨Netscape Navigator 3.012⇨Netscape Navigator. You can also click the Internet toolbar button in WordPerfect, Presentations, and Quattro Pro. Depending on how your system is configured, you may need to connect to the Internet through your service provider's software before you start Netscape.

After you first connect to the Internet, you see a window looking something like the one shown in Figure 17-1. By default, the browser is set up to automatically load the Netscape Web site's home page (a *home page* is the first page you see after you visit a Web site). You can change the initial home page by choosing Options⇨General Preferences, clicking the Appearance tab of the Preferences dialog box, and entering a new URL (page address) in the Browser Starts With option box.

The following list gives you the blow-by-blow of the different components of the browser window:

✔ The status bar gives you information about the status of data being transferred to your computer. This area also displays the address of the page you jump to if you click a particular hypertext link.

✔ The little envelope in the bottom-right corner of the screen is the Mail icon. You can click this icon to get to Netscape's e-mail features, as I explain in the section "Sending Electronic Mail on the Internet," later in this chapter.

Directory buttons   Location box

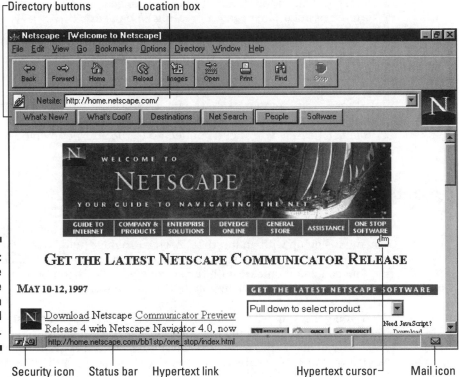

Figure 17-1:
The
Netscape
program
window and
home page.

Security icon   Status bar   Hypertext link   Hypertext cursor   Mail icon

✔ If you pass your cursor over a hypertext link — which could come in the form of a button, graphic, or colored, underlined text — the cursor changes into a little hand with its button-pushing finger extended, as Figure 17-1 shows. Click to jump to the linked information.

✔ The security icon tells you whether you're looking at a *secure document*. Many vendors who sell stuff on the Internet build security precautions into their pages to make sure that cyberthieves can't get their hands on your credit card number or other confidential information. A broken-door key on a gray background, such as the one in the figure, indicates a nonsecure page. A complete key on a blue background tells you that the page is secure. (But keep in mind that even secure pages are sometimes broken into, just like homes with the best security systems.)

✔ The location box at the top of the window shows you the address of the current page. If you know the address of a site you want to visit, type the address in the box and press Enter to move to that site. (See the following section, "Becoming a Page Jumper," for more information on traveling to various Internet sites.)

✔ The row of buttons beneath the location box are the Directory buttons. Each button takes you to another Web page or spot on the Internet.

✔ As do other program windows, the Netscape window offers a menu bar, a toolbar, Close button, Minimize and Maximize/Restore buttons, and a scroll bar. For more information about these window features, see Chapter 2.

You can turn some window elements on and off by clicking them in the Options menu. You may want to turn off the toolbar and Directory buttons at times, for example, so that you can display more of a Web page on the screen at one time.

The various Preferences commands on the Options menu enable you to control many other aspects of Netscape. You can change the font used to display your e-mail messages, for example, and instruct Netscape to launch the mail window along with the main browser window after you start the program. The only options you don't want to fool with are those related to your Internet Service Provider connection. If you don't know what an option means or does, leave it alone or consult your ISP tech support line first.

Becoming a Page Jumper

To view the contents of a Web page, you simply use the scroll bar on the right side of the Netscape window to scroll the page. Most pages contain one or more hypertext links that you click to jump to pages that contain related information. Hypertext links can be indicated by colored, underlined text, buttons, icons, or other special formatting. You know that you've found a link if your cursor changes into the little pointing finger, as shown back in Figure 17-1.

✔ As you jump from link to link, Netscape remembers the addresses of the last several pages you viewed. So if you want to return to the previous page, click the Back button. To go forward a page, click the Forward button.

✔ To go backward or forward several pages, choose the page location from the bottom of the Go menu. Or click the down-pointing arrow at the end of the location box, which displays a list of sites you recently visited. Click a site to jump there.

✔ Clicking the Home button or choosing Go⇨Home takes you to the Netscape home page.

✔ Some pages, such as the one shown in Figure 17-2, have frames, which are like pages within pages. Clicking a link within a frame may jump you to an entirely new page or simply display a new page inside the frame. You can sometimes resize a frame by dragging its border.

Of course, you don't always want to follow a trail of links to travel from one page to another. If you know the URL (address) of the site you want to visit, you can just type it into the Location option box and press Enter.

The information on some Web pages gets updated frequently (on pages offering current stock market quotes, for example). Some pages don't update automatically after you download them, however. To reload the page so that you can view the most current version of the page, choose View⇨Reload, press Ctrl+R, or click the Reload button on the toolbar.

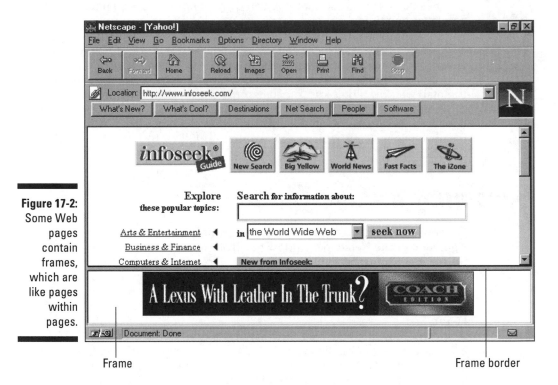

Figure 17-2:
Some Web pages contain frames, which are like pages within pages.

Frame

Frame border

Finding Sites That Interest You

The Web is jam-packed with information to read, products to buy, files to download, and services to use. So many Web sites exist, in fact, that finding the ones that interest you is perhaps the biggest challenge of the Internet. Much of the stuff on the Web is junk — either low-grade content or slimy advertising that tricks you into visiting a site by promising something more than what's really there.

Netscape offers several tools to help you find the good Web sites and bypass the not-so-good:

- ✔ The Net Search, Destinations, and People buttons take you to pages offering links to *search engines* and directories — tools for finding Web sites that deal with a particular topic or tracking down the e-mail addresses of individuals and companies. Figure 17-2 shows you the home page for one popular search engine. You can also access the search engines and directories by choosing the corresponding commands on the Directory menu.

- ✔ Different search tools search different areas of the Internet; some search only for text pages, some search only the Web, and so on. Although each search tool works a little differently, you usually type the topic you want to find in an option box and then click a Search button. You next see a display of links to sites matching your search request. Often, the sites are described briefly and rated in terms of the type and quality of content they offer. To go to the site, just click the link.

- ✔ Directories display links and site information by category. You can click the Arts & Entertainment hypertext link shown in Figure 17-2, for example, to display a list of arts-related sites.

- ✔ Click the What's Cool and What's New buttons to jump to lists of pages recommended by the folks at Netscape.

- ✔ If you find a site that you like and think you may want to visit again, choose Bookmarks➪Add Bookmark or press Ctrl+D. Netscape adds the site or page name to the Bookmarks menu. You then can jump to the page by choosing its name from the menu.

To arrange and delete bookmarks, choose Bookmarks➪Go to Bookmarks or press Ctrl+B to open the Bookmarks window. Drag the bookmarks up or down the list to rearrange them. You can create folders to store groups of related bookmarks, just as you create folders to store related documents in WordPerfect or Quattro Pro. To create a folder, choose Item➪Insert Folder. Inside the Bookmarks window, double-click an item to jump to that page.

One Web site you should definitely check out is the Corel Corporation Web Site, which you can visit at `http://www.corel.com`. The Corel site offers information about Corel's products and the company in general. Also check out Chris Dickman's CORELNET at `http://www.corelnet.com`, which offers discussion areas through which you can share information with other Corel users.

Saving Online Time (And Money)

One of the first things you notice about cruising the Web is that it can take a long time for information to arrive on your computer screen, especially if you have a slow modem. Because many Internet providers base their fees on the number of hours you spend online — and because you've got better things to do than sit and wait for your modem to deliver the goods — becoming a more efficient Webber definitely pays. Here are a few tips to help you make the most of your online time:

- ✔ If a Web site is really popular — which means that many people are trying to download the same stuff at the same time — accessing the site can take a long time. If you get tired of waiting or if you get a page downloaded halfway and realize that it's not what you expected, click the Stop button or press Esc to interrupt the transfer.

- ✔ You can access Web pages much faster if you uncheck the Auto Load Images command on the Options menu. Netscape then downloads just the text parts of a page and displays graphics as little icons. If you want to see the graphics on a particular page, choose <u>V</u>iew⇨Load <u>I</u>mages, press Ctrl+I, or click the Images toolbar button.

- ✔ Instead of taking the time to read a long document on-screen, save it to disk or print it and read it after you log off the Internet. You can find the how-to's in the section "Printing and Saving Pages and Messages," later in this chapter.

- ✔ Oh, and don't compose long e-mail or newsgroup messages while you're online. Instead, compose your messages in Netscape before you log onto the Net, as I discuss in the sections "Sending e-mail" and "Posting a message to a newsgroup," later in this chapter.

Sending Electronic Mail on the Internet

In addition to browsing Web pages, you can send and receive e-mail (electronic mail) over the Internet by using Netscape. To open the Mail window, click the envelope icon in the bottom-right corner of the Netscape window or choose <u>W</u>indow⇨Netscape <u>M</u>ail. A window that looks much like the one shown in Figure 17-3 appears.

Before Netscape enables you to receive or send any mail, it asks you to enter your e-mail password (which your Internet provider assigns you). You can avoid needing to enter this password each time that you open the Mail window by choosing <u>O</u>ptions⇨Mail and News Preferences, clicking the Organization panel in the Preferences dialog box, and checking the Remember Mail Password check box.

Mailbox pane · Message pane · Read/unread · Flag · Message header pane

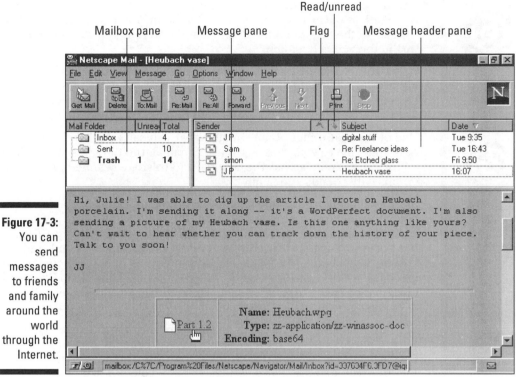

Figure 17-3:
You can
send
messages
to friends
and family
around the
world
through the
Internet.

Receiving and reading your mail

The Mail window has three different panes (refer to Figure 17-3). You can
resize these panes by dragging the pane borders. After you click a folder in
the Mailbox pane, the Message Header pane displays a list of messages in
the folder. Click a message in the Message Header pane to display the entire
message in the Message pane. Here are a few other nuggets of information
about reading your mail:

 ✔ The Message Header pane displays some identifying information about
 the message, such as the name of the person sending the message and
 the subject matter of the message.

 ✔ The little icons to the right of the sender's name can be used to flag a
 message that you want to mark as important. Just click the icon to turn
 the flag on or off. The other icon marks your messages as read or
 unread; a green diamond indicates an unread message. Again, click the
 icon to toggle it on and off.

✔ You can drag the borders between the different column titles to display more or less of the information in that column. You may want to shrink the size of the Sender column, for example, so that you can see more text in the Subject column.

✔ By default, Netscape puts all your messages into a mail folder called Inbox. You can create other folders so that you can store messages by category. Choose File➪New Folder to create a folder. To move a message into the folder, just drag it to the folder.

✔ One of the best things about e-mail is that you can attach a document or graphic file to your message. I use e-mail all the time to send work to editors and clients across the country and to share scanned photographs with friends and family.

After you receive a text document with an e-mail message, the filename typically appears as a hypertext link in the Message pane, as in Figure 17-3. (The hypertext cursor is pointing to the link in the figure.) To grab the document and store it on your hard disk, right-click the link and choose Save Link As. Netscape displays a Save As dialog box that works much like the Save dialog box in WordPerfect, which I discuss in Chapter 5. Choose the folder where you want to store the document and give the document a name, if necessary, and then click the Save button.

Graphics can appear as links or as *inline* graphics, which means that the full image appears in the Message pane. To specify how you want graphics to appear, choose View➪Attachments Inline or View➪Attachments as Links. Whichever way you view a graphic, you can save it to disk the same way that you save a text file: Right-click the graphic or link and choose Save Link As (for graphic links) or Save This Image (for inline graphics).

✔ To delete a message, click it in the Message Header pane and click the Delete button on the toolbar.

After you first Netscape, the program tries to check for any new mail. If mail is waiting for you, an exclamation point appears by the icon. If a question mark appears instead, Netscape couldn't access your mailbox automatically. (Check with your service provider if this problem occurs.)

If you want Netscape to continue to check for messages while you're online, choose Options➪Mail and News Preferences, click the Servers tab of the Preferences dialog box, and change the Check for New Mail option from Never to Every. In the Every option box, specify how often you want the program to check for new mail. Click OK to exit the dialog box.

Even though Netscape checks for mail and alerts you with the exclamation mark that mail has arrived, it doesn't automatically deliver new mail that arrives while you're online. To get that mail or to check for mail between Netscape's automatic checks, click the Get Mail button.

Sending e-mail

To send a new mail message to someone, choose File➪New Mail Message, press Ctrl+M, or click the To: Mail button on the toolbar. The Message Composition window shown in Figure 17-4 appears. In the Mail To box, type the e-mail address of the recipient. If you want to send a copy of the message to other people, enter their addresses in the Cc: box. Type a brief subject heading in the Subject box and then type your message in the message area. Click the Send button to launch your message into cyberspace.

Message area

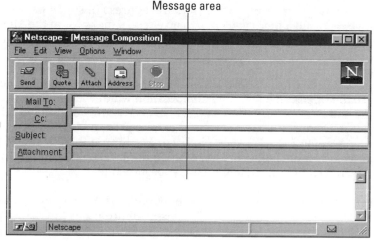

Figure 17-4:
Compose your e-mail messages in this dialog box.

To reply to a message, click the message in the Message Header pane and then click the RE: Mail button. The recipient's name and address are automatically entered for you in the Message Composition window.

Want to send a scanned photograph of your new baby or a copy of your Quattro Pro spreadsheet to a friend or client via e-mail? You can attach the graphic or text document by clicking the Attachment button. Netscape displays the Attachments dialog box, where you're asked to choose whether you want to attach a Location or a File. Choose File and click OK. You're taken to a dialog box that looks and works like the WordPerfect Open File dialog box, which I discuss in Chapter 5. Choose the file and click Open. You return to the Attachments dialog box. Make sure that the As Is button is selected and click OK.

You can compose your messages in Netscape before you log onto the Internet to reduce the amount of time you spend online. Start Netscape but don't connect to the Internet. Create your mail message as usual, but choose Options➪Deferred Delivery before you click the Send button. Netscape stores the message in a folder called Outbox in your Mailbox pane. After you log onto the Internet, go to the Mail window and choose File⇨Send Messages in Outbox or press Ctrl+H to send all the messages in the Outbox folder.

Using the address book

To avoid needing to enter someone's e-mail address every time you send a message to that person, add the address to Netscape's address book. Choose Window⇨Address Book to open the address book, choose Item⇨Add User, and enter the person's name and e-mail address into the appropriate option boxes. Or, to add the address of someone from whom you've received a message, click that person's message in the Message Header window and choose Message⇨Add to Address Book command.

If you want to send a message to someone listed in your address book, choose Window⇨Address Book and double-click the person's name. Netscape opens up a Message Composition window and fills in the person's name and address for you. You can also access the address book inside the Message Composition window by clicking the Address button. Click the person's name and then click the To: or CC: button to indicate whether you want to insert the name into the Mail To option box or the CC option box. Click OK to move ahead and create your message.

Don't confuse the Netscape address book with the Address Book mini - program referred to in Chapter 9. These two programs have the same name but different faces.

Chatting in Newsgroups

Newsgroup is the Internet term for a group of people who exchange messages about a particular area of interest. You can find newsgroups for almost every topic, from using computers to creating craft items.

To see what newsgroups are all about, choose Window⇨Netscape News. Netscape opens a News window that looks similar to the one shown in Figure 17-5. Like the Mail window, the News window has three panes: a Newsgroup pane, Message Header pane, and Message pane. Drag the border of any pane to resize it. Drag the column header borders to resize the columns in the panes.

Newsgroups are organized into folders in the newsgroup pane. Each folder contains newsgroups related to a specific subject. After you double-click a folder in the Newsgroup pane, you see a list of all the newsgroups in the folder. The number in the Unread column indicates how many of the newsgroup messages you haven't read yet, and the number in the Total column tells you the total number of newsgroup messages. A check mark next to a newsgroup name means that Netscape is set up to automatically display the newsgroup in the Newsgroup pane and to keep track of which messages you've read and haven't read.

Catching up on the latest news

After you click a newsgroup name, a list of messages for the newsgroup appears in the Message Header pane. Click a message in the list to display the entire message in the Message pane.

The icons after the sender name indicate the same thing they do in the e-mail window. The first icon flags messages that you want to be able to locate easily later; click the icon to turn the flag on or off. The second icon marks a message as read or unread. After you read a message, the icon shrinks and turns gray. Click the icon to turn it from "read" to "unread" and vice versa.

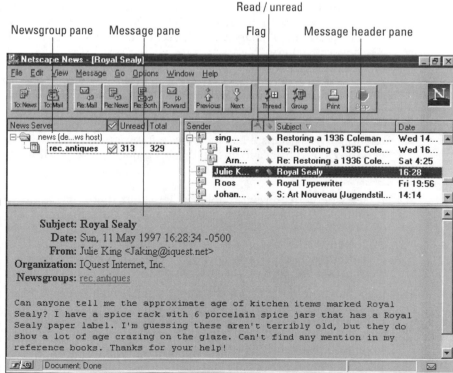

Figure 17-5:
The News window enables you to converse with computer users around the world.

By default, Netscape is set up to deliver 100 newsgroup messages at a time to your computer. After you view the initial 100, choose File⇨Get More Messages to deliver the next 100. Or you can change the number of messages delivered in each batch by choosing Options⇨Mail and News Preferences, clicking the Servers tab, and changing the value in the Get option box at the bottom of the tab.

Replies to a newsgroup message are positioned next to the original message. The original message and all replies are said to be *threaded*, as in strung together. If you click any message in the thread and then click the Thread button, you can mark all the messages in a thread as read (and make a clever rhyme at the same time).

Messages sometimes stretch beyond the width of the Netscape window. To avoid having to scroll the window to view an entire line of text, choose View⇨Wrap Long Lines. Netscape then formats the message to fit the window. (You can turn on this same option in the Mail window, too, by the way.)

Subscribing to a newsgroup

By default, Netscape displays a couple of newsgroups in the Newsgroup pane. To see a list of other newsgroups, choose Options⇨Show All Newsgroups. Then go get a cup of coffee while Netscape downloads the list, which can take several minutes.

You quickly discover, as you scroll through the newsgroup list, that a newsgroup's name often doesn't reveal its subject matter. But you can get a vague idea by looking at the beginning of the newsgroup name. The comp. name, For example, indicates newsgroups dealing with computers; sci. indicates scientific newsgroups; rec. indicates a focus on recreational activities such as hobbies or sports; and soc. indicates groups interested in social interests or socializing.

To see whether you want to join a newsgroup, read a few of the messages. If you like what you see, you can subscribe to the newsgroup. All you need to do to subscribe is check the box next to the newsgroup name in the Newsgroup pane. Subscribing to a newsgroup simply tells Netscape to display that newsgroup every time you open the Newsgroup window — provided, of course, that you turn off the Options⇨Show All Newsgroups command and turn on the Options⇨Show Subscribed Newsgroups command.

The Options menu contains many other settings that you can use to control how and when newsgroup messages appear. You can tell Netscape to show all messages, for example, or show only unread messages.

The View⇨Sort command enables you to specify the order in which newsgroup messages appear — by date, sender, subject, and so on.

Posting a message to a newsgroup

Ready to be bold and put in your two cents worth about the topic at hand? To post a message to the newsgroup, choose File⇨New News Message or click the To: News button. To reply to the message that's currently displayed in the Message pane, choose Message⇨Post Reply or click the Re: News button.

If you want to send a private e-mail message to the author of the message you're replying to, choose Message⇨Mail Reply or click the Re: Mail button. To post a reply to the newsgroup and send an e-mail to the author, click Re: Both or choose Message⇨Post and Mail Reply.

Printing and Saving Pages and Messages

To print the current Web page, e-mail message, or newsgroup message, just click the Print button on the toolbar, press Ctrl+P, or choose File⇨Print. If you're looking at a page that uses frames, the command changes to Print Frame and prints the contents of the currently selected frame only. If you're printing a mail or newsgroup message, the command changes to Print Message(s).

To save a Web page to disk, choose File⇨Save As or press Ctrl+S to display the Save As dialog box. If you select the HTML Files option in the Save as Type option box, the pages is saved as an HTML file, which you can view in Netscape after you log off the Internet by choosing the File⇨Open command, just as you'd open a document in any other program.

If you select the Plain Text option in the Save as Type option box, only the text on the page is saved, and most of the text formatting is lost. You can open the page in most programs, however.

You can save newsgroup and mail messages to disk by choosing File⇨Save As and choosing the Plain Text extension from the Save as Type option box.

If you right-click a hypertext link, you can save the linked page without going to that page. Just choose Save Link As from the menu that appears after you right-click.

Chapter 18

Phun with Photo House

· ·

In This Chapter

▶ Understanding how digital images work

▶ Wrapping your brain around terms like *resolution* and *pixel*

▶ Painting on your pictures

▶ Cropping out unwanted elements

▶ Merging two images together

▶ Adjusting brightness and contrast

▶ Changing image size, resolution, and color mode

▶ Adding text

▶ Saving to the right file format

· ·

Did you ever dream of being a photojournalist? Not the kind that brings back gripping images of war and famine from far-off countries, but the kind that gets the really good assignments, like stalking Bigfoot and other mysterious creatures for those publications that adorn the supermarket checkout lane?

Well, thanks to the advent of digital photography and programs like Photo House, you can! After snapping that picture of a three-headed, nine-footed alien baby, you can scan it, open it in Photo House, crop it and tweak the contrast and brightness, and e-mail it to your editor in no time, scooping the competition. And if you can't track down that alien, no problem! You can create the illusion of an alien inside Photo House by patching together bits and pieces of many photographs and painting in any missing elements. Do we live in a great time, or what!

This chapter gets you started on the road to alien-baby fame by showing you how to edit images in Photo House. It explains how to crop, lighten or darken, and otherwise enhance your images. I also discuss some important background information about digital imagery, including how to choose a resolution and file format.

Image editing is a huge subject, and difficult to present in these few pages. I opted to emphasize the tasks Photo House is best suited for: cropping, resizing, and adjusting the brightness and contrast of images. But I urge you to explore the other Photo House tools, including the painting tools. Check the Key page of the Notebook (described in "Getting Started on Your Image Editing Career" later in this chapter) for tips on how to best use the tools.

Where Do I Get Images to Edit?

Digital images include photographs that you scan into your computer or images from a Photo CD (like the ones stored in the Photos folder on the WordPerfect Suite 8 CD). The clip art drawings in the Suite 8 Scrapbook (discussed in Chapter 16), on the other hand, are vector drawings. You can't edit vector drawings in Photo House. (But you can in Presentations, as covered in Chapter 16.)

Digital images that you can edit in Photo House are stored in special image formats, such as TIFF, JPEG, GIF, and BMP. (See "Printing and Saving" later in this chapter for more information on image file formats.) Vector drawings are stored in different formats, including the WPG format used by WordPerfect and Presentations.

If you want to turn a regular print photograph into a digital image, you can either have it scanned to disk or a Photo CD. If you don't have a scanner, check the Yellow Pages for photo-finishing retailers that offer these services.

You can also buy collections of digital images on CD from companies such as Corel, Digital Stock, and PhotoDisc. In some cases, you pay one fee and then are entitled to use all the images on the CD with no further charge. But other times, you pay a per-use fee for each image.

Finally, if you're really on the cutting edge, you can take pictures with a digital camera and download the images from the camera to your computer. A low-end digital camera runs around $300, but cameras in that price range capture low-resolution images that aren't suitable for anything but online viewing (such as on a Web page). Cameras that offer image resolution acceptable for printed images cost $800 and up, with prices falling every day. If you're not ready to invest in a digital camera yet, you may be able to rent one for about $30 a day from a local camera store.

Extremely Important Resolution Stuff!

With a headline like that, you're expecting some really vital news right now, aren't you? Well, unlike some folks, I live up to the promise of my headlines. The information I'm about to impart is *essential* to your image-editing success. If you want to produce crisp, wonderful digital images, you need to absorb a few basic facts about how images work:

✔ Digital images are comprised of tiny squares called *pixels.* The pixels work like tiles in a mosaic — up close, you can see the individual tiles, but if you move far away, your eyes perceive the tiles as one continuous image. Similarly, if you zoom in on a digital image, you can see the individual pixels. Zoom out, and the pixels blend into a seamless image. See for yourself in Figure 18-1.

Figure 18-1: Zoom in on an image, and you can see the individual pixels (top-left corner). Zoom out, and the pixels blend into a seamless image (right).

✔ The number of pixels per square inch is called the image *resolution.* The resolution determines how good your image looks when viewed on-screen or printed. The higher the resolution, the more pixels per inch (ppi), and the better the image quality, as illustrated in Figure 18-2. But more pixels also means that the image takes up more room on disk.

180 ppi

72 ppi

Figure 18-2: An image with a resolution of 180 ppi looks crisp and clear (left), while the same image at 72 ppi looks soft and gooey (right).

✔ Enlarging the physical size of an image — that is, increasing its width or height — lowers the resolution. Why? Because pixels are always the same size — they're incapable of growing or shrinking. So when you enlarge the image, the pixels simply spread out to fill up the new space.

Think of it this way: If you draw a one-inch square and put 100 pixels inside the square, you have a resolution of 100 ppi. If you draw a two-inch square and put those same 100 pixels inside, you have 50 pixels per inch, or 50 ppi.

You may be wondering why, in this age of computer wizardry, Photo House can't simply perform some digital magic that accounts for the increase in image size. Well, Photo House does try, but it doesn't do a very good job (and neither can any other image editor). The program uses a mathematical formula to attempt to fill in the gaps between pixels by adding new pixels that are similar to the existing pixels. But the results just aren't very natural and usually result in a blurry, blotchy image.

The important thing to remember about all this is that you should avoid enlarging digital images. Scan or open the image at the highest resolution possible so that you have the highest number of pixels to work with. If the image is too large, reduce the width and height as necessary inside Photo House.

✔ You may, however, want a low resolution on some occasions. If you're creating images that will be viewed on a computer monitor — for example, an image on a Web page — 72 ppi is fine. In fact, anything more is overkill, because of the monitor's own resolution limitations. If your image has a higher resolution — the images on the WordPerfect CD, for example, are 96 ppi — you should throw away some pixels (a process called *resampling*). See "Changing the Image Size and Color Mode" later in this chapter for the how-tos.

In general, strive for a resolution of 72 ppi for on-screen images, 90 to 120 ppi for black-and-white images that will be printed on a laser printer, and 120 to 180 ppi for color images that will be printed on a color laser printer or grayscale images that will be printed on an imagesetter (such as the images in this book). Color images that will be printed in a magazine, by contrast, need a resolution of at least 225 ppi. Unfortunately, you can't raise the resolution of the images on the WordPerfect Suite CD from their original 96 ppi without blurring the image — at least, you can't do so in Photo House. Again, see "Changing the Image Size and Color Mode" for more information.

✔ The images in the Photos folder on the WordPerfect Suite CD come in two flavors: Each image is available both as a 256-color bitmap image (look for the file extension .BMP), and a 24-bit (16 million color) JPEG image (look for the JPG extension). See the section "Printing and Saving" later in this chapter for more information about BMP, JPEG, and other file formats. The images have the same resolution — 96 ppi — but the JPEG images are substantially larger, with a physical size of about 8 x 5 inches versus a size of about 1 x 1 inch for the bitmap rendition. The JPEG versions also offer better image quality because they comprise more colors.

Getting Started on Your Image Editing Career

To launch Photo House, click its icon on the DAD bar or choose Corel WordPerfect Suite 8⇨Corel Photo House from the Windows 95 Start menu. The Corel Photo House window appears, as in Figure 18-3. On the left side of the window is the Notebook, which serves as an at-your-elbow guide to the different tasks you can do in Photo House. Separating the Notebook and the image window is a strip of editing tools.

 If the Key tool is selected (just click its icon), the Key page of the Notebook is displayed. The Key page contains buttons that you can click to find out more information about a particular task, as shown in the figure. If you select any of the editing tools, the Key page displays information about using the tool.

The Coloring, Brushes, and Effects pages enable you to change the color applied by certain editing tools, change the size and shape of the tool's nib (tip), and apply special effects. From the Photos tab, you can access images from the WordPerfect Suite 8 CD and the CD that comes with Corel Print House, a companion product to Photo House. (Print House isn't part of the WordPerfect Suite.) Click the page tabs to move from page to page.

If you're a beginner with Photo House, the Notebook is a good way to get your bearings. But if you want to hide it and make more room available for your image, choose View➪Notebook; choose the command again or click the Key tool icon to redisplay the Notebook. All the commands and options available from the Notebook are also available from the menus and toolbar, by the way.

To open an image from the WordPerfect Suite 8 CD (or the Photo House CD, if you have it), click on the Photos tab. The different categories of images available appear on the Notebook page. Double-click a category to display thumbnail views of the images in that category. Double-click on the image you want to open or drag it to the image editing area to the right (the area that holds the cow image in Figure 18-3). Note that the images accessible on the Photos tab are the JPEG versions, not the BMP versions. (See "Extremely Important Resolutions Stuff," earlier in this chapter, for more on this subject.)

If you want to open an image that's not on the CD, choose File➪Open or press Ctrl+O to display the Open dialog box, which works similarly to the one discussed in Chapter 5. Check the Preview box to see a preview of a selected image in the dialog box. Double-click the image that you want to open.

Photo House can open images stored in the FlashPix format, a new digital image format brought to you by Kodak. If you open a FlashPix image, Photo House displays the Import FlashPix Image Properties dialog box, in which you can make several adjustments to your image before opening it. The only options not also found in Photo House proper are the Red, Green, and Blue controls, which enable you to alter the amount of those three colors in the image. Click the Preview button to see the results of your changes. I recommend that you save the other adjustments for later, because you can get a better view of things in the Photo House window than you can inside this dialog box. Click OK to open your image.

If you want to create an image from scratch, choose File➪New or press Ctrl+N. You're presented with the Image Properties dialog box, where you set the size, resolution, and color mode of your new image, as explained in "Changing Image Size and Resolution" later in this chapter.

Choosing Your Weapon

The Photo House image-editing toolbox offers 10 editing tools, as labeled in Figure 18-3, plus one icon for controlling the colors that those tools apply. From top to bottom, the editing tools are:

Notebook   Page tab   Image-editing tools   Peaceful barnyard animal

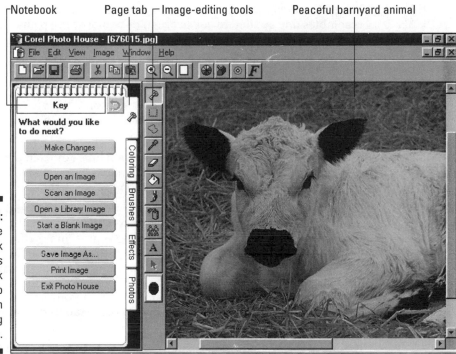

Figure 18-3:
The Notebook provides quick access to information and editing options.

 ✔ Drag with the Select tool to select a portion of your image for editing. A dotted border called a selection marquee appears around the selected area. You can then move the selection, copy it, apply special effects to it, and otherwise manipulate it without affecting the rest of the image. If nothing in your image is selected, any special effects or edits affect the entire image.

 ✔ To select an irregular area of your image — that is, not a square — drag around the area with the Freehand Select tool.

✔ Click with the Eyedropper to lift a color from your image to use as the *foreground color* — the color applied by the Brush, Flood Fill, and Spray tools. Shift-click with the Eyedropper to lift a color to use as the *background color,* which is applied by the Eraser tool. (You can also set the background and foreground colors as explained in "Choosing Your Paint Color.")

 ✔ Drag with the Eraser tool to paint in the background color. Ctrl+drag to paint a straight line.

 ✔ Click with the Flood Fill tool to fill an area of contiguous colors with the foreground color. For example, if I click the cow's nose in Figure 18-3, the nose becomes filled with the foreground color, but the area outside the nose does not.

✔ Drag with the Spray tool to lay down a foreground-colored line that resembles one applied by an airbrush or can of spray paint. Ctrl+drag to spray a straight line.

✔ The Clone tool enables you to duplicate an area of your image. Click the spot you want to clone. A cross-hair cursor appears to show you the area you clicked. Then drag over another portion of your image to reproduce the area under the cross-hair cursor. What you're actually doing is painting one portion of your image onto another portion of your image.

Cloning can be useful for covering up blemishes. For example, see the pieces of straw running from the cow's nose to the ground in Figure 18-3? You could clone some fur from elsewhere on the cow to cover up the straw.

✔ The Change Colors icon indicates the current foreground and background color, which Photo House refers to as the paint color and the paper color, respectively. The inside circle represents the foreground color. To change either color, click the icon to display the Coloring dialog box. Select the Paint color option from the top drop-down list to change the foreground color; select the Paper color option to set the background color. Click the swatch for the color you want to use. You can also change colors by clicking the Coloring tab of the Notebook or clicking the Colors button on the toolbar.

If none of the color swatches suits you, click the More button to display the dialog box shown in Figure 18-4. Click a spot on the color wheel to choose the basic hue; drag the little square inside the shade triangle to make the color darker or lighter. The preview box shows how your changes affect the color.

Color wheel

Shade triangle   Preview box

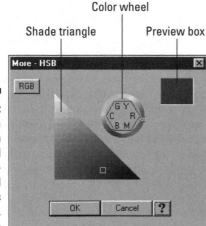

Figure 18-4:
Mix a custom foreground or background color in this dialog box.

If you're creating images that will be viewed on a computer monitor or television set, click the RBG button and mix your color using the resulting R (Red), G (Green), and B (Blue) color sliders. The RGB option creates colors that can be accurately displayed on a monitor. Click the HSB button to return to the standard color-mixing options. (HSB stands for Hue, Saturation, and Brightness, by the way.)

✔ The Text tool and Pick tool work together as a text-creation tag team. You can find out everything you need to know about these tools in "Adding Text to Your Images," later in this chapter.

That sums up the editing tools. But you should also know about a few important buttons on the toolbar at the top of the Photo House window:

✔ Click the Zoom In and Zoom Out buttons and then click your image to magnify and reduce your view, respectively.

✔ Click the Zoom Full button to see your image in its entirety. You can also choose various Zoom options from the View menu.

✔ Click the Color button to open the Color dialog box, just discussed.

✔ Click the Tools button to display a dialog box that enables you to adjust how the selected tool works. If the Brush tool is selected, for example, you can adjust the brush size and make the brush stroke more or less transparent.

✔ The Color Tolerance button displays a dialog box that enables you to control the performance of the Flood Fill tool. If you raise the value in the option box (or drag the slider toward Many Colors), the Flood Fill tool affects a broader range of colors. For example, if you set the value to 0 and click a red pixel, only pixels that are that exact color of red are affected. But if you raise the value, pixels that are similar in color are also affected. No matter what setting you use, however, the Flood Fill tool changes only contiguous pixels (areas of uninterrupted color).

Performing Basic Editing Tricks

The editing tools available in Photo House are fairly limited, so if you plan to do a lot of image editing or need to prepare images for professional publications, you should invest in a more powerful program, such as Corel Photo-Paint or Adobe Photoshop. Photo House lacks some important tools for serious image editing, such as layers. And it's next to impossible to create a precise or intricate selection outline — you can't even select more than one area at a time. But you can perform a few basic editing maneuvers, including these:

✔ To rotate an image, choose a command from the Image⇨Rotate submenu. You may need this command if your image opens up lying on its side, for example.

✔ To crop an image — that is, to cut away unwanted portions — drag around the area you want to *keep* with the Select tool or Freehand Select tool. Then choose Image➪Crop to Selection. The rest of the image is clipped away.

✔ Want to copy a portion of your image to another location or image — for example, to put your head on someone else's body? Select the area you want to copy using either of the Select tools and press Ctrl+C (Edit➪Copy). Then do one of the following:

- Open the image where you want to place the copy. Then press Ctrl+V or choose Edit➪Paste➪As New Selection. Photo House pastes the copied selection and keeps the selection outline active. That means that you can drag the pasted selection around the image without harming the underlying image. To set the selection in place, click outside the selection.

- To create a new document and paste the selection into it, choose Edit➪Paste➪As New Document.

- Stay away from the Paste Into Selection option on the Paste submenu. This option pastes the copied area into an existing selection outline. The problem is that Photo House enlarges or shrinks the copied area to fit the selection outline, which can result in a blurry mess.

✔ To move a portion of an image from one spot to another, select it and drag the selection to its new home. Photo House fills the area left behind with the background color, as shown in Figure 8-5.

Notice the top left boundary of the moved bus in Figure 8-5. When I selected the bus, I also grabbed part of the building in the background. Drawing a selection outline precisely is very difficult in Photo House, so you'll probably find yourself in a similar pickle often. A good way to fix the bus image would be to clone a similarly colored area of sky over the building remnants at the top of the bus. Of course, that still leaves the problem of the bus-shaped hole to the left — maybe I can find some images of the royal family to fill the gap.

✔ To fill an area with the background color, select it and press Delete.

✔ To cancel a selection outline, click outside the selection.

✔ Goof up? Press Ctrl+Z to undo your last editing move. You can undo up to three edits; just keep pressing Ctrl+Z. Or, if you want to go back to square one, choose File➪Revert to Last Saved. Any changes made since the last time you saved the image are wiped out.

Figure 18-5:
I selected
the bus and
moved it to
the right,
leaving a
bus-shaped
hole in the
image.

Enhancing Your Images

Although Photo House can't turn a lousy image into a terrific one, you can make small improvements to the focus, brightness, and contrast of an image. The keys to enhancing these aspects of your image lie on the Image⇨ Touch-Up Effects submenu.

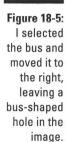

If you select a portion of your image before choosing any of the following commands, the command affects the selected area only.

✔ Choose the Brightness/Contrast/Intensity command to display the dialog box shown in Figure 18-6. Drag the three sliders to adjust the brightness, contrast, and color intensity of the image. Click the Preview button to see the results of your changes in the After box.

If you're preparing images for print, you should generally adjust your images so that they appear a little too light on-screen. Images have a way of darkening when printed.

✔ Inside the effects dialog boxes, you can zoom in on your image by clicking in the Before preview box. (Your cursor becomes a hand, as shown in Figure 18-6.) Right-click to zoom out. Drag to reveal areas of the image not visible in the box.

✔ You can sometimes improve the focus of blurry images by using the Sharpen command, which displays a dialog box similar to the one in Figure 18-6. Raise the sharpening value to bring out the *edges* in your image — areas of high contrast — which can sharpen up soft focus, as in Figure 18-7. The left image in the figure shows the unsharpened original; the right image shows the effect of a sharpening value of 4. The sharpening effects are most noticeable around the hairlines and eyes of our revered ex-presidents.

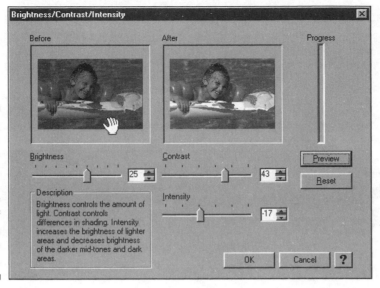

Figure 18-6:
You can
control the
brightness,
contrast,
and color
intensity of
your images
all in one
dialog box.

Don't raise the sharpening value too high, or you'll get a grainy effect.

✔ The opposite of the Sharpen command is the Reduce Speckles command. This command softens edges, which can fix the speckled look created by some scanners.

The effects on the Image⊅Cool & Fun Effects don't enhance your image; they distort it. For a look at some of these effects in action, see "Play with Special Effects in Photo House" in Chapter 20. "Turning Someone's Face Green with Envy" in that same chapter introduces you to the Replace Colors command, which you can use to swap all occurrences of one color with another color.

Changing the Image Size and Color Mode

The Image Properties dialog box, shown in Figure 18-8, contains all the controls for changing the physical dimensions, resolution, and color mode of your image. Here's what you need to know:

✔ To change the color mode, select a mode from the Color Mode drop-down list. No surprise there, eh? Keep in mind that if you reduce the number of colors — going from, say, 16 million to 256 — you not only reduce the size of the image on disk, but also reduce your image quality. You see, Photo House has to decide which colors to keep and which to throw out, and the program just isn't up to the job. If you need

Original

Sharpened

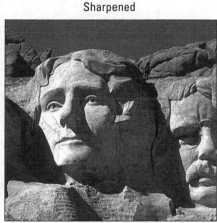

Figure 18-7: Sharpening the original image slightly brought out the contrast around the eyes and hairlines in this close-up view of Mt. Rushmore.

Image Properties

Color mode: 16 million color

☐ Transparent Background

Image size

Type: Custom

Width: 7.95 inches

Height: 5.26

☑ Maintain aspect ratio

Resolution

Horizontal: 96 dpi

Vertical: 96 dpi

☑ Identical values

Image Size: 1157.5 KB

OK   Cancel   ?

Figure 18-8: To change the size, resolution, or color mode, open up the Image Properties dialog box.

to convert your image to 256 colors — for example, to save the image in the GIF format, explained in the next section — don't do the conversion in Photo House. Instead, ask a friend with Photoshop or Photo-Paint to do the job for you.

You can safely convert an existing image from color to grayscale or black and white. Or, if you're printing your image using a professional, four-color printing process, select the CMYK mode.

✔ Adjust the width and height values to change the physical dimensions of your image. Check the Maintain Aspect Ratio check box to retain the image's original proportions.

The preset size options in the Type drop-down list are designed to mesh with printed materials you create with Corel Print House. Don't worry about these options; choose the Custom option and set your own image dimensions.

As discussed in the first section in this chapter, enlarging the image dimensions lowers the image quality. So, to get the best quality, always start with a large image and reduce it to the final print or display size you need.

✔ To lower the resolution of an image, use the Horizontal and Vertical resolution option boxes. Be sure to check the Identical Values box — you definitely want to use the same value for both the Horizontal and Vertical resolution. Remember that the lower the resolution, the lower the image quality. Refer to the section "Extremely Important Resolution Stuff" earlier in this chapter for suggestions on appropriate resolution values for different image uses.

By the same token, you can't raise the resolution without lowering image quality. Photo House attempts to add in pixels to create your desired resolution, but the results are far from satisfactory. Try it for yourself to see what happens: Open an image, raise the resolution, and watch the image blur before your very eyes. Press Ctrl+Z to undo the change.

More powerful image-editing programs enable you to safely raise resolution by reducing the Width and Height values. Photo House doesn't. When you reduce the Width and Height values, Photo House simply throws away pixels as needed to maintain the current resolution. If you really need a higher resolution for your image, make nice with a pal who uses a more sophisticated image editor.

✔ If you're preparing images for distribution on the World Wide Web, try to get your file size as small as possible (by lowering the resolution or the Width and Height values) to reduce the time it takes Web surfers to download your image. A resolution of 72 ppi is acceptable for Web images.

✔ Notice that the resolution value in the Image Properties dialog box is labeled in terms of dpi, which stands for dots per inch. DPI is technically reserved for measuring printer resolution — the number of dots per inch the printer can print. PPI refers to the resolution of digital images and monitors, which display images using pixels. Photo House doesn't make a distinction between the two, which is why you see dpi instead of the more accurate ppi in the dialog box.

If you create an image from scratch (by choosing File⇨New), you see the same Image Properties dialog box. In this case, you can choose whatever settings you want without worrying about mucking up the image with a resolution snafu. Pick whatever image size, resolution, and color mode you want the finished image to have.

Adding Text to Your Images

Want to add a caption to your photo? Photo House offers a basic text tool that may suffice, as long as you don't want anything too fancy. To add text to your image, as in Figure 18-9, click with the text tool on your image. A vertical line, known as the *insertion marker,* appears. Type your text, pressing Enter to start a new line if necessary. If you make a mistake, use the arrow keys to move the insertion marker to the offending characters. Press Delete to lose the character to the right of the insertion marker; press Backspace to toss the character to the left of the insertion marker.

After you type the caption, click the Pick tool icon in the toolbox. Your text becomes surrounded by square selection handles, just like a text box in Presentations. To reposition the text, drag it. To enlarge the text, drag the handles. Drag a corner handle to retain the characters' original proportions.

If you click a second time with the Pick tool, the selection handles are replaced by arrows. Drag the corner arrows to rotate your text. Drag the side, top, or bottom handles to skew (slant) the text.

Don't like the font or color of the text? To change the font, click the Font button, which displays the Text Style dialog box. In this box, you can pick a new font as well as set the size, alignment, and type style. To change the text color, click on the Color button on the toolbar and pick a new foreground (paint) color.

If necessary, you can switch back into text-editing mode by clicking the Text tool again. The insertion marker reappears, and you can edit the text as needed.

When you have your text the way you want it, switch to any tool but the Text or Pick tool. Your text then becomes forever merged with your image. If you change your mind, press Ctrl+Z immediately to get rid of the text.

You can't go back and edit your text after you merge it with the image. So always make a backup copy of your image before you apply text. That way, if the text needs to change, you can simply create the new text on the backup copy.

Figure 18-9:
Give your
image a
caption
using the
Text tool.

Printing and Saving

Printing an image from Photo House works the same as printing from any other program: Choose File⇨Print, select the number of copies you want, and click OK. (For more on basic printing, see Chapter 5.)

To save an image, choose File⇨Save or File⇨Save As (use Save As if you want to save the image under a different name than you previously saved it, change the file format, or save to a different folder or drive). If you're saving an image from a Photo CD, you need to go the Save As route and select a location on your hard drive; you can't save back to the CD.

You can choose from several different file formats, and the best format depends on how you're going to use the image:

✔ Choose TIFF Bitmap for images that you want to be able to open in other programs or share with other users, including those who work on the Mac. To compress the image data so that it takes up less space on the disk, choose the LZW option from the Compression drop-down list. LZW is a compression scheme known as *lossless,* which means that you don't sacrifice image quality for reduced file size. After you click the Save button, a dialog box may appear, offering the option to save the image in the CIELab color space. Ignore the option and click OK, or press Enter to save your image.

✔ Choose Windows Bitmap (BMP) if you plan to use your image as a Windows system resource, such as a desktop pattern or image in a Help file. Otherwise, choose another format. And if you do save in BMP, don't select the RLE Compression option in the Save dialog box, or Windows won't be able to recognize your image as a system resource.

✔ JPEG (JPG) is a good option for images that you plan to put on a Web page or send to others over the Internet. This format is available only for 16 million color (24-bit) and grayscale images. When you save the image, a dialog box appears that demands your input on some strangely worded options. The only one you need to worry about is the Quality Factor slider, which controls how much your image is compressed on disk. JPEG uses *lossy* compression, which means that the more you compress the image, the more image details you lose (although you may not be able to notice the difference in your image). Choose a higher quality setting to retain as much image data as possible. The higher the quality setting, the larger the file size, naturally.

Each time you save your image, it gets compressed again, losing more and more image detail each time. So save to JPEG only after you're completely finished with an image. Until then, save in TIFF.

✔ Another popular format for Web images is CompuServe GIF. This format is available only for images that have 256 colors or fewer. When you save to this format, you get a dialog box that asks you to select from one of two radio buttons: 87a Format or 89a Format. Choose 89a Format to create a *transparent* GIF. With a transparent GIF, the background Web page shows through the transparent portions of the image. Inside the dialog box, click the color that you want to make transparent. Choose the Interlaced option if you want your image to display at low quality as soon as the image begins to download. The image display gradually improves as more and more image data arrives. If you don't choose the Interlace option, the image doesn't appear until all image data is downloaded.

You can also save in the Photo-Paint (CPT) and PaintBrush (PCX) formats. But unless you specifically want to open your image in one of those programs, choose one of the other options. Photo House also enables you to save to the FlashPix format, a new format developed by Kodak and used with some digital cameras. Because few other programs support this format yet, don't save to it if you want to be able to open the image outside Photo House.

Chapter 19
Using Everything Together

● ●

● ●

*I*magine coaching a team of basketball players who all refused to play if they weren't the one with the ball. The minute one player got the ball, all the other players stomped off the court and sat on the bench.

Well, in the old days of computing, programs worked just like that. If one program was active, all the others rushed to the sidelines. But today, programs know how to play together as a team. And unlike some NBA superstars who shall remain nameless, the players in the WordPerfect Suite don't charge into the stands to beat up fans, cover themselves with tattoos, or otherwise behave like unruly children.

This team-computing philosophy means that you can call on the collective strengths of all the programs in the WordPerfect Suite to create a single document. Suppose that you want to create a report that contains text and a data chart. You open a WordPerfect document and create your text. You then tell WordPerfect that you want to create a chart, and it passes the digital basketball to Quattro Pro, which is, after all, the team member best equipped for creating charts. After you build your chart, Quattro Pro passes the ball — and your chart — back to WordPerfect.

Although you can get good results by working with each member of the WordPerfect team individually, you can accomplish a whole lot more in less time if you learn the art of tag-team document creation. At the risk of carrying the sports analogy one step too far, this chapter gives you the game plan for doing just that.

You're about to encounter some scary technical lingo such as *Object Linking and Embedding* and *OLE server.* If these words make your eyes glaze over — as they rightly should — just skip them and follow the steps for accomplishing the various tasks. If you want to understand more about how and why a feature works — which can be helpful in figuring out the best way to get something done — take a deep, relaxing breath and dig in to the text marked with the Technical Stuff icons. The information isn't really that difficult to grasp, just a little dry. Okay, a lot dry. But it's useful information just the same.

Saving Time and Effort with OLE

The key to getting your programs to work together is Object Linking and Embedding, which is called OLE (pronounced olé). OLE isn't a command or a tool; it's a background technology built into many Windows programs, including those in the WordPerfect Suite.

OLE enables you to do several things:

✔ Create data in one document, put a copy of that data into another document, and have the copy automatically updated any time you make changes to the original. For example, you can create a chart in Quattro Pro and then copy it into a WordPerfect document. When you update the chart in Quattro Pro, it's automatically updated in the WordPerfect document as well. (You can turn off this automatic updating if you want to keep the two charts separate.) The upcoming sections, "Making Linked Copies that Update Automatically" and "Linking Copies without Automatic Updating," tell all.

✔ After copying data from one program into another program, you can just double-click the data to edit it in the original program. Say that you create a drawing in Presentations and copy it into a WordPerfect document. If you want to edit the drawing while you're working in WordPerfect, you just double-click it. Windows opens the drawing in a Presentations window for you. When you're finished making changes, the Presentations window closes, and your edited drawing appears in WordPerfect. This magical editing process is discussed in the section "Editing without Leaving Home," later in this chapter.

✔ You can use different programs to create the different elements of your document without leaving the confines of your primary program. Suppose that you're working in WordPerfect and decide that you want to create a simple drawing to illustrate your point. You can launch Presentations, create your drawing, and place it into WordPerfect — all without ever venturing outside WordPerfect. For the inside scoop, see the section "Embedding Objects on the Fly," later in this chapter.

OLE can be a great tool for sharing data not just between programs in the Suite, but between Suite programs and other Windows 95 programs. But not all programs support OLE or all the OLE features discussed in this chapter. If a particular feature or command doesn't seem to be working — or even available in the program you're using — chances are that the program doesn't offer OLE support. Even without OLE, however, you can usually copy data between documents using the Cut, Copy, and Paste commands, as I discuss near the end of this chapter in the section "Sharing Data without OLE."

Deciding Whether to Link, Embed, or Copy and Paste

You can create two kinds of objects with OLE: *linked* or *embedded.* When you create a linked object, Windows establishes a link between the *source* program (the program you use to create the object) and the *destination* program (the program where you place the object). Chipheads sometimes refer to the source and destination programs as the *OLE server* and *OLE client,* respectively.

With linking, the object is automatically updated in the destination document anytime you make changes to it in the source document. Linking can be a great way to make sure that all your documents contain the same version of some text or graphic that changes frequently. If you decide that you don't want the object to be updated automatically, you can change the link settings so that you can update the object manually or sever the link altogether.

The drawback to linking is that if you want to share your document with other people, you need to give them a copy of the source documents for any linked objects along with the destination document.

With embedding, all the information you need to display and edit the object is placed — embedded — in the destination document. If you embed a Quattro Pro chart in a WordPerfect document, for example, you can edit the Quattro Pro chart from within WordPerfect even if you no longer have access to the original Quattro Pro file. It's way cool, but embedding also eats up a great deal of space on your computer's hard drive or floppy disk. And when you edit the original object in the source program, the changes aren't automatically made to the object in the destination program as they are with linking.

If all you want to do is copy or move some data from one document to another and you don't want or need to take advantage of the OLE features just I describe, you can simply use the Cut, Copy, and Paste commands, as I describe near the end of this chapter, in the section "Sharing Data without OLE." Cutting, copying, and pasting between documents using these commands is the same as cutting, copying, and pasting within the same document.

Making Linked Copies that Update Automatically

You create a chart in Quattro Pro to illustrate your company's annual sales figures. You copy the chart into a WordPerfect document, where you're writing an executive summary to justify the dismal sales performance to the board of directors. You also copy the chart into a second WordPerfect document, in which you're creating the company's annual report, and then into a third document, in which you're creating a letter to convince stockholders that things aren't as bad as they appear.

What's all this talk about OLE objects?

The term *OLE object* refers to any data — whether it's text or graphics — that you copy or create in one program and place into another using OLE. The computer people found it tiring to keep using the phrase "text or graphics that you copy or create in one program and place into another using OLE," so they came up with a new term. Either that, or they just wanted to make you feel bad because they knew a word that you didn't.

Just when you get the chart copied into all three documents, your boss says that management wants to make a few minor changes to the sales figures. You could leap up, grab the boss by the collar, and snarl, "Not in this lifetime, pal!" Or you could smile enthusiastically and say, "Sure, no problem at all," secure in the knowledge that you can easily update all the copies at the same time through the wonder of OLE linking.

Of course, if you want to find yourself in this happy, enthusiastic place, you have to create your copies using OLE linking in the first place. The following steps show you how to use OLE linking to copy a Quattro Pro chart into a WordPerfect document and have that chart update automatically when you make changes to the data in Quattro Pro. The process is the same no matter what programs you're using, as long as those programs support OLE — some programs don't. (You can't link a Presentations slide show file or an object in a slide show file to another program. You can link a Presentations drawing file, however.)

The source document contains the data you want to copy. The destination document is the one that receives the copy.

1. **Make sure that the source document has been saved to disk.**

   You can't link data from a document that hasn't been saved to disk.

2. **Select the data you want to copy and choose Edit⇔Copy.**

   If you don't know how to select stuff, look in this book's index for information related to the specific program that contains the data you're copying.

3. **Switch to the document where you want to place the copy.**

4. **Click the spot where you want to put the copy.**

5. **Choose Edit⇔Paste Special.**

   The dialog box shown in Figure 19-1 appears.

6. **Select the Paste Link radio button.**

   If the button is dimmed, either the source or destination program doesn't support linking. (Or you may have forgotten to save the source document as I begged you to do in Step 1.) You can click the Paste button to create an embedded object, as explained in "Creating an Embedded Copy," later in this chapter, or perform a simple copy and paste, as explaine in "Sharing Data without OLE," near the end of this chapter.

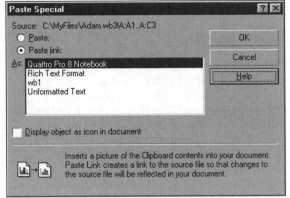

Figure 19-1:
If you want
the copy to
be updated
every time
you make
changes to
the original,
select the
Paste Link
option.

Sometimes, you get several file format choices in the As list box. The computer automatically selects the best format for you, so you don't need to fool with this option unless you experience problems.

7. Click OK.

The copy appears in your destination document.

Congratulations — you just created a linked OLE object. Any changes you make to the data in the source document are automatically made in the destination document as well. The next time you open the destination document, the program alerts you if the linked data has been changed in the source document and gives you the option of updating the copy or leaving the copy as is.

Linking Copies without Automatic Updating

If you don't want your linked copies to be updated automatically when you change the original, you can change the link so that you can update the copy manually when needed. Here's how to do it in WordPerfect:

1. Open the document that contains the copy.

Make sure that no text or graphics are selected.

2. Choose Edit⇨Links.

The Links dialog box shown in Figure 19-2 appears. Each linked object in the document is listed in the dialog box.

3. **Click the linked object whose link you want to change.**

4. **Click the Manual radio button.**

5. **Click the Close button or press Enter.**

If you later change the original and decide that you want to update the copy to reflect the changes, just open the Links dialog box and click the Update Now button. (If the copy doesn't update, try closing and then reopening the document that contains the copy. Then try updating the link.)

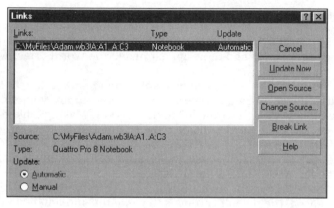

Figure 19-2:
The Links
dialog box
lets you
automatically
or manually
update
linked
copies.

The Links dialog box also offers some other options you may find useful:

- ✔ Click the Open Source button to open the source document. You may want to do this to check out the source data to see what changes were made since you last updated the copy.

- ✔ Click Change Source to link the copy to a different source document.

- ✔ Break Link severs any and all ties between the copy and the source document.

To edit links in Presentations, you follow these same steps. In Quattro Pro, similar link editing commands appear on a submenu when you choose Edit⇨ Linked Document rather than in a separate dialog box. (The commands have slightly different names in Quattro Pro.) To turn off automatic updating, right-click the OLE object (the pasted data) and choose Properties from the QuickMenu. Then deselect the Automatic Updating check box on the OLE Object tab of the OLE Object dialog box.

Creating an Embedded Copy

When you embed an object through OLE, you copy all the data the computer needs to display and edit the object into the destination document. Say that you create a chart in Quattro Pro and embed it into a WordPerfect document on your desktop computer. You then save the document to a floppy disk so that you can work on it on your laptop computer during your business trip to Tasmania. (Hey, as long as you're traveling, you may as well travel somewhere exotic.)

Anyway, assume that you forget to bring along a copy of the original Quattro Pro file. As long as you have Quattro Pro installed on your laptop, you can still edit that chart on the road. You double-click the graphic, and all the Quattro Pro commands and tools appear inside the WordPerfect window.

With that ridiculous build-up, you probably expect embedding to be a very mysterious and complicated process. Sorry to disappoint you. To embed an object, just follow steps 2 through 7 in the section "Making Linked Copies that Update Automatically," but select the Paste radio button rather than Paste Link in step 6.

If you embed a spreadsheet from Quattro Pro, be sure to select the Quattro Pro 8 Notebook item in the As list box inside the Paste Special dialog box. For some reason, the default setting is to paste the spreadsheet in the Rich Text Format, which doesn't keep your formulas and Quattro Pro formatting intact.

With embedding, the copy doesn't get updated if you change the original. Also, files that contain lots of embedded objects can take up lots of disk space.

Embedding Objects on the Fly

The preceding section explains how to embed an existing object into your document. But you can also create embedded objects as you work on a document. You can open up a second program, create the object, and embed it without leaving the comfy confines of your first document window. The following steps show you how to create an embedded Presentations object when you're working in WordPerfect. The steps are similar for other programs.

1. **Make sure that nothing is selected in your document.**

2. **Choose Insert⇨Object.**

   The dialog box shown in Figure 19-3 appears.

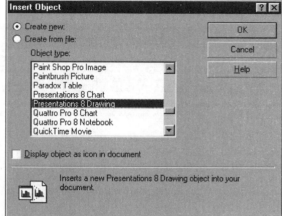

3. Select the Create New button.

4. Select the type of object you want to create from the Object Type list box.

5. Click OK or press Enter.

After some grinding noises from your computer, the WordPerfect menu and tools are transformed into the Presentations menu and tools, and a drawing window appears right on your WordPerfect page, as shown in Figure 19-4.

6. Create your object.

7. Click outside the object boundaries.

Or, in some programs, you can click a Return to Document button on the toolbar, labeled in Figure 19-4. Your drawing is embedded in WordPerfect and appears selected in the WordPerfect window.

WordPerfect offers some special commands that give you another way to create an embedded Presentations drawing or data chart. To create a drawing in Presentations, choose Insert⇨Graphics⇨Draw Picture. If you want to create an embedded Presentations data chart, choose Insert⇨Graphics⇨Chart. Choosing these commands lets you bypass the Insert Object dialog box. Everything else works the same as in the preceding steps.

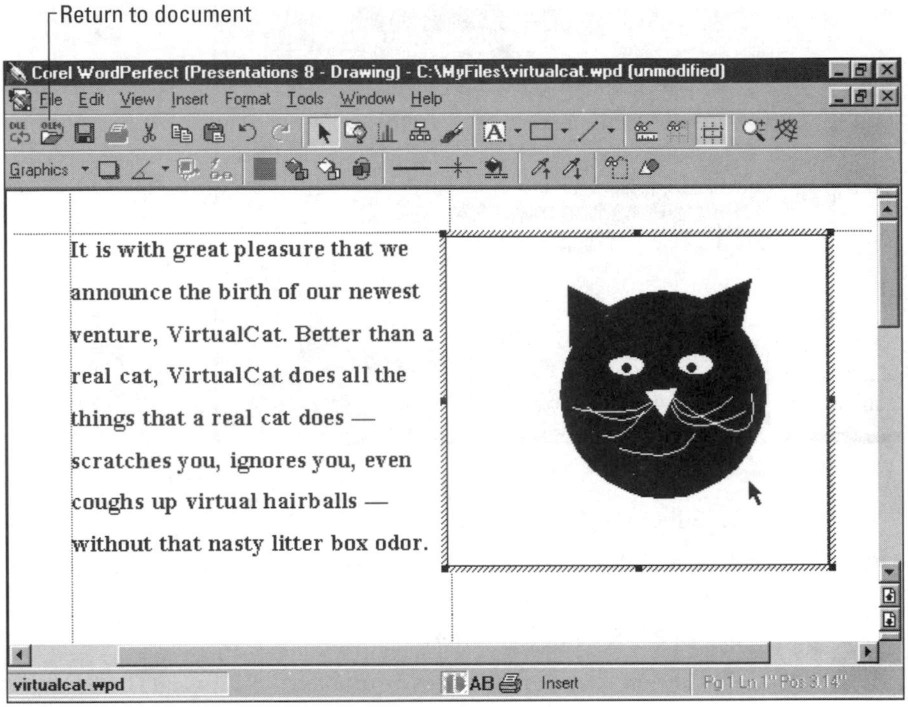

Return to document

Corel WordPerfect (Presentations 8 - Drawing) - C:\MyFiles\virtualcat.wpd (unmodified)

File Edit View Insert Format Tools Window Help

Graphics

It is with great pleasure that we announce the birth of our newest venture, VirtualCat. Better than a real cat, VirtualCat does all the things that a real cat does — scratches you, ignores you, even coughs up virtual hairballs — without that nasty litter box odor.

virtualcat.wpd   AB   Insert   Pg 1 Ln 1" Pos 3.14"

Figure 19-4:
You can access all the Presentations drawing tools while working in WordPerfect.

Dragging and Dropping between Programs

Many programs — those in the WordPerfect Suite included — allow you to drag and drop data from one program to another. You can use drag and drop to create a linked copy, to create an embedded copy, or to move data from one document and embed it in another. Here's the 1-2-3:

1. **Open both the source document and the destination document.**

2. **Select the data you want to copy or move.**

3. **Drag, Ctrl+drag, or Shift+Ctrl+drag the data from the source document to the destination document's button on the Windows 95 taskbar.**

Dragging deletes the data from the source document and embeds it in the destination document. Press Ctrl as you drag to copy the data and embed it in the destination document. And press both Shift and Ctrl as you drag to create a copy that's linked to the source document rather than embedded.

When you drag the object to the taskbar, don't release the mouse button — just pause for a second until the destination program window appears.

4. **Drag the object from the taskbar into place inside the destination program window and release the mouse button.**

When dragging and dropping a selection in Quattro Pro, place your cursor on the border of your selection. When you see the four-headed arrow, press the mouse button. The border should turn blue, indicating that you can now drag and drop.

You can't create a linked copy unless you've saved the file that contains the data you're copying.

Embedding or Linking an Entire Document

If you want to embed or link an entire file into your document, first make sure that nothing is selected in the document. Then choose Insert➪Object to display the Insert Object dialog box and select the Create from File option. Enter the name of the file you want to copy or click the Browse button to locate your file. (In some programs, including WordPerfect, that little white box at the end of the filename option box serves as the Browse button; in other programs, you see a button labeled Browse.) If you want to copy the file as a linked object, select the Link option box. If you want to copy the file as an embedded object, deselect the Link button. Click OK to make the copy.

Editing without Leaving Home

One of the advantages of OLE linking and embedding is that you can edit an OLE object by simply double-clicking it. The process varies depending on whether you double-click an embedded or linked object:

✔ If you double-click a linked object, the source document launches and your object appears in its own window, ready for editing. Make your changes and then save them in the source program. Then choose File➪Exit to close the source program and return to the destination document or just click outside the source document window to return to the destination document and keep the source program open.

> ✔ If you double-click an embedded object, the menus and tools of the source program become available in the current window. Make your changes and then click outside the object boundaries.

Sharing Data without OLE

You don't *have* to use OLE to share data between programs. You can also copy and move data using the Cut, Copy, and Paste commands. If you go this route, you lose some of the advantages of OLE: The copy doesn't get updated when the original changes, and you may not be able to double-click the copy to edit it in the source program. Then again, you don't have to tax your brain with all that OLE linking and embedding rigmarole, either.

Inside the major programs in the WordPerfect Suite, you can sometimes double-click to edit in the source program as long as the source program was also a major Suite program (Quattro Pro, Presentations, and WordPerfect). For example, if you paste a Presentations drawing into a WordPerfect document, double-clicking the chart makes the Presentations tools available to you.

At any rate, the following steps show you how to copy a Quattro Pro chart into a WordPerfect document. You can use the same steps to copy data between any two programs or documents.

1. **Open the document that contains the data you want to copy.**

2. **Select the data you want to copy.**

3. **Press Ctrl+C or click the Copy button on the toolbar.**

   If you're a menu-lover, choose Edit⇨Copy instead. The data scurries away to the Windows Clipboard, where it hangs out until the next time you choose the Copy or Cut command.

4. **Open the document where you want to place the copy.**

5. **Click the spot where you want to insert the copy.**

6. **Press Ctrl+V or click the Paste toolbar button.**

   If you like choosing things from menus, you can choose Edit⇨Paste instead.

You can paste the same copy repeatedly if you want. Just keep clicking the spots where you want to put the copy and continue choosing the Paste command. The copy is available to be pasted until the next time you choose the Copy or Cut command, at which time the Clipboard chucks its current contents to make room for the incoming material.

You can use these same steps to move data between programs. Just choose Edit⇨Cut, press Ctrl+X, or click the Cut button on the toolbar in Step 3 instead of using the Copy command.

 You can copy and move data between documents in the same program by dragging the data from the source document to the Application Bar button for the destination document. Don't let up on the mouse button when you reach the Application Bar — wait until the destination document appears on-screen and then drag the data into place and release the mouse button. Drag to move the data; Ctrl+drag to copy it.

Part V
The Part of Tens

In this part . . .

Welcome to the short-attention-span part of the book. The next three chapters contain tidbits of information that you can digest in minutes — seconds, really, in some cases. You discover ten cool tricks to amaze and astound your friends, ten shortcuts you can use to get things done with less effort, and ten tips to trim some time off of your workday. If you need a quick fix of information or inspiration, look here first.

Chapter 20

Ten Cool Tricks to Try on a Slow Day

*I*t's 4:00 on a Friday afternoon, the boss is gone, and you're sitting around trying to kill time until you can shut the door on another long workweek. You could fire up one of those games that comes with Windows 95, but frankly, you're a little tired of losing to a machine.

That's the time to check out the ten features described in this chapter. Tucked inside the menus and toolbars of various programs in the WordPerfect Suite are some pretty nifty tools that I haven't covered elsewhere because they're not the sort of features most people need on a regular basis. They are, however, lots of fun to play with — heck, they may even prove useful now and again.

Start Off with a Drop Cap

Many magazines, newsletters, and other publications begin articles with a *drop cap*. A drop cap is a letter that's enlarged and dropped down into surrounding lines of text, as shown in Figure 20-1.

WordPerfect makes creating a drop cap easy. Just click anywhere inside the paragraph you want to start with a drop cap and choose Format⇨ Paragraph⇨Drop Cap or press Ctrl+Shift+C. WordPerfect turns the letter into a drop cap. Click to the left of the drop cap to display Property Bar buttons that enable you to change the drop cap's style, font, and position.

To remove the drop cap formatting, click to the left of the drop cap, click the Drop Cap Style button, labeled in Figure 20-1, and select the No Cap option from the drop-down list (the one with the X through the drop cap icon).

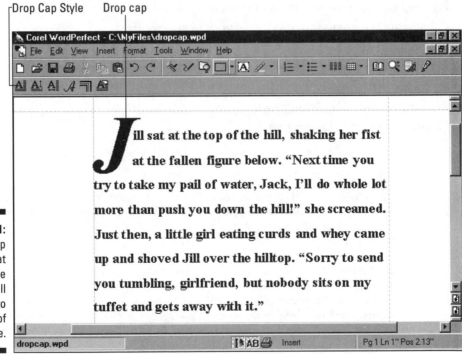

Figure 20-1: A drop cap is a great device to call attention to the start of an article.

Twist and Stretch Your Words

TextArt lets you turn ordinary words into graphic masterpieces, as shown in Figure 20-2. You can access TextArt from inside WordPerfect, Quattro Pro, or Presentations. Try it out:

1. **Click the spot where you want to add a TextArt object.**

   Or select the word that you want to manipulate.

2. **Choose Insert⇨Graphics⇨TextArt.**

   A TextArt window appears, as shown in Figure 20-2. The word you selected appears in a TextArt box, or, if you didn't select a word, the word *Text* appears in the box. The TextArt dialog box also opens.

3. **Play with your text.**

   The panels in the TextArt dialog box are full of options that let you stretch, shape, color, outline, and add other cool effects to your text. Most of the effects are self-explanatory, but a few require some instruction:

   • If you want to edit your text, do so in the Type Here box.

   • To change the shape of your text, click one of the icons in the Shapes option box. Click the More button to display more shapes.

   • Click the Rotation button on the 2-D Options panel to display four little handles around your text. Drag a handle to rotate the text. Or double-click the Rotation button and enter a specific angle of rotation in the resulting dialog box.

   • Unless you're trying to create text with jagged edges, select the Very High setting from the Smoothness drop-down list.

4. **Click the Close button in the TextArt dialog box.**

   Your TextArt object is inserted into your document. To edit it, double-click the image. You can move, copy, and resize the TextArt object as you can any graphic in WordPerfect.

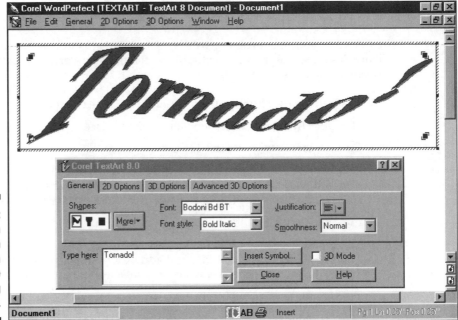

Make Your Letters Sing

If your computer is equipped with a sound card and microphone, you can record your voice as a sound clip and insert the clip into your WordPerfect documents. Anyone viewing the document on a computer that has a sound card can click the clip to hear it. Here's how to record your favorite song and insert it into a WordPerfect document:

1. **In your document, choose Insert⇨Sound to display the Sound Clips dialog box.**

2. **Click Record.**

   The Windows Sound Recorder launches.

3. **Record your song.**

   The Sound Recorder controls work pretty much like those on a regular tape recorder; click the red Record button to start your recording and click the black Stop button to stop recording. Use the Rewind and Play buttons to preview your clip.

4. **Choose File⇨Save in the Sound Recorder and save the clip to disk.**

   Then close the Sound Recorder window.

5. **Click the Insert button in the Sound Clips dialog box.**

The dialog box shown in Figure 20-3 appears. Enter the path name of the sound clip file in the File option box. (For more about path names, see the sidebar, "What's a path name, anyway?" at the end of Chapter 5.) Select the Store in Document radio button if you're going to send the document to someone else — otherwise, the clip can be played on your computer only.

6. **Click OK.**

The dialog box closes and your sound is inserted into your document.

Figure 20-3:
You put
sound in
your letters
through this
dialog box.

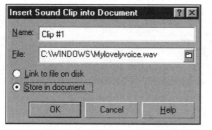

> **Insert Sound Clip into Document** ? ☒
>
> Name: Clip #1
>
> File: C:\WINDOWS\Mylovelyvoice.wav
>
> ○ Link to file on disk
> ● Store in document
>
> [OK]   [Cancel]   [Help]

To play the sound clip, just click the speaker icon in the left margin of the document. Or choose Insert⇨Sound and click the Play button in the Sound Clips dialog box.

If you insert two sound clips right next to each other, you see a little balloon with quotation marks in the margin instead of a speaker icon. Click the balloon to display the speaker icons for each sound clip and then click the one you want to play.

In addition to sending your friends and coworkers a clip of yourself singing *Don't Cry for Me, Argentina,* you can insert digital (.WAV) and MIDI sound files into your document. Follow the preceding steps, but skip Steps 2 through 4. Enter the file's path name into the File option box in Step 5.

Save by Refinancing a Loan

Trying to decide whether or not you should refinance that mortgage? Don't tax your brain; tax Quattro Pro instead. Choose Tools⇨Numeric Tools⇨Analysis to open the Analysis Experts dialog box. Choose the Mortgage Refinancing item from the Analysis Tool list box and click Next. In the Output Cells option box, enter the cell address of the top-left corner of the block where you want the results to appear in your spreadsheet. Enter your current remaining mortgage term, balance, and rate. Then enter the proposed new rate and any financing fees and click the Finish button. Quattro Pro creates a spreadsheet that spells out your potential savings or loss if you refinance the loan.

Figure Out How Many Days Until . . .

Counting the days till your next day off? Instead of using your calendar — which could look a little obvious to anyone walking by — use Quattro Pro to make the calculation for you. To figure out the number of days between the current date and another day, enter this formula into a cell in a Quattro Pro spreadsheet:

```
@CDAYS(@TODAY,@DATE(year,month,day),1)
```

When you enter the formula, replace *year, month,* and *day* with the date that you're looking forward to. For example, to find out how many shopping days until Christmas 1997, enter 97,12,25.

The 1 at the end of the formula, in case you care, tells Quattro Pro to count days using the actual number of days in a year rather than using some other arbitrary calendar in its databank.

Play with Special Effects in Photo House and Presentations

In addition to the image-correcting effects covered in Chapter 18, Photo House offers several effects that enable you to distort images. These special effects, a few of which are shown in Figure 20-4, enable you to wreak all kinds of havoc on images of friends, enemies, and coworkers.

The special effects are found on the Image➪Cool & Fun Effects submenu. When you choose one of the effects commands, Photo House displays a dialog box that enables you to adjust the effect by playing with various options. Small values typically distort an image just enough to elicit a few yucks, as in the Swirl and Emboss examples in Figure 20-4, while large values apply the effect so liberally that the result bears no resemblance to the original image, as in the Ripple example. Click the Preview button to see what mayhem your choices will create, and click OK to apply the effect to your image.

If you select a portion of your image before choosing the command, the effect is applied to the selection only. In the top-right example of Figure 20-4, I applied the Swirl effect to the girl's face, but left the rest of the image untouched. Hmm, that hair suits her new face better, I think.

Original

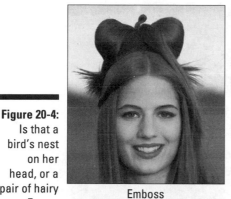

Swirl, face only

Emboss

Ripple

Figure 20-4:
Is that a
bird's nest
on her
head, or a
pair of hairy
Easter
eggs?
Either way,
this dropout
from the
Ace
Academy of
Hair is just
begging for
some
special
effects.

Can't find an effect you like in Photo House? See if the ones in Presentations appeal to you. After inserting an image into your drawing or slide show (Insert⇨Graphics⇨From File), double-click the image to open the Bitmap Editor. Choose Tools⇨Special Effects to display the Special Effects dialog box, shown in Figure 20-5. The preview in the top-right corner of the dialog box shows the entire image. The previews at the bottom of the dialog box give you before and after views of the portion of the image surrounded by the selection box in the full image preview. Drag the box to move the preview.

To see what an effect looks like, click it in the Effects list box. Then click the Apply button. If you like the result, click OK to apply the effect to the image and return to the Bitmap Editor. Or choose another effect and click Apply. After you return to the Bitmap Window, choose File⇨Close Bitmap Editor to save your edits and return to your drawing.

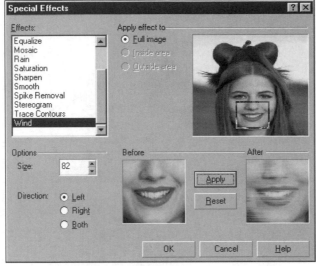

Figure 20-5:
Presentations also offers some image-editing effects.

Send an Object into the Third Dimension

The Presentations Quick3-D command adds instant three-dimensional depth to a drawing or text object. Select any object in Presentations and then choose Tools⇨Quick3-D. Up pops the Quick3-D dialog box, where you can add depth to an object, change the perspective, and rotate the object around the X, Y, and Z axes. Figure 20-6 shows a rectangle before (top) and after (bottom left) I applied 3-D effects. I created the bottom-right image by applying the Tools⇨QuickWarp command to the top rectangle. Like the Quick3-D command, the QuickWarp command gives you some interesting ways to distort and reshape an object.

Wrap Text around a Circle

With the Contour Text command in Presentations, you can adhere text to a circle, curved line, or any other shape. In graphics circles, this process is known as *fitting text to a path*. Here's how it's done:

1. **Click the shape to select it.**

2. **Shift+click the text block to select the text, too.**

3. **Choose Tools⇨Contour Text.**

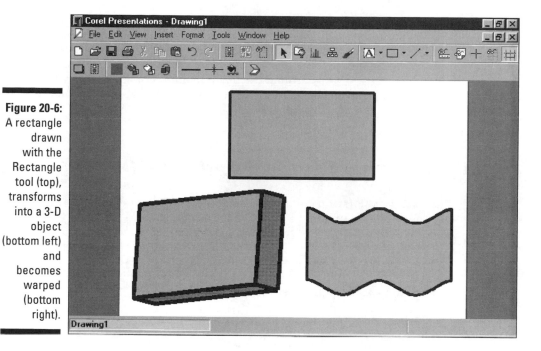

Figure 20-6:
A rectangle drawn with the Rectangle tool (top), transforms into a 3-D object (bottom left) and becomes warped (bottom right).

The Contour Text dialog box appears. Here, you can choose the position of the text relative to the shape. You can also specify whether you want to see the shape itself after you contour the text. Turn on the Display Text Only check box to hide the shape. Deselect the check box to see both shape and text, as in the example on the left.

4. Click OK.

Presentations welds the text to the shape. If you don't like the results, press Ctrl+Z, choose the Contour Text command again, and try different settings.

To separate the shape and the text, right-click the shape and choose Separate Objects from the QuickMenu.

If the text clings too closely to the shape, press Ctrl+Z to undo the contouring or right-click the graphic and separate the text and shape. Then give the shape a thick border in the color of your background, as explained in Chapter 16. The result is an invisible border that serves as a separator between the shape and the text. If you really want your circle to have a visible border, draw a second circle, slightly smaller than the first, and drag it on top of the first circle. Then apply the border to the top circle.

You can't choose the Contour Text command when a piece of clip art or bitmap image is selected — the command is only available for shapes and lines that you draw using the Closed Object and Line tools. But you can make it *look* as though the text is fit to the clip art or image: Use the Freehand tool to draw a line around the portion of the graphic where you want the text to appear. Select the line, select the text, and apply Contour Text, making sure that the Display Text Only check box is selected.

Turn Someone's Face Green with Envy

Here's a trick to try on color images in Photo House: You can use the Replace Color command to replace all similarly colored pixels with a different color.

Suppose that your arch enemy is foolish enough to let you snap his or her picture. After scanning the picture, you can open it in Photo House and turn the person's face bright green, as follows:

1. **Drag around the face with the Freehand Select tool.**

2. **Choose Image⇨Touch-up Effects⇨Replace Colors.**

   The Replace Colors dialog box, shown in Figure 20-7, appears.

3. **Click the eyedropper icon and then click your enemy's face inside the Before preview box.**

   In the figure, I clicked the woman's forehead, for example. Clicking with the eyedropper tells Photo House what color you want to replace.

Figure 20-7:
The
Replace
Colors
dialog box
is the
secret to
swapping
one color in
your image
with
another.

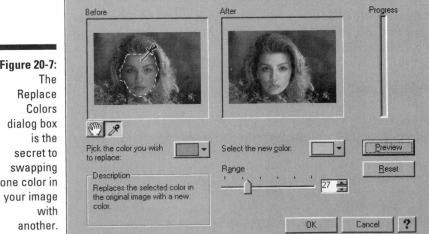

4. **Choose a lovely shade of green from the Select the New Color drop-down palette.**

   This color is the color that you want to use as the replacement color.

5. **Adjust the Range slider to affect more or fewer pixels.**

   If you use a low value, only pixels that are very close in color to the pixel you clicked with the eyedropper are replaced. The higher the value, the more pixels affected.

   To see the results of your settings, click the Preview button. If you don't like what you see, adjust the Range slider and click Preview again.

6. **Click OK to do the deed for real.**

If you don't select an area of the image before choosing the Replace Colors command, the command affects the entire image. By selecting the face in step 1, you guarantee that only the face pixels are replaced.

Play with PerfectExpert Templates

For still more fun adventures, click the Corel PerfectExpert icon on the DAD bar or choose Corel WordPerfect Suite 8➪Corel New Project from the Windows 95 Start menu. A dialog box appears, listing all the available PerfectExpert templates (formerly known as QuickTasks and now sometimes called Experts). As discussed in Chapter 3, the templates create most or all of the text and graphics for certain common documents. You can edit the documents to customize them as you see fit. Some of my favorite PerfectExpert documents are:

- ✔ **Award:** This one helps you create an official-looking certificate, perfect for proclaiming yourself Employee of the Month.

- ✔ **Graph Paper:** Ideal for those times when you want to sketch out the floor plan of your dream home, this template creates a piece of graph paper.

- ✔ **Hangman Game Sheet:** Tired of wasting time playing computer games? Print out a hangman game sheet and waste some time the old-fashioned way!

- ✔ **Gift Tag:** When you don't care enough to buy the very best, use this template to create a homemade gift tag to adorn that cheap present you bought. Really, you just can't say "I celebrate the wonderful person you are" any better than this.

Some PerfectExpert templates use graphics stored on the Suite CD-ROM. So if you see a dialog box complaining that the PerfectExpert can't access a required file, slip the CD into your CD-ROM drive and try again.

Chapter 21

Ten Shortcuts You Can Use All the Time

In This Chapter

▶ Opening existing documents and creating new documents

▶ Closing documents

▶ Moving around in documents and dialog boxes

▶ Cutting, copying, and pasting data

▶ Printing documents

▶ Saving your work

▶ Undoing mistakes

▶ Making text bold, underlined, or italic

▶ Getting help

▶ Quitting a program

*W*hen I was a kid, I was fascinated by the notion that Samantha Stevens, the magical mom of TV's *Bewitched,* could do her household chores simply by twitching her nose. I thought that if I concentrated hard enough, I, too, could make my bed, clean my room, and do other tedious tasks by wrinkling my nose. Alas, I never acquired the touch, or should I say, the twitch.

Imagine my delight, then, when I discovered that computers have built-in shortcuts that enable you to perform certain jobs in one quick step instead of working your way through menu after menu to dig out the commands you want. This chapter shares some of the keyboard shortcuts and buttons you can use in WordPerfect Suite 8, as well as many other Windows 95 programs, to get your work done faster and with less effort. It's not magic, mind you, but then again, you don't have to worry about the side effects that so often plagued the Stevens household, where people were forever getting turned into barnyard animals because of a glitch in a twitch.

Not all programs offer all the toolbar buttons shown in this chapter. But you can always create your own toolbar button for a command or feature that you use frequently, as I explain in Chapter 22.

Creating and Opening Documents

To create a new document, press Ctrl+N or Alt+F, N or click the New Document button.

To open an existing document, press Ctrl+O or Alt+F, O. Or, if you prefer clicking to pressing keys, click the Open Document button.

Closing the Current Document

To close the current document, press Ctrl+F4 or Alt+F, C. You can also click the Close button for the document window. If you haven't already saved the document to disk, you're prompted to do so.

Moving Around Documents and Dialog Boxes

To jump quickly to the end of your WordPerfect document, press Ctrl+End. To jump to the beginning of the document, press Ctrl+Home. Press Home to move to the beginning of the current line and press End to move to the end of the current line. These shortcuts also work in most other word processing programs.

In Quattro Pro, pressing Ctrl+Home moves you to the first cell on the first page in the notebook; pressing Home moves you to the first cell on the current page.

To move from one option to the next inside a dialog box, press Tab or press Alt plus the underlined letter in the option name. To move to the previous option in the dialog box, press Shift+Tab.

Pasting Data

graphic, select it and then press Ctrl+C or
rots off to the Windows Clipboard, where it
ose the Copy or Cut command.

love it to the Windows Clipboard, press
The data remains on the Clipboard until you

lipboard into your document, click the spot
a and press Ctrl+V or click the Paste button.
tents as an OLE object, as explained in Chap-
ial command from the Edit menu instead.)

contents in multiple places if you want; just
here you want to paste the data and pressing

ts

ument, press Ctrl+P or Alt+F, P. Or click the Print

Saving your work

To save the current document to disk, press Ctrl+S or Alt+F, S or click the Save button. The first time you save, a Save File dialog box appears, and you're asked to give the document a name, specify a file type, and choose where you want to store the document. The next time you press Ctrl+S or click the Save button, the document is saved using the same Save settings; the dialog box doesn't appear. If you want to save the document using different settings, choose File⇨Save As or press Alt+F, A.

Undoing Mistakes

Screw up bigtime? You can erase all evidence of your mistake by pressing Ctrl+Z or Alt+E, U or clicking the Undo button. Undo can reverse most, but not all, actions; you can't undo saving a file, for example.

If you change your mind about that Undo, press Ctrl+Shift+R or Alt+E, R to reverse your decision. Or click the Redo button. Choose Redo *immediately* after you choose Undo, though, or this feature may not work.

Making Text Bold, Underlined, or Italic

 If your data's looking dull, give it some flair by applying character formatting. First, select the text you want to format. Then press Ctrl+B to make it bold, Ctrl+U to underline it, or Ctrl+I to italicize it. Or click the **B**, *I*, or <u>U</u> toolbar buttons. Press the shortcut or click the button again to turn the formatting off.

Getting Help

If you're stumped as to how a particular feature works, click it and then press F1. A Help window appears, displaying information about the feature.

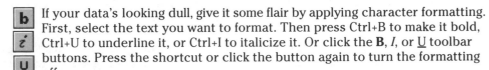 In WordPerfect, Quattro Pro, and Presentations, you can also click the PerfectExpert button or choose <u>H</u>elp⇨PerfectExpert to display the PerfectExpert window, a special Help feature explained in Chapter 3.

 Some dialog boxes include a question mark button. Click the button and then click a dialog box option to find out more about that specific option. Or click the button labeled Help to get information about the dialog box contents in general.

Quitting a Program

When you've had all you can take of this computing business, press Alt+F4 or Alt+F, X to shut down the current program. Or simply click the program's Close button. If you have any open documents, you're prompted to save them before you exit the program.

Chapter 22
Ten Ways to Save Time

In This Chapter

▶ Using the mouse to reach commands faster

▶ Creating buttons for commands you use all the time

▶ Taking advantage of Quick commands

▶ Using styles to speed up formatting

▶ Protecting yourself from losing data if the power goes out

▶ Creating data once and reusing it in other documents

▶ Dragging and dropping stuff from here to there

▶ Sharing ideas and information on the World Wide Web

▶ Getting assistance from technical experts

▶ Swallowing your pride and reading the book

*T*ick tick tick tick . . . Recognize that sound? It's not a bomb — at least, I don't think so, unless you offended a mobster lately or something like that. No, that sound is the clock on the wall, reminding you that there are only so many minutes in a day, and you haven't even begun to accomplish all the tasks slated for this day's minutes.

With so much to do and so little time, what you need is a way to make your computer work faster. (Certainly *you're* already going as fast as you can go.) With that thought in mind, this chapter continues Chapter 21's time-saving theme by bringing you ten more ways to speed things up. Put these tips into practice, and you may even make up for all that time you spend tooling around the Internet when no one's looking.

Click Once Instead of Twice

Whenever possible, avoid hunting through menus to access commands. Instead, choose a command by clicking its toolbar button, selecting it from a Property Bar drop-down list, or pressing its keyboard shortcut. (Chapter 21 provides a rundown of buttons and shortcuts for the most frequently used commands.)

You can also save yourself some time by right-clicking to access QuickMenus, which contain commands related to the text, graphic, or other element you right-clicked.

Create Your Own Toolbar and Property Bar Buttons

If a program doesn't have a toolbar or Property Bar button for a command you use often, you can make your own button. The following steps show you how to create a button in WordPerfect 8. The command names for creating and editing buttons may vary slightly in other programs; you should find specifics in the Help menu for the program you're using.

1. **Right-click the toolbar or Property Bar and choose Edit from the QuickMenu.**

   The Property Bar Editor dialog box, as shown in Figure 22-1, appears. (If you're editing the toolbar, the dialog box is named Toolbar Editor instead, but works the same.)

2. **In the Features list box, click the command you want to turn into a button.**

   Commands are organized by menus; you can switch to a different menu by selecting it from the Feature Categories drop-down list.

3. **Drag the highlighted command to the toolbar or Property Bar.**

   You can also click the Add button or double-click the command to add the button to the end of the toolbar.

4. **Click OK to make your addition permanent.**

To remove a button from the toolbar or Property Bar, press Alt as you drag the button off the bar. You can also rearrange buttons and move buttons by holding down Alt and dragging them.

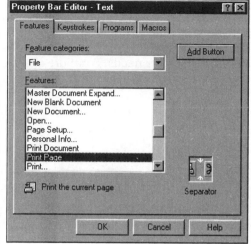

Figure 22-1:
Create
your own
toolbar and
Property
Bar buttons
for com-
mands you
use often.

 If you don't like the button face that WordPerfect assigns to a command, you can change it. With the Property Bar or Toolbar Editor dialog box open, double-click the button you want to change. You see a dialog box in which you can change the name of the button and specify what QuickTip text you want to see when you pause the mouse cursor over the button. Click the Edit button to display a dialog box that lets you edit the colors and design of the button. (Click the button face display in the zoomed area of the dialog box to change the colors of the pixels that make up the image.)

Use Quick Thinking and Templates

The WordPerfect Suite offers several different speed-it-up features that begin with the word Quick: QuickCorrect, QuickWords, and so on.

Using QuickCorrect, for example, you can correct typing errors on the fly and also set up the equivalent of a keyboard shortcut, as explained in Chapter 6, in the section "Letting WordPerfect Correct Mistakes for You." (QuickCorrect works similarly in other programs in the suite.)

Different programs offer different Quick commands — work your way through the menus looking for commands related to the project you're doing. Be sure to also right-click your way around the screen to display different QuickMenus, which are mini-menus containing commands related to whatever you right-click.

PerfectExpert templates, formerly known as QuickTasks, help you blaze your way through various routine tasks, such as creating fax cover sheets. The templates provide the basic building blocks for documents, handling formatting and entering some text and graphics automatically. You can then edit the document to customize it to your needs. For more on using templates, see "Using PerfectExpert Templates" in Chapter 3.

Work in Style

Especially in WordPerfect, it pays to use *styles*. Styles enables you to automatically apply many different formatting attributes at once, instead of choosing them one by one from various menus. Styles also ensures that the different components of your document — headlines, body text, and so on — have a consistent look.

For more information about using styles in WordPerfect 8, see "Using Styles to Speed Up Formatting Chores" in Chapter 9. For information about using styles in other programs, check out the Help index in each program.

Keep Automatic Backup Turned On

Most programs offer a feature that automatically saves your document every so often to protect you from losing all your work should the power to your computer go out unexpectedly. But, in many cases, you have to turn this automatic backup feature on before it can do its job.

Where you activate automatic backup depends on the program. In WordPerfect, choose Tools⇨Settings, double-click the Files icon, click the Document tab, and make sure that the Timed Document Backup check box is selected. In Presentations, use the same steps, but click the Backup tab. In Quattro Pro, choose Tools⇨Settings and click the File Options tab of the resulting dialog box to find the automatic backup option. To locate the option in another program, consult the program's Help system.

Teach Your Programs How to Share Data

Don't recreate the same data over and over again; create it once and then use OLE commands or the normal Cut, Copy, and Paste commands to copy and move it into other documents. If you want, you can use OLE to create copies that automatically get updated when you update the original data.

You can find out more about these options in Chapter 19 and also in the editing sections of chapters discussing individual programs in the WordPerfect Suite.

Practice the Art of Drag and Drop

If you want to copy or move data, you can select the data, choose the Cut or Copy command, click the spot where you want to place the data, and then choose the Paste command. Or, you can make life easy by simply selecting the data and drag it to its new home using your mouse.

You can drag and drop data within the same document, between two open documents in the same program, and, in some cases, between two open documents in different programs.

In most programs, you drag to move data between documents and press Ctrl while dragging to copy data. For more information, see the section "Dragging and dropping" in Chapter 6 and "Dragging and dropping a copy" in Chapter 13. You can use the techniques presented there to drag and drop stuff in most programs.

When dragging between programs, Ctrl+dragging embeds the data as an OLE object and Shift+Ctrl+dragging links the data, as explained in Chapter 19, in the section "Dragging and Dropping between Programs."

Seek Out Online Help

Corel Corporation maintains a site on the World Wide Web at `http://www.corel.com`. This site is a great place to find out about the latest Corel products and programs and access technical support. (See Chapter 17 for more information.)

Don't Be Shy about Calling for Help

I can't tell you how many hours I lost trying to research and solve my own computer headaches before I finally wised up to the benefits of calling tech support. In some cases, I would have never been able to find a solution myself because the problem was related to some software or hardware bug known only to the folks at tech support.

So if you encounter a problem that you just can't seem to solve, don't waste endless hours trying to track down a solution on your own. Instead, pick up the phone and call the technical support department for the software or hardware that's causing you fits.

In some cases, you may pay a small surcharge for technical support — and you may have to wait on hold for some time before you get to speak to a real, live person. But if you weigh those drawbacks against all the time you lose if you try to fix things yourself, you almost always come out ahead.

When All Else Fails . . .

Many people seem to feel that they should be able to install and use a new piece of software just like that, with no instruction and no information about how the program works. They refuse to read the manual that came with the program or any other references, such as this book. As a result, they never learn to use the program to even a bazillionth of its capacity — which means they plunk down a lot of money for a meager return. They also spend much more time than necessary getting things done, because they don't know how to put the program's power to work for them.

Of course, I know that *you* don't fall into this category, because you bought this book. But just in case the book was a gift (or was anonymously put on your desk by someone who was tired of hearing you yell at your computer), understand that it is no reflection on your intelligence that you can't learn how computer programs work by osmosis. Heck, you didn't learn how to tie your shoes by osmosis, did you? (Oh . . . is that why you're wearing loafers?) So swallow your pride and let this book show you how to use the WordPerfect Suite. If you spend just five minutes a week reading, you can pick up techniques and tricks that will save you hours in the future.

Appendix
Installing WordPerfect Suite 8

● ●

*I*nstalling the programs in the WordPerfect Suite is relatively painless — the Suite setup program walks you through the entire process. The biggest problem you're likely to face is not having enough space on your computer's hard drive to hold all the programs. Installing all the components in the Suite requires more than 300MB of hard drive space.

Before you install the suite, read the first two sections in Chapter 1 to determine whether you want to install all the programs. If you don't think you have any use for a particular program, don't install it — save your hard drive space for something else. Remember that you can always go back later and add components that you didn't install the first time.

The WordPerfect Suite runs on Windows 95 and Windows NT 4.0 only. You also need a computer with at least a 486/66 processor and 8MB of RAM; you do much better with a faster processor and 16MB or more of RAM, however.

Installing over Older Versions

The setup program for the WordPerfect Suite doesn't automatically overwrite or remove pre-Windows 95 versions of WordPerfect or other programs in the suite. If your hard drive space is limited, you may need to delete the old programs to make room for the new versions. You can remove the old programs by clicking the Windows 95 Start button and then choosing Settings⇨Control Panel. Double-click the Add/Remove Programs icon to access the Windows 95 uninstaller and select the programs you want to remove. You can also delete the program files using the Uninstall utility that came with the original program, if one was provided.

If you're upgrading from Version 7, don't install the Envoy 7 program that comes with Version 8. In Version 8, Corel provides the Viewer component of Envoy only, whereas in Version 7, the full Envoy program is provided. (With the full program, you can create Envoy documents as well as view them.) If, on the other hand, you have Envoy 1.0 or 1.0a installed, you need to remove it before you install Envoy 7.

If you want to be able to use any of the files you created in earlier versions of the Suite programs, copy the files to a floppy disk or a folder on your hard drive before you remove the old programs. If you're uncertain of how to do this, ask a Windows 95 guru for help.

Doing a Standard CD-ROM Installation

To install the core components of the WordPerfect Suite — WordPerfect, Quattro Pro, Presentations, DAD, Photo House, and Envoy — from the Suite CD-ROM, just follow these steps:

1. **Insert the WordPerfect Suite 8 CD-ROM into your CD-ROM drive.**

   After a few seconds, the Corel WordPerfect Suite 8 screen appears automatically.

2. **Click Corel WordPerfect Suite Setup.**

3. **Click the Release Notes button.**

   Clicking this button displays a window detailing any last-minute installation information from Corel. Software companies use release notes to advise users about any reported problems with certain types of computers and other potential problem areas. Chances are, you won't find anything worth worrying about, but it's always good practice to check. When you click the Release Notes button, the Help system cranks into gear, displaying the available release documents in a standard Help window. (For an explanation of how to navigate a Help window, see Chapter 3.) After you scan the notes, click the little X button in the upper-right corner of the Help window to close it.

4. **Click Next.**

   A dialog box appears, asking you whether you agree to the terms of the software licensing agreement.

5. **Click Yes to signal that you're A-okay with the terms of the agreement.**

6. **Enter your name, company name (optional), and program serial number and then click Next.**

   You can find the serial number on the software proof of purchase form. Be sure to keep this number stored somewhere safe; you'll need it if you ever contact Corel's technical support staff.

7. **Choose an installation type and click Next.**

   You have four installation options:

- **Typical** performs a standard installation and requires about 100 MB of empty hard drive space.

- **Compact** installs the minimum number of components required to run the program. It takes only about 40 MB of free hard drive space, but you won't be able to take advantage of many program features if you choose this option.

- **Custom** lets you pick and choose which components you want to install. The amount of disk space required depends on how many components you install. Information about custom installation is provided in the next section of this appendix.

- **Run from CD-ROM** lets you install just a few program files on your hard disk and then actually run your programs from the CD-ROM. This option requires 48MB of hard drive space, but you'll find that your programs run really, really slowly. Also, you must always have the WordPerfect Suite CD-ROM in the CD-ROM drive to run programs.

8. **Specify the drive and directory where you want to install the suite.**

   Typically, the default options that the Setup program picks are fine. But you can change the installation drive and directory if you want.

9. **Click Next.**

   A dialog box appears, listing all the components that are installed by default. If you don't want to install a particular program, click its check box to deselect it. (A check mark indicates that the program is selected for installation.)

10. **Click Next and then click Install.**

    The installation process takes a few minutes.

When the installation is finished, the Setup program displays a dialog box announcing that you're ready to roll and asking permission to restart your computer. Press Enter to give the Setup program the go-ahead. After the Setup program restarts the computer and does some final tweaking of your system, the Setup window reappears, telling you that you made it successfully through the installation process. You should find the WordPerfect Suite 8 program menu on the Windows 95 Start menu. To put away the Setup program, click the Close button (that X button in the upper-right corner of the screen).

Netscape Navigator is not installed as part of the regular WordPerfect Suite installation. To install Netscape Navigator, click the Netscape Setup button on the screen that appears when you first slide the Suite CD into your CD-ROM drive. The installation steps are the same as for installing the core Suite programs.

Performing a Custom Installation

If you want to install just some components of the suite — or install high-end components not installed via the Typical installation option — follow the preceding Steps 1 through 8, and choose the Custom option in Step 7.

The setup program displays a dialog box listing all the major components you can install. If you see a check mark in the box next to a component, that component will be installed. Click the box to turn the check on and off.

At the bottom of the dialog box, the setup program indicates how much disk space you need to install the currently selected components. Each time you select or deselect a component, the disk space information is updated.

For each component, you can click the Components button to display a second dialog box of options related to that particular component. Click the options that you want to install. Some components have several layers of options; keep clicking Components to find all the possible options that you can turn on and off. Click OK to work your way back to the first layer of components.

 When a box is shaded, only part of the component is installed by default. Click the item and then click Components to access the other parts of the component and turn them on or off.

When you're finished selecting all the components you want to install, click Next and then click Install.

Adding and Removing Installed Components

After you do the initial Suite installation, you can go back at any time and install additional components. Just follow the instructions for performing a custom installation, as described in the preceding section.

To remove a program, click the Windows 95 Start button and choose Corel WordPerfect Suite 8➪Setup & Notes➪Corel Remove Program. The Corel Remove window appears. Click Next and select the programs you want to remove. Click Next and then click Remove.

Note that the Corel Remove program can't remove Netscape Navigator. To dump Netscape, choose Settings➪Control Panel from the Windows 95 Start menu. Double-click the Add/Remove Programs icon, click the Netscape item, and click the Add/Remove button.

Index

IDG BOOKS WORLDWIDE REGISTRATION CARD

Visit our
Web site at
http://www.idgbooks.com

ISBN Number: __0-7645-0187-9__

Title of this book: __WordPerfect Suite 8 For Dummies__

My overall rating of this book: ❑ Very good [1] ❑ Good [2] ❑ Satisfactory [3] ❑ Fair [4] ❑ Poor [5]

How I first heard about this book:

❑ Found in bookstore; name: [6] _____

❑ Advertisement: [8]

❑ Word of mouth; heard about book from friend, co-worker, etc.: [10]

❑ Book review: [7]

❑ Catalog: [9]

❑ Other: [11]

What I liked most about this book:

_____
_____

What I would change, add, delete, etc., in future editions of this book:

_____
_____

Other comments:

_____

Number of computer books I purchase in a year: ❑ 1 [12] ❑ 2-5 [13] ❑ 6-10 [14] ❑ More than 10 [15]

I would characterize my computer skills as: ❑ Beginner [16] ❑ Intermediate [17] ❑ Advanced [18] ❑ Professional [19]

I use ❑ DOS [20] ❑ Windows [21] ❑ OS/2 [22] ❑ Unix [23] ❑ Macintosh [24] ❑ Other: [25]_____

(please specify)

I would be interested in new books on the following subjects:

(please check all that apply, and use the spaces provided to identify specific software)

❑ Word processing: [26]

❑ Data bases: [28]

❑ File Utilities: [30]

❑ Networking: [32]

❑ Other: [34]

❑ Spreadsheets: [27]

❑ Desktop publishing: [29]

❑ Money management: [31]

❑ Programming languages: [33]

I use a PC at (please check all that apply): ❑ home [35] ❑ work [36] ❑ school [37] ❑ other: [38] _____

The disks I prefer to use are ❑ 5.25 [39] ❑ 3.5 [40] ❑ other: [41]_____

I have a CD ROM: ❑ yes [42] ❑ no [43]

I plan to buy or upgrade computer hardware this year: ❑ yes [44] ❑ no [45]

I plan to buy or upgrade computer software this year: ❑ yes [46] ❑ no [47]

Name: _____ Business title: [48] _____ Type of Business: [49]

Address (❑ home [50] ❑ work [51]/Company name: _____)

Street/Suite# _____

City [52]/State [53]/Zip code [54]: _____ Country [55]

❑ **I liked this book!** You may quote me by name in future
IDG Books Worldwide promotional materials.

My daytime phone number is _____

IDG
BOOKS
WORLDWIDE
THE WORLD OF
COMPUTER
KNOWLEDGE®

❏ YES!

Please keep me informed about IDG Books Worldwide's World of Computer Knowledge. Send me your latest catalog.

TECHNICAL BOOKS

BESTSELLING
BOOK SERIES
FROM IDG